More Praise for Re-

"Captures in a most marvelous way the 'enchantment of the Tibet saga, and how it has been 're-enchanting' our dreary, dangerous post-industrial world. . . . By far the best of the recent popular books exploring the amazing impact of Tibetan Buddhism. Paine's witty, erudite, flowing prose creates a memorable album of many characters—saints, rascals, and ordinary folks. He glosses over nothing, is ruthlessly critical where it is deserved, but also secure enough to appreciate the beauty and the power of the 'magic and mystery': the profound practical wisdom and compassion of Tibetan civilization gonè global." —Robert Thurman, Jey Tsong Khapa Professor of Indo-Tibetan Buddhist Studies at Columbia University

"Riveting . . . immensely readable . . . performs a much needed service. These authoritative sketches reflect Paine's fluency with the essentials of some of Buddhism's thorniest ideas, from emptiness to bodhicitta." —Askold Melnyczuk, *Boston Sunday Globe*

"In this new page-turner narrative, Jeff Paine gives us an insider's view of many of the chief players in the exciting drama of Tibetan Buddhism's journey to the West. From David-Neel to Lama Thubten Yeshe, from Trungpa Tulku to Richard Gere, we follow the stories of the exceptional characters who made it happen. This is a great story and Jeff Paine is a great storyteller." —Jan Willis, professor of religion, Wesleyan University, and author of *Dreaming Me: An African American Woman's Spiritual Journey*

"[Paine] presents lively cameo portraits of some leading characters. . . . Thoroughly engaging." —Charles Allen, *Washington Post Book World*

"An enlightening and charming book full of fascinating characters, wonderful stories, and irresistible ideas. Paine's original insights are articulated here with sensitivity, probity, and wit."

—Lee Siegel, author of *Love and Other Games of Chance*

"Memorable anecdotes, great storytelling and keen observations mark this cogent exploration of the explosive growth of Tibetan Buddhism in the West."

—*Publishers Weekly*, starred review

"A richly informative, hugely entertaining account of Tibetan Buddhism's arrival in the West. I recommend this lucid, thoughtful, and lively book to everyone interested in the remarkable story of how the East met (and changed) the West in the twentieth century."

—Charles Johnson, author of *Middle Passage*

"*Re-enchantment* is a page-turner. A masterful storyteller, Paine combines wit and sobriety in recounting tales of the Western encounter with Tibetan Buddhism."

—Holly Gayley, *Buddhadharma*

"[A] splendid and illuminating survey of the coming of Tibetan Buddhism to the West. Paine does a fine job of covering individuals who discovered Tibetan Buddhism and allowed it to transform their lives. [His] commentary on the contributions of the Dalai Lama to this tradition is thought-provoking."

—Frederic and Mary Ann Brussat, *Spirituality & Health*

"A fascinating account. . . . Paine manages the unlikely feat of chronicling the more troubling and outlandish incidents in Tibetan Buddhism's short Western history without obscuring the positive effect its teachings appear to have had on so many adherents."

—Ed Halliwell, *Observer* (London)

"Paine has assembled a wonderful cast of characters, from the enlightened to the merely eccentric. Lucid and slyly humorous, Paine's effortless prose is that of a writer who knows his material extremely well and can make the reader share his respect and fondness for the practices of one of the fastest growing religions in the United States."

—Sudhir Kakar, author of *Shamans, Mystics and Doctors*

"Paine's enthusiasm radiates from the page. . . . He weaves all strands into a web of understanding and appreciation of the amazing accomplishments of Tibetans in exile. . . . It would take a heart of stone to read this book and not want to seek out the nearest lama."

—Jeff Preslaff, *Winnipeg Free Press*

RE-ENCHANTMENT

Tibetan Buddhism Comes to the West

Jeffery Paine

W. W. NORTON & COMPANY · NEW YORK · LONDON

For information about permission to reproduce selections from this book, write to
Permissions, W. W. Norton & Company, Inc., 500 Fifth Avenue, New York, NY 10110

Manufacturing by Quebecor World, Fairfield
Book design by Mary McDonnell
Production manager: Amanda Morrison

Library of Congress Cataloging-in-Publication Data
Paine, Jeffery, date.
Re-enchantment : Tibetan Buddhism comes to the West / Jeffery Paine.
p. cm.
Includes bibliographical references and index.
ISBN 0-393-01968-3 (hardcover)
1. Buddhism—Tibet. 2. David-Neel, Alexandra, 1868–1969—Journeys—China—
Lhasa. 3. Tibet (China)—Description and travel. 4. Buddhism—China—
Tibet—Doctrines. I. Title.
BQ7604.P35 2004
294.3'923—dc22

2003018278

ISBN 0-393-32626-8 pbk.

W. W. Norton & Company, Inc., 500 Fifth Avenue, New York, N.Y. 10110
www.wwnorton.com

W. W. Norton & Company Ltd., Castle House, 75/76 Wells Street, London W1T 3QT

1 2 3 4 5 6 7 8 9 0

That great historic process in the development of the
world, the de-enchantment of the world . . . came
[in Protestantism] to its logical conclusion.

—Max Weber
The Protestant Ethic and the Spirit of Capitalism

CONTENTS

Book IV

BUDDHA: THE SCREEN TEST

Book V

IN SEARCH OF THE ORDINARY: 3 VISITS

CONCLUSION

RE-ENCHANTMENT

Tibetan Buddhism Comes to the West

introduction

•

A Thousand Years
in the Eye of God

I

TIBET HAD VANISHED, so far as the world's attention and concern went. After the Dalai Lama and his followers had escaped their Chinese-occupied homeland in 1959, they established a capital-in-exile in the small Indian Himalayan town of Dharamsala, determined not to fade away in the night. But governments everywhere, with an eye to China's markets, ignored Tibet's plight, and countries like France and the United States denied the Dalai Lama a visa even to visit. Now a decade later, in autumn of 1968, Dharamsala was astir with excitement because an important American might soon be arriving.

Rumor had it that America's most celebrated Catholic intellectual, Thomas Merton, known for his vast sympathies, was on his way there. Merton already felt such empathy with Taoism and Zen that on the plane he scribbled in his journal that this, his first trip to Asia, was "a homecoming." His sure-to-be enthusiastic response to Tibetan Buddhism might supply that religion and its people a lifeline to the larger world, or so it was reckoned in Dharamsala. To prepare himself, the Dalai Lama had studied films about the Cistercians, the Catholic order of priests to which Merton belonged.

It thus came as a shock in Dharamsala when, after his arrival, Merton announced that he had no intention of meeting the Dalai Lama. So little was then known about the Dalai Lama that Merton assumed he was merely a popelike bureaucrat, a type to be shunned. So little was then known about Tibetan Buddhism that Merton dismissed it as a degraded quasi-religion, made up of black magic and superstition. Before Merton left the States a book just off the press, Lucien Stryk's *World of the Buddha*, broke new ground by actually offering a chapter about Tibetan Buddhism. Of the book's twenty-seven chapters, it is the shortest, and in it Stryk concludes that Tibetan Buddhism "is still very much of a mystery"—"a compound of yoga, nature worship, [and] magic," preoccupied with sexuality and the gaining of supernatural powers. Stryk's view, like Merton's, somewhat resembled the one in Chinese Communist propaganda: The religion of Tibet was unsavory old mumbo jumbo, which the advance of progress and material betterment should leave behind.

Merton's attitude might have remained unchanged had he not ventured out to take photographs one crisp Himalayan morning. When he returned, he was in a state of exhilaration; the words couldn't pour out of his mouth fast enough. Nobody asked for an explanation. Merton had obviously run into Sonam Kazi, the Dalai Lama's official translator. Sonam Kazi had a genius for discussing Tibetan Buddhism, and when he did it changed people's outlooks, instilling an intimation that life contained larger possibilities than hitherto imagined. In talking about Buddhism, he would look with his dark brown eyes into the other person's eyes and the other person would think *he knows*: He knows that a human being is extraordinary beyond words, and you can personally exceed any previous measure you have set for yourself.

Overnight, after this first heady taste of Tibetan Buddhism, Merton's wariness lessened, and he fantasized about devoting the rest of his life to studying this unknown religion. Others in Dharamsala remarked on his enthusiasm. The young American who served as his guide (named Harold Talbott, the only American then living there) recalls Merton's being in "a state of utmost exuberance, absorbing with delectation every moment of every experience and every person that passed. He was on a roll, on a toot, on a holiday from school. He radiated a sense of 'This is an adventure and here I am, folks.' "

His young guide detected Merton's sense of excitement but not the reason for it. Talbott considered Merton an admirable Catholic, who had come to Asia to attend a conference on Monasticism East and West. Before leaving America, however, Merton had read a Ph.D. dissertation about his work, and seeing his religious development summarized, he concluded that he had simply not gone far enough. Attending the ecumenical conference was a pretext, and Merton confided in his journal his real reason for the Asian trip: to "find something or someone who will help me advance in my own spiritual quest." Merton's quest encompassed more than personal salvation, though, and was undertaken on behalf of contemporary Christianity. He had watched his faith adapt to an increasingly prosperous and secular America mainly by joining in the party and, in the process, diluting its most vital traditions. "We need the religious genius of Asia to inject a dimension of depth into our aimless threshing about," Merton wrote in his journal. "May I not come back [to America], without having settled the great affair."

Outwardly Merton appeared a model Catholic in Dharamsala, waking at 2 A.M. to say the Christian prayers appropriate to that hour and waking again at 4 A.M. to pray to Jesus. Merton had no thought of abandoning the priesthood or abjuring Christianity; it was as a good Christian that he decided to emulate the Tibetan Buddhists, if the others were at all like Kazi. And they probably were. Merton noted the Tibetan exiles in Dharamsala laughing and singing, full of "intensity, energy, and also humor," despite the fact that the Chinese communists were enslaving their countrymen and destroying every trace of their beloved faith. He intuited that the source of resilience of these people derived from their religion. If he could extract that elixir of vitality from Tibetan Buddhism, it might help restore religion back home to its former vigor. His quest in Dharamsala now began in earnest, as he searched out those characters, some of them truly rum customers, who could explain their strange religion to him.

Only the adventurous would seek out, as Merton now did, Chatral Rinpoche. A *rinpoche* (literally "precious jewel") is a high reincarnated lama, but Chatral Rinpoche was a jewel whom the cautious avoided; he was so wild there was no predicting what he would do. "Ah, a Jesus lama!" he greeted Merton affably enough. "You know, I have never been able for the life of me to get a handle on Christianity. Is it true," Chatral asked Merton, "that Jesus Christ rose from the dead?" In Tibet when a dead man pulled that stunt, a lama was called in to pray and get the corpse to lie down again. "Has Christianity erected an entire religion around a ghoul?"

Merton cleverly responded to Chatral in tantric terms, explaining that Jesus' resurrection was proof that sickness, fear, even death can be transformed into life radiant. The transformation of negative conditions into positive energies is the very heart of Tibetan Buddhism, so Merton's answer made sense to Chatral. "At last I understand something about Christianity," he said. Soon the two men, despite their religious and cultural differences, were talking animatedly and laughing—so much so that Chatral paused and commented, "There must be something wrong here." What was wrong, or unprecedented, was that a Christian monk was asking a lama to teach him Tibetan Buddhism. Indeed Merton was asking not for a basic introduction but for Chatral to teach him advanced practices that many lamas never attempt. What was wrong was that Chatral accepted Merton's far-fetched proposition on the condition that Merton do the preliminary practices first. But in Tibetan Buddhism those groundwork practices (or *ngondro*) are done in units of a hundred thousand—a hundred thousand prostrations, a hundred thousand mantra recitations, etc.

What was wrong was that, without batting an eye, Merton consented, and they discussed his finding a solitary cabin or cave in Bhutan for this year-long feat of spiritual gymnastics. Since Chatral did not consider himself "enlightened" (no rinpoche would ever admit to being so), these two men decided on a contest, a race to see who could reach the ultimate realization first. "This is the greatest man I ever met," Merton thought to himself, and Chatral thought, "That foreigner is a natural buddha."

What Merton had asked Chatral Rinpoche to teach him is revealing. Merton showed little interest in the metaphysics of Tibetan Buddhism, or its ethics, or its concept of ritual, or its communal organization. Rather he homed straight in on the Tibetan methods of connecting directly with the numinous or "divine" within oneself. Merton had previously written about Christian, Sufi, Zen, and Taoist mystics, but he now suspected that Tibetan Buddhism might be the most mystical of all the religions. Its *bodhisattva* ideal—that you achieve enlightenment not for yourself but to help all sentient beings—gave personal sainthood a universal dimension. Its concept of *tonglin*—of taking on others' pains and returning to them your happiness—erased the boundaries between you and others in a vast interconnected web of compassion. Its practice of *dzogchen*—which holds that beneath ingrained, accumulated habits everyone's nature is already perfect—emptied out the neurotic contents and made room for a sense of holy capacity within oneself. In meeting Sonam Kazi and Chatral Rinpoche, in being introduced to heady matters such as *tonglin* and *dzogchen*, Merton felt his trip to Asia was becoming the pilgrimage he had long dreamed of undertaking: "a journey to a mysterious unknown but divinely appointed place, which was to be the place of the monk's ultimate meeting with God."

His encountering one lama, Chatral Rinpoche, had whetted Merton's appetite to discover what the most fabled lama of them all would be like. In the jeep on the way to meet the Dalai Lama, Harold Talbott informed Merton that to ask His Holiness about advanced esoteric practices would be considered improper and constitute a breach of etiquette. After an exchange of courtesies, however, Merton explained that to learn such practices was why he had come to the Dalai Lama. Instead of being offended, the Dalai Lama, who by tradition occupied a high throne elevated above all others, squatted on the floor, the better to demonstrate to Merton the lotus posture, the posture of the back, breathing techniques—instructions that began with the ABCs of meditation and sometimes ended, Merton thought, in realms unimaginable where men and deities exchange places. The Dalai Lama wore his red and yellow robes, Merton his white Cistercian habit with the black scapular, so that they resembled a Giotto painting in which two pilgrims meet at a crossroads.

Many years later when the Dalai Lama was asked what Merton hoped to learn from Tibetan Buddhism, he recalled that the Christian monk wanted "the systematic methods, how to develop step by step, mentioned in Buddhist scriptures." Merton liked the fact that Tibetan Buddhism came with a detailed set of instructions; for once mysticism appeared straightforward, matter-of-fact. For the "poetry" of religion, he thought that the Taoists could hardly be matched; for asceticism and devotion, that the Christian Desert Fathers could not be surpassed. But the Tibetans appeared to have mastered the operative techniques of spirituality, of mapping the actual route from earth to heaven, as it were. Kazi, Chatral, the Dalai Lama himself were the evidence Merton needed that those techniques could transport you at least into the vicinity of sainthood or enlightenment. "The Tibetan Buddhists are the only ones at present," he noted in his journal, "who have a really large number of people who have attained to extraordinary heights in meditation and contemplation." Merton's notebooks (published as *The Asian Journals*, 1973) are pervaded by his astonishment that this all-but-unheard-of sect that was practical when it was most mystical, feet on the ground when its head was in the clouds, might spiritually reanimate the West.

As he began preparing to leave India, Merton confided to several people that, after a scheduled lecture in Thailand, he would return to India or Bhutan to begin the yearlong preliminary practices. The friend who escorted him to the airport remarked, "I suppose you'll be writing a book about Tibetan Buddhism now." A safe assumption, for Merton's pen was like an old gossip reporting the latest tidbit, except in his case it was reporting his last intellectual discovery. No one doubted that Merton would plunge into Buddhism and the Tibetans would get their book, a famous writer sounding the alarm that a great (if little-known) religion and culture were in danger of extinction.

There was one lama, however, who had a vision that none of this would come to pass.

Before he left India, Merton wanted to meet one Tibetan monk whom Harold Talbott had intriguingly depicted as "a way-out lama, a very wild man who is a tremendous troublemaker and extremely rollicking in an unpredictable way—a top-flight, wonderful yogi." This lama, Chogling Rinpoche, upon meeting Merton asked him straight off whether he believed in reincarnation. "Well, I think it's a very, very fascinating, persuasive proposition," Merton answered, "but I wouldn't say I believe it. No." "In that case, I can't teach you," Chogling replied. But then Chogling's thoughts appeared to drift off into another sphere, and when he snapped to, he said, "Okay, let's just say you believe it, and then I can teach you." What Chogling Rinpoche taught Merton was a Tibetan technique that no beginner is ever taught. He instructed him in phowa, or how (supposedly) to shoot consciousness out of the fontanel at the time of death. Merton could scarcely credit this propelling consciousness like a geyser out of the skull: "I'm not sure about all this consciousness and shooting it out the top of the head," he noted in his journal. "I'm not sure this is going to be very useful for us."

A few weeks later in Thailand, Merton slipped coming out of the shower. Evidently he tripped and fell against the floor fan. It electrocuted him instantly. Chogling Rinpoche had a premonition that Merton would die quite soon, which is why he had taught him phowa. With his death so imminent, nothing else would be of any use to him. Merton's quest thus reached, unexpectedly, its abrupt end: His offhand remark about a homecoming in Asia had come true in the Christian sense, as he entered his lasting home.

Merton's premature death put his whole Asian journey in a different light: It was not one more passage, but the final peak in his lifelong spiritual ascent. When news of his death filtered backed to India, to Dharamsala, it registered a shock, a personal loss, and something more. Had Merton lived, any book he wrote on Tibetan Buddhism would have supplied that religion a much-needed lifeline to the larger world. Yet as the Chinese communists relentlessly pursued their methodical eradication of Tibetan culture, any significance that Merton's "lost" book would have had for Tibetan Buddhism (had he written it) would likely not have occurred in politics but in another arena entirely.

For we do know that in Dharamsala Merton struck a fairly new note in the history of religion. For centuries adherents of one faith knew about other faiths only enough to ignore, slaughter, or convert their followers. More recently, a disaffected Englishman or alienated American—Christopher Isherwood, say, or Gary Snyder—has sworn allegiance to an alien persuasion from the East. But Merton planned to devote his remaining life to Tibetan Buddhism (or so he said), even as he continued to abide by the Cistercians' strict rules and to obey his father superior with whom he invariably disagreed. More than even he knew, he was concocting an untried recipe for a new religious future.

Indeed Merton was a harbinger of things to come. In a few days, he had gone from viewing Tibetan Buddhism as a superstitious sect to considering it a great repository of spirituality. Similarly, in one historical moment, in a few decades, Western attitudes in general toward that religion underwent a "conversion." In 1968, the year Merton died, had you ransacked the West, you would have located only two Tibetan Buddhist centers, one in Scotland, the other in Vermont. By the end of the century every American city of any size had such a center, with Washington, D.C., hosting eight, Boston around twenty-five, and New York forty. In 1968 anyone curious about Tibetan Buddhism would have been lucky to scavage a handful of books—W. Y. Evans-Wenz's works, Lama Govinda's *Foundations of Tibetan Mysticism*—replete with inaccuracies and unreadable jargon. Now each year scores of books on the subject pour off the presses. By the year 2000, France counted one in every thirty-five citizens a Buddhist, and will soon have more Buddhists than Protestants or Jews. In the United States Buddhism keeps doubling its numbers faster than any other religion, and the fastest-growing form of it is Tibetan Buddhism. Though no one recognized it at the time, this flourishing had already began with one man, during Merton's "homecoming" in Asia.

Dharamsala, India, was the final act of Merton's story, the grand finale, in which a "Jesus lama" demonstrated how an obscure, ancient faith might renew a modern person's inner life. It also opened the first act— the out-of-town trial run, as it were—of Tibetan Buddhism in America.

II

IN 1959 WHEN THE DALAI LAMA and his followers escaped Tibet, any success their religion might achieve abroad lay in the future—a quite unimaginable future. The Tibetans strayed into the second half of the twentieth century from a country so backward it didn't even have wheeled vehicles (except prayer wheels). Nothing had prepared them for life in modernity. They didn't even have words for it. The advanced industrial nations were then characterized by a term missing in the Tibetan language (for to nothing in Tibet could it correspond): *secular*.

Beginning with the French philosophers like Voltaire and continuing through the nation builders such as Nehru and Attaturk, modernity had come to be synonymous with secularization. About the time the Dalai Lama escaped Tibet, an article in the *American Anthropologist* declared: "To a modern intellectual, religion is probably the most unfamiliar subject in the world." Mid-twentieth-century intellectuals—economists and other bright academics—depicted a world progressing into a global prosperity, whose satisfied citizens would have no need of the consolations of faith.

Even if religion did provide a useful kernel of moral teachings, they argued, its irrationality voided its usefulness. Of all faiths Tibetan Buddhism was suspected of being the most irrational: Its highest goal was to go meditate in a cave. What kind of a career move is that? In short all religion, but especially Tibetan Buddhism, was considered an endangered species.

During his own lifetime Merton had watched his countrymen's religion increasingly reduce to a disguise for politics or ethnic identity or psychotherapy. By contrast, in Dharamsala he had glimpsed a faith that did not relegate sacred wonder to one item in the bric-a-brac of one's routines, but on the contrary, it was synonymous with the whole of life. Tibetan Buddhism's appeal to him, and to Americans subsequently, was that it promised them a way to reenter that earlier stage of religion that Max Weber had described, when spirituality was charismatic, overflowing, and molten. (And yet Tibetan Buddhism, with its thousand years of peaceful history, seemed worlds away from the religio-political fundamentalism that would soon ravage the globe in civil wars and holy wars.) If Merton felt that he had stumbled back beyond both secularism and modern politicized fundamentalism—had in fact stumbled back into the Middle Ages—he was not alone. When the mythologist Joseph Campbell met an exiled lama in America, he too marveled that two such different eras had collided. "If a European scholar-monk of the period of, say, Abelard were to appear in today's New York . . . the miracle would be scarcely more remarkable," Campbell declared, "or important for the students of political and religious history."

Suppose during the sixteenth century, as the Incas and Aztecs perished in their homelands, Londoners had started proclaiming themselves neo-Incans and Parisians attending worship at the Church of Quetzalcoatl? Scholars to this day would be using that episode to reinterpret what religion is. A twentieth-century equivalent to that counterintuitive implausibility actually occurred, however, when Tibetan lamas in exile, who had grown up never hearing of America, began attracting American students by the hundreds and then thousands. To win a place in the modern world, those Tibetans had to cross a thousand years of religious development, and do it in double time. In effect they recapitulated the history of religion—went from the Abbey of St. Denis to downtown Manhattan, as it were—in a single generation. Nothing quite like this had happened before, and with no other indigenous religions left intact, nothing like it will happen ever again.

This, then, is the question: How did Tibetan Buddhism make its thousand-year overnight voyage to modernity—particularly since all the social scientists and bright academics had already concluded that nothing remotely like it could be done?

III

TO BEGIN WITH, amid endless misfortunes, there was something fortunate in the chronology. If Tibetans were in the wrong place after 1959, they were at the right time. Not long after the Dalai Lama fled Tibet there began not the sixties but The Sixties! The decade was overrun with such earnestness, such naïveté, so much wide-eyed conviction that life was to be used for discovering the meaning of life, and then living by it. A young American composer studying in Paris, Philip Glass, chanced upon a few books on Tibetan Buddhism (by Evans-Wenz), and wondered whether there were any living Tibetans left. Just on the chance there might be, Glass traveled overland to India to study with them. A generation of young "rebels" like him, many with wilder and woolier fancies, launched a protest against the perceived despiritualization of contemporary life. Hippies and other middle-class youth joined the protest against what they considered the unenlightened policies of their society (e.g., racial discrimination, war in Vietman), often by turning to the East to pursue a different kind of enlightenment. Probably at no other time, before or since, could Tibetan Buddhism have thus landed on American shores and enjoyed such a welcoming reception. If the Tibetan State Oracle could have divined the most opportune moment for his religion to venture westward, he might have said—as he said to the Dalai Lama that fateful day in 1959—"Go! Now!"

If Tibetan Buddhism in America had only been a hippie phenomenon, however, it would soon have vanished along with other remnants of the sixties (such as Indian gurus like the Maharishi). Some Tibetan lamas like Chögyam Trungpa intuited early on that their youthful American followers displayed more enthusiasm than endurance, and they quietly guided them back to the social norms that the hippies had hoped to escape. Tibetan Buddhism's real intersection with Western history occurred at a deeper level, arriving as it did after—and as a counter to—the long withdrawing of "the Sea of Faith" (in Matthew Arnold's phrase), that is, after the sphere of religion had been contracting for over two centuries, ever since the time of the English Deists and French *philosophes*. By the latter twentieth century the old authoritarian character of Western religion, chipped away by science and cross-cultural information, was eroding, often replaced by a hospitableness to novel kinds of experience.

Nineteen hundred and fifty and the year 2000—though only a few decades apart, not even by a human lifetime separated—are really two distinct eras in the common knowledge of different cultures and religions. Most Americans in 1950 knew only one faith intimately, and may never have seen or talked to an Oriental in person. By 2000 their children usually went to school with Asians or Asian-Americans, and Americans flew off to the East (which was becoming the West by another name) not to encounter the unknown but for a casual week of business or vacation. A Rip Van Winkle who fell asleep in 1950 probably wouldn't have been able to tell you much about Buddhism, but waking fifty years later he would find ample elucidations on the best-seller lists.

This intermingling of cultures and religions created a practically unprecedented situation in the West. When Thomas Merton realized he could remain a Catholic yet benefit from Buddhism anyway, he approached spiritual life in a relatively novel way (certainly for a priest).

An analogy to language may illustrate this new approach to religion. People who speak only English or only Chinese can roll it off their tongues with great conviction, but someone who knows more than one language will better understand how language itself works. By analogy, if you know only one religion, you voice it—that is, you believe (or reject) it. But if you become familiar with a second religion, you likely won't consider it the only tongue God speaks. Instead you may discover there are ways to benefit from that other religion, besides bowing down and praying to it. Merton, or the hippies, or later the buyers of popular books about Buddhist (Hindu, Sufi, etc.) spirituality usually had no intention of converting. They could "practice" a second religion merely by being interested and understanding it, by reading about it and trying out a ritual or meditation they liked (while ignoring those they didn't). It was as a "second religion," unofficial and without any authority at all, that Tibetan Buddhism could steal into the United States.

In exile Tibetan Buddhism thus initiated its own novel experiment of a religion voluntarily surrendering its power to prescribe conduct and to dictate a cosmology of existence. It had little choice, for if it did not relocate at least partially to America and Europe, it would likely perish. Tibetan spiritual leaders during the 1970s began exploring what in their religion was universally valid, and what was merely "Himalayan dogma" and which therefore could go. Beginning with Chögyam Trungpa, Tibetan lamas began to learn European languages as well as master Western psychology.

By the late 1980s, the Dalai Lama himself would sometimes stop in midsentence, and reverse a thousand years of Tibetan precedent before he reached the next period. Some gay reporters once quizzed him about his stance on homosexuality, for example, and the Dalai Lama voiced the typical Buddhist condemnation of it. He paused however, thought, and centuries of prejudice went out the window: "If the two people have taken no vows [of chastity], and neither is harmed," he declared, "why should it not be acceptable?" Similarly, the Dalai Lama comes from a tradition that opposes birth control, but he recognizes the dangers in overpopulation, and believes that one can no longer forbid it. He has even said, "If the words of the Buddha and the findings of modern science contradict each other, then the former have to go." (Try to imagine the Pope or an ayatollah making a similar statement about the New Testament or the Koran.) In dozens of such instances, the Dalai Lama has remodeled an ancient faith for use today. For the first time, an Asian religion was willing to meet the West on the West's own terms.

In the United States and Europe, those Tibetan lamas in exile thus quietly inaugurated the greatest revolution in the history of their religion. They relocated their form of spirituality from the province of monks and monasteries—its center in old Tibet—to the middle of personal, private life. In updating or "secularizing" their faith, they went further than the popularizers of Zen, who had introduced Buddhism into America during the 1950s. Alan Watts had propped his best-selling *The Way of Zen* (1957) on two elegant propositions: (1) Zen is a storehouse of Eastern wisdom, and (2) it offers a respite from, it is the antithesis of, the crass modern world—the very points Tibetans in exile came to reject. The lamas, once they acclimatized to America or Europe, insisted there was nothing particularly Asian about their religion and that it suited the present age as much as it did any supposedly golden past. Many Tibetan teachers began not by teaching metaphysical truths, Eastern or Western, but instead by instructing their pupils in meditation, which supposedly requires no more faith than a medical inoculation does to be effective. By giving them tangible, nondogmatic things to do, those lamas caused their new Western pupils to experience the psychological effect of religion without necessarily its theological cause. Tibetan Buddhism could thus appeal to lapsed Christians (and Jews) who no longer attended church and were exposed to the elements, figuring out life's key puzzles on their own.

Was that, then, the secret of Tibetan Buddhism's success in America and other Western lands? In *The Varieties of Religious Experience* (1902) William James forgot theology and bypassed ecclesiastical organizations to define religion "as the feelings, acts, and expressions of individual men in their solitude"—that is, to make salvation a personal, psychological affair. Tibetan Buddhism could furnish such "individuals in their solitude" a way of being spiritual: Contemporaries who cannot believe in an organized church can have their share of the Promised Land, too. A century after James a sociological survey, Robert Wuthnow's *After Heaven: Spirituality in America since the 1950s* (1998), found ever more Americans claiming that "they are spiritual but not religious, [that] their spirituality is growing but the impact of religion on their lives is diminishing." Yet no one is trained to mint a spiritual practice on his or her own: So for help in this pilgrim chore some people turned to the lamas, who were out of work, and to Tibetan Buddhism, which seemed up for grabs.

While Western governments after 1959 ignored the plight of the Tibetans, some private citizens thus appear, in retrospect, almost waiting for their services. Journalists, concentrating on politics, still tend to dismiss Buddhism as a fluke or fad in America, while historical observers, considering longer-term social trends, speak of a fated niche, an inescapable rendezvous. "The coming of Buddhism to the West," declared historian Arnold Toynbee," may well prove to be the most important event of the Twentieth Century." As for the future, religion will have to "cope with modern scientific needs" and "should transcend [a] personal God and avoid dogma and theology," Albert Einstein observed in a similar spirit and added pointedly, "Buddhism answers this description." Prophecies like those of Toynbee's and Einstein's suggest that Buddhism's arrival in the West may contain besides the personal drama involved something else: necessity.

Strangeness and necessity are the twin themes of this book (hardly surprising in a work investigating the nature of religion). Peculiar was the very beginning, a millennium ago, when the militaristic warrior society of Tibet imported Buddhism to initiate one of the longest reigns of peace in history. But it seems equally odd today, when that guide for living on those high sparse plateaus has migrated into today's modern cities, where

for some hemmed-in residents it adds a sense of spaciousness and meaning to their lives. Tibetan Buddhism thus stands planted at the opposite
ends of the spectrum: there in an underpopulated, ancient, untamed landscape, and here in contemporary, overcrowded, man-made environments.
And between those two poles run the wires, the lines, of the following
strange but necessary story.

Book
I

TIBET,

BEFORE

chapter I

●

Was

IN THE LONG YEARS before Tibetan Buddhism met the West, foreigners, and modernity, few Westerners and certainly only viceroy of India ever managed to cross into Tibet proper. When in November of 1923 some minor government business took the then-viceroy, the Earl of Lytton, to the Tibetan border town of Phari (or Pharijong), he found himself gazing upon the loveliest mountains he had ever seen. He readjusted his priorities; he realized what he must do. He instructed his interpreter to procure a guide for a skiing party the following morning.

The interpreter returned apologetic, stammering. No, skiing was perhaps not the ideal diversion here. The natives regarded these hills as sacred terrain, and to scar the face of them with skis would insult the goddess. Lytton replied, Tut tut, insulting goddesses was hardly unusual in his line of work. He ordered the porters and guide to be ready at dawn.

Snow blanketed the mountains through the night, yet the next morning when Lytton peered out the window, the choice slope he had his heart set on was, unaccountably, the only ground where no snow had fallen. Not one to be deterred, the Earl directed his party in the opposite direction, where a deep snowfall lay beckoning. By the time they reached that spot, however, the sun had entirely melted the snow. As Lytton's gaze chanced back, he noticed—strange weather in this part of the world—now the original slope, barren this morning, was whitely pelted in new snow. Too late, damn it, the day was already lost.

The viceroy shrugged his shoulders, returned to Phari, conducted his business, and went back to India. Lord Lytton, a man of the world, had little inclination to ponder aberrations, and merely dismissed the day's oddity with "Who will dispute that Tibet is a land of mystery!"

IT IS A CLICHÉ that has been repeated a thousand thousand times. That November of 1923, through the whole of Tibet, only one Western woman was to be found anywhere. Her reflections resembled Lord Lytton's. "The reputation enjoyed by the 'Land of Snows' [is] for being a country of wizards and magicians, a ground on which miracles daily occur." This Frenchwoman, a Madame Alexandra David-Neel, wondered why "Tibet has been credited with being the chosen land of occult lore and supernormal phenomena?"

Mystery, wonders, had always been Tibet's chief item of export. The few travelers who smuggled themselves into that country later smuggled out the most outlandish reports of it. Even missionaries bent on unmasking Tibet's charlatan religion, even die-hard rationalist explorers returned with trunkfuls of unwanted tales of wonders. In the mid–nineteenth century the French priest Evariste Huc barged into the monastery of Kumbum, to disprove the myth of a tree that supposedly grew there imprinted with holy Tibetan letters on its leaves. "We were filled with an absolute consternation of astonishment," Huc reported dumbfoundedly, "at finding that, in point of fact, there were upon each of the leaves well-formed Tibetan characters, all of a green color, some darker, some lighter than the leaf itself. . . ." A half century later, when the Swedish explorer Sven Heden went to map the Tibetan land, he wanted to be spared the magical mumbo jumbo. When his young Tibetan guide died along the way, and it later turned out that the guide's brother who'd stayed behind already knew what had happened (having seen it in his mind's eye, the brother claimed), Heden was incensed: First, the guide's inconsiderate death had frustrated his journey, and now his brother's clairvoyance uprooted Heden out of a civilized world governed by rationality. Add up the travelers' reports of all the Hucs and Hedens, and you get a country existing on the other side of the moon, ruled by laws (or the absence of them) unto itself.

The Frenchwoman Madame Alexandra David-Neel (1868–1969) was certainly a class of visitor above Huc or Heden: She stayed longer and she saw more with eyes that were neither a missionary's nor a narrowly focused explorer's. She was called a disciple of Descartes, and though not cynical, she was empirical, almost scientific in her approach, and yet, for all that, she was genuinely intrigued by Tibetan religion. Her approach to it was to accept nothing on faith, but to search for a plausible explanation, and in absence of such explanation or unimpeachable witness, to discount the phenomenon. She demonstrated why the Abbe Huc's miracle tree at Kumbum could not even grow under the conditions described. She argued case by case that most instances of telepathy could have some more rational explanation. Yet, with her open mind, she conceded that so-called occult phenomena warranted the same scientific scrutiny as any other reported physical happenings.

When Alexandra David-Neel told Tibetans she was from Paris, they assumed she meant Phari (where the viceroy visited), since for them beyond their borders the world's geography ended. As though in agreement, she claimed she was not really a foreigner. The Tibetan word for foreigner usually referred to Englishmen who had to cross several seas to reach Tibet, while from France she could (theoretically) reach Tibet's capital, Lhasa, the way any Tibetan did, by repeatedly setting one foot in front of the other. Her joke that she was thus technically a Tibetan contained one tiny grain of truth to it. She had mastered the Tibetan language and customs sufficiently to pass herself off in numerous disguises, from a lama to an old Tibetan beggarwoman, and thus she could spend a dozen years off and on in Tibet, while other foreigners one after another were expelled.

Such an odd contradiction—that so modern and rational a mind as hers would immerse itself in old, otherworldly Tibet. But in fact it was Alexandra's intellectual modernity that allowed her to penetrate Tibet in a way that an older European outlook could not. Earlier missionaries and explorers, with their colonial mindset, dismissed Tibetan culture and religion as superstition, something the new highway to progress had bypassed. But though she was not an anthropologist, Alexandra shared anthropologists' values of field study and culture-free judgment; although she was not a Freudian, she took a psychological approach to understanding the unconscious and its symbolism. Alexandra David-Neel could thus accept Tibetan Buddhism as having its own cultural integrity and psychological validity, and so by her, for the first time, Tibetan Buddhism became studied by a Westerner as a valuable living reality.

As she traveled up and down that vast land, where often no foreigner had set foot previously, she was a kind of ambassador of modern consciousness to an earlier age of religion. Her subsequent books supply, beyond all the old fables and wild surmises, the first realistic account of Tibetan or tantric Buddhism. Later, after 1959, after the Chinese communists burned libraries and monasteries, intending to reduce Tibetan culture to rubble, if one wished to reenter its vanished world, her writings provided the visa. She was "the first to introduce the real Tibet to the West," the present Dalai Lama said, and added with understatement, "Much of what David-Neel describes is now lost forever, which only increases the value of her account."

Something of old Tibet rubbed off on her pages, and a larger-than-life quality hovers over the descriptions of her daredevil journeys across the highest mountain ranges in the world. This woman who so logically investigated (and often defrocked) supposed wonders became in time a wonder herself—a last legend added on to a legendary and now largely extinct Tibet.

AN ENDANGERED CULTURE MAY, at the last moment, attract an alien witness who records its unique way of life before it perishes. So the desert Bedouins in Arabia, before the discovery of oil obliterated their ancient customs, attracted Wilfred Thesiger; so Canada's inland Eskimos, when there were but two women of childbearing age left in their villages, attracted Farley Mowat. But to preserve Tibet's story, Alexandra David-Neel was, obviously, the wrong person entirely. First of all, she was exactly that, she, a woman, who undertook excursions and perils in which men perished like swatted flies. A trained athlete in prime condition could hardly have endured the ordeals she encountered, yet when she began her mad march to Lhasa she was fifty-five, then considered the threshold of old age. Well-provisioned expeditions had perished on those treacherous wintry routes, but Alexandra embarked on them with a single companion and with no provisions at all. Her subsequent account, My Journey to Lhasa, describes a Parisienne on an insouciant lark, but her jaunty attitude played down the actual facts—starvation; threats from brigands; danger from wild beasts; uncharted icy wastes—that made every day a game of Russian roulette. Later journalists and feature writers, puzzled how she survived at all, invariably resorted to some variation of (to quote one account) "It was the most remarkable journey a white woman has ever made."

Upon her return from Tibet acclaim rained down upon her—the gold medal of the Société Géographique, the silver medal of the Belgian Royal Geographic Society, the Chevalier of the Legion of Honor, etc. In old age she wrote (though did not publish) her memoir, Le Sortilège du mystère, to fathom how such an unlikely destiny had fallen to an ordinary French girl. Yet she, like others subsequently, searched in vain for how that daughter of an aging schoolteacher and a vacuous younger woman, born in a mid-nineteenth-century Paris suburb, became the opposite of everything her upbringing intended her to be. Well, she did find one clue: When growing up, Alexandra repeatedly ran away from home, which in retrospect she thought augured that one day she would become an explorer. Tibetans (including, it seems, the thirteenth Dalai Lama) had a different explanation for her puzzling career: Alexandra was a Himalayan soul who had reincarnated in a Western body, to preserve their culture when history threatened to obliterate it. But Alexandra was too levelheaded ever to claim that that was the mystery beneath her mystery.

But if she wasn't a Tibetan offshoot growing in the wrong flowerpot, what is the explanation? In the beginning: When the young girl Alexandra ran away from home, she had something to run from. Like several nineteenth-century prodigies, she was the late and only child of a vastly unhappy marriage, where the mother and father were chiefly linked by the detestation each felt for the other. The social conventions for which she was predestined—marriage, children, church, bourgeois society, moral duty—were made unattractive by her parents' mismanagement of them. And love? Even in her nineties, Alexandra would lecture her housemaid, "What does 'love' mean? Isn't it just a word that imbeciles repeat?" (She uttered this contempt even as she refused to set traps for the mice, not wishing to harm living creatures.) As Rainer Maria Rilke, likewise an offspring of an unhappy marriage, observed of the social arrangements for which he (and Alexandra) was earmarked: "Who can enter a doll's house on which the doors and walls are only painted?"

Her earliest formative years did have one defining event. When she was hardly more than a baby, Victor Hugo bounced her on his knee. Her father, a disciple of the great Romantic writer, bequeathed as his main legacy to his daughter a Hugoésque longing for *la grande passione*. She grew to young womanhood in the hothouse atmosphere of fin-de-siècle Europe, when new ineffable urges, longings for a magical redemption, were sprouting up outside of (and as replacements for) the Christian traditions. Years would pass before Alexandra David-Neel introduced Tibetan

Buddhism to her European audiences, but the latent receptivity to it was perhaps already there. Yet if nineteenth-century Romanticism constituted half Alexandra's character, the other half was a twentieth-century capacity for critical self-scrutiny. Before there was Freudian psychoanalysis, she subjected herself to as ruthless a self-analysis as ever occurred outstretched on a Viennese couch. In it she ruled out marriage and motherhood, thus subtracting from her possibilities the roles then available for women. She condemned herself to settling for less even as inwardly she cried out for more. This mixture of metaphysical longing while intellectually exhausting the West made her pine for some ultimate spiritual elsewhere—anticipating those Americans who would "discover" Eastern religions the better part of a century later.

Alexandra inadvertently became a new kind of rebel: Hers was a "suburban rebellion" that did not grandly challenge the political or social order but merely expressed discontent with the satisfactions of bourgeois life. A generation later suburban rebels (as represented, say, in the novels of Colette or D. H. Lawrence) would live out their quiet mutiny in an overtly erotic sphere and work out their discontents partially in sexual terms. But Alexandra arrived too early for such erotic defiance and sexual compensations. (Neither Balzac's evil antiheroines nor Rilke's overidealized lovers suggest an actual course that a woman of her class might pursue.) She had to solve her vexations in some puzzling larger arena—in blank "white space" where she scarcely knew what to ask for. It is thus not entirely unfitting that she would one day find herself in a place like Tibet, one of the last white spaces left on the map.

At age eighteen Alexandra had no interest in a temporary job in a fabric shop and then a husband, which is how her mother envisioned her future. As she grasped at every straw, she happened to read some writings about the occult. The occult was then in fashion: Victor Hugo employed mediums to contact his drowned daughter; Queen Victoria herself dabbled; William James judged science and the occult equally valid approaches as the new century began. For this young Parisienne, the occult was not merely a hobby or intellectual study, however; it was one of the few "occupations" available to her. Her impractical vision for herself was to read everything mystical—which included anything she could get her hands on about Asian religions—and then to travel to the East to experience it personally. She practically sequestered herself in the Musée Guimet, the Asian museum in Paris, where under a statue of the Buddha she could study the classical Asian texts in scholarly quiet.

At this crucial moment in her career (or lack thereof) Alexandra inherited a legacy from her godmother, which her own mother sagely counseled her to invest in a small tobacconist's shop that would ensure her a safe small income as the decades rolled inexorably by. She followed her mother's advice so far as to smoke something (though not tobacco) to try to obtain a vision of the future. In a hashish reverie she beheld herself trapped within her parents' nauseatingly claustrophobic house. After that vision, Alexandra "squandered" her legacy and immediately booked a year's passage to India.

Her fellow passengers aboard ship, all on colonial assignment, questioned the young woman why such a pretty, delicate bird was flying to harsh old India. Alexandra replied, with supreme disdain, that she intended to study Sanskrit, and her shipmates were too intimidated to inquire, though some were unsure, whether Sanskrit was a language, a region, or a tribe. From the Musée Guimet she had fantasized an India of sages, Hindu Socrateses meditating in perfumed gardens or melodious forests. She disembarked instead into a land scorched by drought and ravaged by famine. Undeterred, she settled down to mastering Sanskrit and Indian religions, and in Benares a naked guru taught her yoga and Vedanta. During that year of 1892–93 all the heat and famine and poverty could not deflect Alexandra from realizing that she herself was the only woman she had known who'd succeeded at studying at the feet of India's holy men. Yet even as her appetite for the East increased, her finances diminished, and all too soon she was back in Europe, facing the world's oldest dilemma—an empty purse.

Her choices were grim, which came down to becoming either a dreary governess or (to her) that even drearier specimen of humanity, a petit bourgeois's wife. Her fine singing voice allowed her to escape or at least postpone that choice as she obtained parts in light operas. The career had its moments: Jules Massenet praised her role in his *Manon*; she returned to Asia as the *première chanteuse* in the Opéra-Comique's touring company. But the older a *chanteuse* became, the further she was exiled to companies in the outer provinces. After a decade Alexandra found herself beyond the beyond, in Tunisia, where her operatic career dribbled to extinction. There in Tunis, with every other option foreclosed, she committed (to her) the "suicide" worse than suicide.

Old enough to know better, why were Alexandra David and Philippe Neel so foolhearty as to marry each other? The answer is not hard to produce. Neel, the French engineer and bachelor dandy working in Tunisia, had kept lower-class mistresses, but his affair with Alexandra was his first liaison with a woman of his station and respectability. Should he want family and children, it was now or never. Alexandra, too, at thirty-six felt she was at the end of things at the end of the world. "We have made a singular marriage, more out of malice than tenderness," she told her husband two months after their wedding *sans* honeymoon. "It was foolish, without doubt, but it is done." Philippe had at least wanted what goes with marriage—family, children, home—while Alexandra was more culpable, knowing in advance that she did not. A few months after her marriage, an unexplained lethargy replaced her former vivacity, and she succumbed to a serious but undiagnosable disease. "Old age is overtaking me quickly," she declared. "My life is over and I feed on what I was."

No physician in North Africa could diagnose her malaise or prescribe a remedy. But Philippe diagnosed what no doctor was able to, and prescribed what few husbands would have been generous enough to. The sure cure to restore her would be, in a word, India, and he proposed to pay for her to journey there as long as twelve months. Relieved, renewed, Alexandra thanked her dear, dear Mouchy (her pet name for him), and dashed off to Paris, to take courses at the Sorbonne in preparation. The professors had much to teach her—grammar, philology, culture—but she rejected their example. "There are great men at the Sorbonne who know all the roots of the words and the historical dates," Alexandra said. "But I wish to live philosophy on the spot and undergo physical and spiritual training, not just read about them."

In mid August, 1911, Alexandra embarked on what she anticipated would be a yearlong visit to India. It would be fourteen years before she saw husband or Europe again.

* * *

> A lady explorer? A traveler in skirts?
> The notion's just a trifle too seraphic:
> Let them stay and mind the babies, or hem our ragged shirts,
> But they mustn't, can't, and shan't be geographic.

The British humor magazine Punch published this ditty just as Alexandra was beginning her Asian peregrinations, not satirizing her (she was not well known enough) but those women, few in number but larger in notoriety, who tramped off on their own to Africa and the Middle East. In 1912, however, Alexandra had no intention of becoming "geographic" or an explorer. Nor did she dream that writing about the strange affinities between ancient East and modern West that would one day make her world famous.

Before she departed for India, however, Alexandra contracted with several French publications to write articles about India and occasionally about Buddhism—a religion that was perhaps best known in Europe (to the extent it was known at all) mainly through the writings of philosophers like Schopenhauer who approved of Buddhism for its pessimism. Schopenhauer had lauded Buddhism for rooting itself realistically in life's inherent disappointments and suffering and for having as its ultimate goal nirvana, the suspension of human personality and its traffic with daily concerns. As for the Tibetan variety, experts such as Dr. L. A. Waddell in his *The Buddhism of Tibet* (1895) called it Lamaism and dismissed it as an animistic creed full of dark gods and black magic. Although Alexandra merely planned to write an occasional article, by the end of her career she, more than anyone else, had stood all these assumptions on their head.

Thanks to those articles, we can pinpoint the precise moment when Tibet entered Alexandra's musings and also the person who insinuated it there. In 1912 the Dalai Lama was in exile in India, escaping (as his successor would a half century later) an invading Chinese army, and she conjectured that a story about him might entertain readers of *Mercure de France*. The difficulty was the Dalai Lama would see no Western women. (Many Asians then thought that white people, though wizards at technology, were otherwise mentally deficient.) But the Dalai Lama made an exception for such a nonpareil, a European woman reputedly learned in Buddhism. "If I had vanished into space while talking with him, he would have been less astonished," she noted after her interview, in which her knowledge of Buddhist doctrines had impressed him. She astonished him further when she revealed that her Buddhism was learned not from an Oriental master, as he could only suppose, but from a Tibetan text translated into French before she was born.

"Ah well," the Dalai Lama muttered. "if a few strangers have really learned our language and read our sacred books, they must have missed the point of them."

That would have signaled the end of the interview, except for the cleverness of Alexandra's response: "It is precisely because I suspect that certain religious doctrines of Tibet have been misunderstood that I have come to you to be enlightened." Delighted with her reply, the Dalai Lama agreed to answer any question she had. The rest of the interview, and a subsequent one, went swimmingly. The Dalai Lama's last words to her were: "Learn Tibetan!"

Tibetan is spoken only in Tibet, however, and Tibet was closed to for-

eigners. Did the Dalai Lama intuit or perhaps wish that she would penetrate into his country and become a voice for Tibet when its time of troubles would begin? (He issued dire prophecies predicting China's brutal
conquest of his country.) The Dalai Lama confided to others that this
Frenchwoman might actually be a reincarnation of the legendary holy
woman Dorje Phagma ("Thunderbolt Cow"). Indeed, when Alexandra
questioned him, "What is the path of salvation, of clairvoyant wisdom?"
he answered her: "You already know."

Interviews with a Dalai Lama were unprecedented; how could Alexandra surpass that experience? A young and handsome Himalayan prince,
Sidkeong Tulku, heir to the throne of Sikkim, invited her to his little
Himalayan kingdom in the clouds, where Tibetan Buddhism was the state
religion. A short visit there, she mused, might net her an essay that could
be published in the *Annales du Musée Guimet*. When she arrived at Gangtok,
Sikkim's tiny capital, the thirty-three-year-old prince greeted her in his
golden brocade robes, "a genie from a fairy tale," ruling over the court so
exquisite and delicate that a harsh wind, she thought, might disperse it
into air. Educated at Oxford, Sidkeong Tulku had constructed in the royal
gardens a rustic English country house, and there he and Alexandra discussed Tibetan Buddhist philosophy, as between them flowed the tea in
jade cups, and also flowed something less tangible but equally delicious.
This woman who only a few years before had reckoned herself prema-
turely old and finished now remarked, "There are days when I don't recognize myself in the mirror. The years have been erased from my
features."

Philippe suspected that his wife and the prince were sexually intimate; the British authorities, who kept a watchful eye over their little
maharajah, entertained a similar suspicion. But many nineteenth-century
women such as Queen Victoria—and indeed Alexandra—were educated
only darkly about sexuality if at all, and they had more important things
to do. Philippe had provided her a bourgeois household; the prince was
offering her, in effect, earth and the heavens. She joined Sidkeong Tulku in

reforming Buddhism in Sikkim, where the monks were typically coarse, ignorant, and drunk. Alexandra, now outfitted in priestly robes, began touring monasteries, lecturing those monks about their own religion, as people crowded around begging for her blessing. Perhaps, she speculated, her and Sidkeong's relationship was not love but Love, not sexual passion but an embodiment in a man and a woman of the harmonic music of the spheres. Friendship and metaphysics, affection and high purpose— Alexandra, instead of dashing off an article for the *Annales du Musée Guimet*, had stumbled into living the philosopher's dream.

Here began her real introduction to Buddhism, not as professors back in Europe taught it, but by stepping off the European spectrum of experience entirely. Her interpreter told her of a hermit lama who was stabbed in his cave by his one disciple, who coveted his few possessions. When a traveler chanced upon the dying lama wrapped in a blood-stained blanket, the lama forbade him to report the crime. If reported, his murderer would be caught and likely executed, before he had a chance to repent and thus would suffer in lives to come. Then the lama begged his visitor leave, for his agony was unbearable, but when he meditated he did not feel pain. So one's religious practice can suspend acute pain! Alexandra thought. Hearing such stories, she began to see religion not as a matter of God and sin and salvation but something that began in one's own body. Tibetan Buddhism might not be all mystical reveries and magical propitiations, as rumor painted it, but rather something like medicine, a "science" or study of empirical phenomena.

Traveling about Sikkim, she chanced upon two young monks in the forest, attracted by their loudly yelling "Hik!" From behind a tree she spied on them, noting how the Hik! arose from their bellies and shook their very being, and afterwards they would stick a piece of straw in one another's hair. It would be months before she learned they were mastering *phowa*—what Chogling Rinpoche attempted to teach Thomas Merton—where success came when a tiny hole in the fontanel was created in which a straw could be inserted. Seeing such occurrences, Alexandra further understood that religion was not necessarily a business of preaching and precepts and prayers, but it began with techniques, honed skills, which could serve you practically. Just as a gymnast or dancer strengthens and makes agile the body, so a religious practitioner strengthens and makes supple the psyche, or "soul." Gradually a revolution was occurring in the way Alexandra thought of religion.

It did not lessen the inducement to learn such rites that she would have a king (Sidkeong Tulku had inherited the throne in 1914) to practice them with. When Sidkeong became betrothed to a princess from Burma, any jealousy Alexandra might have felt was sublimated into a vision of herself chaperoning the royal couple to all the Buddhist courts of Asia. Sidkeong himself was troubled by the engagement, however, which led him to consult a lama-oracle, who sank into a trance and rasped, "Trouble not yourself. The decision will never need be made." Nonsense, thought Sidkeong Tulku; he must give or withhold his consent promptly. Or he would have, had not the lama proved unexpectedly prescient when an inexplicable illness cut short Sidkeong's life soon thereafter.

In her grief, Alexandra learned firsthand the fundamental Buddhist lesson of impermanence, that too great attachment is the prelude to suffering. She also discovered that her vision of the future was voided—she was no longer the honored guest in Sikkim but simply a foreigner in an alien land. "Everything is so closed, so secret," she began to complain of Himalayan Buddhism; "the people and things themselves are so reticent." Over the horizon—it might as well have been on the moon—lay the legendary monastery-cities of Tibet. Beyond them, higher up, impossibly remote, holy hermits were sequestered in caves who, rumor said, mentally influenced the world they had left behind physically. Only a few Europeans had ever visited those monasteries. None had ever managed to apprentice himself to a fabled hermit-master of esoteric wisdom. Could Alexandra do that she would, in a single step, surpass in knowledge and experience every other Westerner who had fantasized about Tibet.

An infinitely wise sage in a cave, meditating at the edge of the world: Shelley's poetry depicts such a holy solitary; Yeats dreamed of meeting such a sage face-to-face. But does that archetype really exist, or would hunting one be like tracking the Yeti, leading into chimeras, into nowhere?

Sikkim reputedly had such a wise recluse. Rumors of him so beguiled Alexandra that she determined to seek out this elusive man called the Gomchen of Lachen (literally: the Hermit of the Great Pass). As she labored the mountainous ascent to his remote hermitage, she recalled stories about how such anchorites repulsed would-be disciples. The Gomchen, when she finally reached his cave, looked fiercer than the legends, and more frightening. He wore a necklace made from human skulls and an apron from carved human bones; his hair descended in a plaited braid to the ground; his eyes were afire like lit coals. When she beseeched him for instruction, he objected that he knew too little: "It was useless for me to stay in such an inhospitable region to listen to an ignorant man," Alexandra recorded him saying, "when I had the opportunity of long talks with learned lamas elsewhere." The Gomchen's refusal sounded strangely perfunctory, however, and soon enough he accepted her "not exactly as a pupil, but on a trial as a novice, for a certain time," providing she never left their retreat without his permission. Alexandra did not suspect then that, far from considering her an unwelcome intrusion, the Gomchen had postponed going on a three-year retreat specifically to instruct her.

Below the Gomchen's cave Alexandra set up house in her own cave, converted by makeshift carpentry into a cabin. If there were four seasons at Lachen, winter was three of them, when month after month barricaded her in unbroken snowy monotony. She developed cabin (cave?) fever, and other fevers as well: as influenza and rheumatism wracked her, her daring to leave ordinary life behind appeared a horrible mistake. The Gomchen's talk still struck her as "marvelous, audacious, frightening" (she half suspected him of being a wizard), yet fed up, sick, she thought that this truly ugly, filthy man and she had "nothing in common but the color of our robes." The weary monotonous months wore on, or perhaps time had stopped, frozen in its tracks. By the time the spring thaw came, however, with the rhododendrons blooming everywhere, Alexandra felt that, unobserved even by herself, a quiet change had gradually transpired in her:

> Mind and senses [she afterwards noted] develop their sensibility in this contemplative life made up of continual observations and reflections. Does one become a visionary or, rather, is it not that one has been blind until then? . . .

At the end of her life, when her crippled ninety-plus-year-old body seemed a curse to her, Alexandra would sigh and wished she had died—not when Sidkeong Tulku did; not when she attained Lhasa; not at the height of her fame—but before she ever left the Gomchen's company and the snowy pass, where the basis of everything that followed had been realized and existence had shown itself most pristine.

"What were the fruits of my long retreat?" Alexandra reflected. "I should have found it difficult to explain." Actually the fruits seem rather easy to describe. She learned Tibetan by talking with the Gomchen and with the help of dictionaries. Together they read the lives of Tibet's famous mystics, which he interrupted with similar personal stories of his own— a phantasmagoria of palaces and ascetics' caves and meetings with hermits and sages—which gradually built up in Alexandra a solid knowledge of Tibet's inhabitants, customs, and thoughts. And what more esoteric matters did she learn? The Gomchen discouraged her from writing a book about what he taught her. "Waste of time. If you speak about profound Truths people yawn," he told her, "but if you tell them absurd fables they are all eyes and ears." Yet, long after he was dead and she herself an old woman, Alexandra did write that book, calling it The Secret Oral Teachings (1951). (After she left, Gomchen did hint to others that he quietly intended her to publicize Tibetan Buddhism to the larger world.) What The

Secret Oral Teachings is truly secretive about, however, is Alexandra herself and her mastery of self-discipline.

She mentions, for example, that learning of a new Tibetan practice, she went into solitary retreat for several months to perfect it. Solitary retreat; several months!—her casualness makes it seem she was attending an evening lecture. As she listened to the Gomchen's long "evening lecture" which lasted from spring to winter to spring again, she slowly became the first Westerner to ransom the legendary feats of Tibet from impossible rumor and to test them out experientially. The practice she referred to above was *tummo* (or *tuomo*). The Gomchen, witnessing his disciple succumb to wintry flu after flu, realized he had to teach her this meditation that raises bodily temperature and allows the practitioner to withstand the harshest winter wearing only the lightest clothing. Graduation day in *tummo* came when the Gomchen sent Alexandra out in late autumn, when the temperature was nearly freezing, and had her bathe in an icy stream and then meditate naked till dawn. She did come down with a cold, but she also conquered a lifelong aversion to harsh weather. Later on her trek to Lhasa, when she marched in snow for nineteen hours at a stretch or had no means to start a fire, if she had not recalled how to practice *tummo*, she might well have perished.

Before Alexandra David-Neel, Western occultists had evoked Tibet (without ever having been there) to validate their daydreams of mystic, magical powers. Unlike them, Alexandra was not interested in magic. She liked to repeat the story of the ascetic who boasted to the Buddha that after twenty-five years' occult practice he could walk across the river. "My poor fellow," the Buddha answered, "the ferryman will take you across for a small coin." At Lachen, fantasy and magic ended and an accurate knowledge of Tibetan practices began to replace them. (*Tummo* may seem on a par with the Indian rope trick, but Harvard scientists have subsequently verified under laboratory conditions its ability to regulate the body thermometer.) Alexandra deliberated remaining at Lachen, until she attained the mind's final illumination. But after a year the servants who fetched fuel and water and cooked for her refused to remain any longer. In 1915, realizing her apprenticeship there was at its end, she gazed out her cabin-cave as though trying to glimpse the future.

Time to return to Europe, she thought with a sinking heart? In the distant landscape stretching out below her, at the far end of her gaze, beyond an unmarked border, lay the beckoning land, Tibet. What she most wanted was what was most forbidden her—to travel in that country proper. It would always be possible to return to Europe, but now might be the only chance to do the impossible, it lying so nearby at hand. Her apprenticeship done, Alexandra decided to dare a "triple journey": into a forbidden geography, a strange religion, and, perhaps the deepest mystery of all, herself.

THE DOOR TO TIBET was doubly sealed against foreigners, first by the Tibetans from the inside and then from the outside by the British authorities, wary of other nations' influence. When Alexandra had earlier complained to a Tibetan lama that his country was closed to her, he responded, "Ridiculous." An animal could slip over its immense border, and was not a human being cleverer than a cat? What had she to lose? She was leaving Lachen, and suppose she were caught and expelled after entering Tibet—she would have at least tasted the forbidden dish. Be daring, she encouraged herself, as from Lachen she headed toward the nearby Sikkim-Tibetan border and the *terra incognita* beyond.

Trespassing the unmarked boundary, Alexandra obtained a preview of Tibet, and it enchanted her beyond measure. The Tibetan monks she now met were more refined than those in Sikkim, and the monasteries were great religious universities, veritable palaces of learning. Her 1915 excursion into Tibet was brief, confined to the border areas, but she nonetheless had to pinch herself that it was really happening. "In a few minutes," she half thought, "I shall wake up in a real bed, in some country not haunted by genii nor by 'incarnated Lamas' wrapped in shimmering silk. A country where men wear ugly dark coats and the horses do not carry silver inlaid saddles on golden-yellow cloths." The Panchen Lama invited her to become "his permanent guest" in that enticing world, but Alexandra realized he lacked the power to make good his hospitality. She convinced herself that her luggage, notes, and collection of photo negatives left behind needed rescuing. In fact she was not ready to plunge into such demanding and unknown terrain: "How great was the mental transformation necessary to enable me to become a joyful tramp in the wilds of Tibet," she declared years later, after she had made that transformation. So she returned to Sikkim, where the British authorities were waiting for her. For her unauthorized trespassing, they gave her fourteen days to quit Sikkim with orders to return nevermore.

Alexandra fumed, this was not England, they had no right to issue such orders. How better slap the face of absurd British authority, she decided then, and demonstrate the worthlessness of their edicts than one day for her to parade boldly through the streets of Lhasa? One day. With Tibet and Sikkim both now closed to her, she deliberated returning to Europe, which for a year she had been promising Philippe to do.

"You will think the best thing [for me] to do would be to stop my Asiatic peregrinations and rejoin you," she wrote Philippe, who was financially supporting her in a life he objected to. Her letters to him invariably professed undying affection, and invariably postponed acting upon it. After posting this letter to him, she boarded a ship in Calcutta, but one going in the opposite direction. She had decided to tour the Buddhist countries Burma, Japan, and Korea. By October 1917 she had reached Peking, which opened up a backdoor route to Tibet (and one this time with no British roadblocks in the way).

Finally on the road to Tibet, she lived an adventure story such as boys used to thrill to read in the safety of their bedrooms. Only she was a fifty-year-old woman enacting such a story amid dangers quite real. Civil wars were raging across China, and Alexandra might bed down at an inn, only to wake the next morning to find the courtyard filled with decapitated human heads on spikes. When she camped, she stretched a rope across her tent entrance, and with the gun kept under her nightgown shooed away the robbers who tripped over it. Barely five feet in stature, she would separate the brawling men in her party using her whip. Seven months and two thousand miles of such travels brought her to the Chinese-Tibetan frontier. Her comment on this impossible, exhausting trek: "There is no more effective fountain of youth."

Just across the Chinese-Tibetan frontier was the legendary monastery of Kumbum. In entering Kumbum, she stepped into a gigantic white-washed gold-roofed beehive where three thousand maroon-clad monks buzzed through its corridors and alleyways. Alexandra would spend the next three years "in the lulling calm of this monastic citadel," although it can seem surprising that she managed to spend three days there. Kumbum was a monastery and she was a woman. But her great age (fifty-plus years) neutralized her gender, her Buddhist learning canceled out her for-eignness, and her having known both the Dalai Lama and the Panchen Lama did the rest. Those years were consumed in her studying and trans-lating ancient Buddhist texts, in meditation retreats, and for diversions going on "little excursions." She described one such jaunt in a letter to Philippe: "I walked forty-four days, crossed a dozen peaks with snow up to my knees, slept in icy caves like a prehistoric woman, without food, almost barefoot, the soles of my moccasins being worn out by the rocks in the road." On outings nearer the monastery, she wore the golden vest inlaid with silver that the Panchen Lama had given her, and the sick begged her to heal them, others besieged her to foretell their future, and almost everyone prostrated before her.

Back in North Africa, Philippe rubbed his eyes as he read her letters: Was this the flirtatious little woman he had married? He had observed, after their marriage, his wife outstretched languid on her divan, suffering one undiagnosed malady after another, fretting her life was over. Now, a decade later, she suddenly possessed the vigor of a teenager. What bargain with Lucifer, he wondered, had produced this transformation?

Outwardly, when Alexandra wasn't hunched over her translations, she might be seen sitting cross-legged, following her breath, and mastering practices intended to reinvigorate the body. Inwardly, she learned to quiet the field of perception, in meditational exercises meant to "stabilize" her mind, so that even hardships and unpleasantness wash through it without leaving much after-trace. But Alexandra's main tutorial at Kumbum, if reduced to a phrase, taught her the surprising fluidity of identity. A few years before Alexandra arrived at Kumbum, for example, a great lama had died and the steward of his estates usurped his wealth for himself. One day outside Kumbum the steward was taking snuff from the old lama's jade snuffbox, when a little boy demanded, "Why do you use my box? Give it back to me at once!" Was the boy the old lama's reincarnation? Alexandra was present when the child was led into the old lama's quarters, where he knew passages that had been since sealed off and could name objects stowed away so long ago no one else remembered them. Such phenomena made her wonder about the narrowness and limitations often assumed about the "self." Ordinarily, people have a certain self-image—the way after her marriage she saw herself as a finished woman— an image that often requires a lot of psychological maintenance. But phenomena like the boy-lama reincarnation made her suspect that we are a nexus of subtly interconnected forces that are as much ourselves as the limited, idealized self-image that we have set up on a pedestal.

As her sense of "I," her self-centeredness, became lighter, Alexandra felt more leeway in her responses to what happened to her. Such malleability was what the great lamas at Kumbum had been urging: She must take the "bad" that came her way—sickness, hardship, misfortune, mistreatment—and cease labeling it agreeable or disagreeable but see each as something valuable whose value was momentarily obscured. Had Alexandra not taken this lesson to heart, she could never have made her later journey to Lhasa; a change in outlook and identity was her boot camp wherein she trained to march where no Western woman had gone before.

"Objectively," she was now a woman in her mid-fifties, incapable of such a journey. "Realistically," the obstacles she would encounter on the way were so formidable, she could have spared herself the trouble and jumped off a cliff. Instead Alexandra regarded the difficulties involved as small hurdles that make the race more interesting, part of the gaiety of the voyage. In *My Journey to Lhasa* (1927) her heedlessness comes off as a Parisienne's insouciance, but that nonchalance masked a mind and body trained in the Himalayas to withstand the hazards of fortune with cool neutrality.

All those months and years at Kumbum, during that tranquil and happy period, Lhasa was never long absent from her thoughts. On the surface, Alexandra declared herself content to stay in Kumbum's monastic calm for the next thousand years, but, really, three years was pressing it. Funds from Philippe could reach Tibet only with difficulty, when at all, and it was after all a monastery, to which she as the female of the species could never fully belong. In 1923, physically hardened, emotionally steeled, grown more visionary, she resurrected her vow to show the British what a Frenchwoman could do, and to show mankind what a woman was made of. If a Westerner was barred from the roads to Lhasa, she would disguise herself as a Tibetan. If a caravan and supplies would call attention to herself, she would avoid main-traveled routes and travel with a single companion (her young protégé-servant, Yongden, who she later adopted as her son). "I cannot imagine any danger I could not successfully circumvent by my wits alone," she declared, hardly unaware that well-equipped expeditions, Sven Heden's or Prince Henri d'Orleans's, had failed to reach Lhasa, and most explorers, such as Dutreuil de Rhins or Louis Dupont, had simply perished on unmarked routes, the wind as their gravestone. Alexandra was confident and jaunty—though not so confident as to overlook composing a farewell letter to the world (posted c/o Philippe):

Tell yourselves they [i.e., she, along with Yongden] are mad. But whatever you may think, you have to admire their courage. If it happens that their strength fails them and they don't return from their adventure, keep in your mind a miniature portrait of these explorers who tried something their glorious confreres, with famous names, didn't have the heart to undertake.

But don't worry, things will go well. It's a long walk, that's all.

A LONG WALK, *c'est tout.* The only certainty about her walk is that it could not be made. *My Journey to Lhasa,* for all its gaiety and charm, is a catalogue of ways to die: starvation, freezing, bandits, accidents, no medical help, hopelessly lost, wild beasts, etc. What made their trek to Lhasa sheer suicide was the need to avoid established (i.e., relatively safe) routes and populated areas (i.e., sources of food and aid), which would have led to their detection and expulsion. To survive at all, Alexandra and Yongden needed to be a witch and wizard, which they often pretended to be—in order to frighten brigands off or to scare food out of the miserly as well as to make people practice better compassion and hygiene. Since they could take no retainers or supplies, they usually posed as *arjopas,* or beggar pilgrims, Yongden passing for a poor lama (which he in fact was) and Alexandra as his feeble-witted mother who was too stupid to be bothered with questioning. They had chosen that pose by necessity, but "Why should I not confess it?" she wrote, "the absolute freedom of the *arjopa* . . . free from the care of servants, horses, luggage, sleeping each night where he pleases, attracted me greatly. . . . I deem it to be the most blessed existence one can dream of." Were she expelled from Tibet, Alexandra claimed her plight would be worse than Eve's banished from Eden. Eve had already explored all paradise's pleasures, "but I, her little great-granddaughter, although I had wandered for years in my fairyland, I was far from having exhausted its interests."

After six bruising months of unmitigated ordeal, as she surmounted the last mountain pass descending into Lhasa, Alexandra yelled the traditional Tibetan cry of victory, "*Lha gyalo!*" ("The gods have won!") Anyone who so desires can still join her on her thousand and one adventures, recorded in *My Journey to Lhasa,* which she wrote in English (an American publisher offered the biggest advance). Not the least of the book's charms is how lightheartedly she recounts her frozen ordeals and icicle-draped tortures as part of a "Parisian joke to play on those who tried to stop me." In reality, after she reached Lhasa, when she rubbed her body, she felt only a thin layer of skin barely covering her skeleton. As she stopped taking the stimulants, e.g., homeopathic strychnine, that had allowed this fifty-six-year-old woman to accomplish her march, fever and pains ravaged her. She confessed to Philippe that her excursion had been "pure madness for a woman my age." "If I were offered a million to begin the adventure over again, under the same conditions, I would refuse it." In her published work Alexandra appears invariably amused and intrepid; in her private correspondence she gives a truer picture of what a hero is: someone who in the aftermath does not swagger or gloat but licks her wounds, half puzzled that it really happened. Yet even as one journey, across the unknown landscapes of Tibet, was ending, another journey—that of transposing that country's unknown culture and religion ("a world still more amazing than the landscapes I had beheld") to paper, to understanding—was just beginning.

Alexandra's travels had not taken her merely through geography; they were also a voyage through an unexplored metaphysics. For her to ship her tales of travel back to Europe, she had to create a new understanding of religion in which to ship them. Specifically, if she was to write anything other than an adventure story, she needed to accomplish three literary tasks.

(1) She had to describe Tibet. Western literature has not lacked idealized "others," from Voltaire's Chinaman and Montesquieu's Persian to Samuel Johnson's wise Abyssinian, but these were European puppets, Western inspirational figures dressed in exotic costume. By contrast, Alexandra had to make Tibet a creditable country (like France or Sweden), not some cardboard stage set for a morality play. And indeed, the Tibet that emerges from her dozen books overflows with an earthy, almost Shakespearian cornucopia of very human virtues and foibles. The Tibetans one

encounters in her pages are, above all, sturdy, good-humored, and sensible, as though the moral to her tale was: If you plan to peer mystically into the clouds, plant both feet firmly on the ground first.

(2) She had to establish herself as a creditable witness whom the reader can trust. To be a good travel writer, a writer must first be good company, somebody you want to go roaming with. Alexandra is a good companion for the trip—levelheaded, humorous, so resourceful she enjoys even the obstacles, with a healthy appetite for whatever may lie around the next turn. She does not rank among the first tier of travel writers, however. If she lacked the comedic touch by which Mark Twain, Evelyn Waugh, and Redmond O'Hanlon convert foreign countries into a delightful Zany Fair, she possibly had something more pressing to write than comedy. If she could not paint a grand social canvas the way Wilfred Thesiger, Michael Asher, and Peter Goullart do, her task was in some ways more challenging than theirs.

She needed to delineate a country outwardly and inwardly; she had to bring to life not simply its geo-historico-eco-sociological conditions but also its "spiritual psychology." Travelers like Madame Blavatsky or Paul Brunton who explore the spiritual or mystical often fall down a rabbit hole, never to be seen by the respectable again. Alexandra's job was to convert magic into mundane explanations, into natural, reproducible phenomena. She wrote critically of reincarnated lamas who misused their power, observing that the rigors of rebirth had evidently exhausted all their holiness. She also brought the legendary flying monks of Tibet down to earth. On the three occasions Alexandra witnessed these monks, they were not flying at all but speeding by gracefully, effortlessly, their feet bouncing lightly off the ground rather the way rubber balls do. She then sought out the centers where the monks trained in the muscle control that allowed this believable marvel (as opposed to an unbelievable one). Western modernity is also a magic show—people flying through the air, living underwater, seeing events thousands of miles distant, conversing with friends an ocean away—except we know the planes, submarines, televisions, telephones, etc., that make it credible. The Tibet that emerges from Alexandra's pages does extend the perimeters of the possible, but she reveals the mechanisms that make that enlargement plausible.

(3) Finally she needed to make Tibet not merely a geographical collection of quaint customs and exotic lore, but a country of the mind as well. For centuries Europeans had encountered native peoples, from the Aztecs to the Zulus, each with their own beliefs, which promptly got deposited into the waste receptacle reserved for backward superstitions. Alexandra had to show that Tibetan Buddhism was relevant for modern Westerners, maybe strange or alien but potentially as meaningful to them as their own nightly dreams.

Could she make, for example, the Tibetan practice of chöd appear anything other than insanity to Western readers? Chöd is done alone in graveyards or charnel grounds at night, in which the practitioner so fervently offers up his body as a feast to imaginary demons that they become real and they (or his imagination of them) can actually destroy them. If she could make such a bizarre practice sensible to her readers, then Tibetan Buddhism might clear the hurdle and take its place among the useful arts and activities of humankind.

Alexandra first encountered chöd when she was camping in central Tibet, and daily there passed near her encampment a young lama so sickly and emaciated that she tried to press medicines on him. No medicines, he yelled, and scurried away like a frightened rabbit. Some nights later out wandering, she spied near a makeshift burial ground the young lama, self-hypnotized or otherwise in a trance, writhing in agony, imagining fiends were devouring him. Seeing Alexandra, he screeched, "Come, angry one, feed on my flesh!" mistaking her for another monster in the ghoulish crew. "Drink my blood!" Obviously he was out of his mind. She determined to find the young lama's guru, so he could end this practice before the practice ended his young disciple.

At the teacher's dwelling place, a cave not far away, she reported his disciple's desperate condition: "He really appears to feel himself being eaten alive." As Alexandra listened to the holy man's explanation, *chöd* began to make sense and have a purpose. The explanation: In performing *chöd* the practitioner offers the parts of his body as a meal not only to evil spirits but to everyone he owes a karmic debt to, and in doing so, this voluntary self-mortification supersedes the natural order. We think our instinct for self-preservation protects us, the old man told her, but it actually increases our suffering by isolating us in a self-centered armor, by making an "I" in opposition to "them." By summoning up what we most dread and offering what we most cherish, he told her, we cut the double bondage to our bodies and our egos. "Methods to reach *tharpa* [supreme liberation] are many," he concluded. "You may follow a method less coarse than that suited to the man whom you pity, but if it is effective, it will be equally hard."

Liberal European thought of that period urged everyone to pursue his rational self-interest, which Adam Smith's "invisible hand" or Jeremy Bentham's democratic calculus would somehow reconcile into the public good. After learning about *chöd* or the *tonglin* practice of assuming another's pain, Alexandra thought "rational self-interest" an oxymoron. The compassion in those Tibetan practices enlarged one's humanity beyond instinctual self-centeredness, into something interconnected and more luminous. Could she import that exotic Buddhist understanding of a larger human world back to Europe, she reckoned, she would secure Tibet a place in modernity. In the middle of Tibet, five thousands miles from Europe, Alexandra had her vision of what she must do when she returned, and a sense of mission grew upon her.

ALEXANDRA HAD SPENT fourteen years in Asia, she had entered forbidden Lhasa, and done what no other white woman had ever done, and it was now time to introduce the lessons she had learned to Europe. She had entered Tibet on foot and empty-handed, carrying no provisions that would attract attention, but she left with a caravan of horses loaded with rare books. To the monotonous plop-plop of the horses' hooves, all during the slow route back, she mused on what her role should be, once in Europe. She determined to avoid all Madame Blavatsky–like claims boasting occult prowess; she would barely allude to having experimented with *tummo* or *chöd* personally. Indeed, because she was so reticent about herself, Alexandra David-Neel is far less well-known today than equivalent explorers like Sir Richard Burton. (There is no and probably never will be an adequate biography of her because, simply, all intimate materials are lacking: Her companions in Asia like the Gomchen and Yongden left no memoirs, and her thousands of letters to Philippe are mainly a begging for money, disguised as affection. Some plays and novels have attempted to evoke her, the best being perhaps the German novelist Antje Windgassen's *Alexandra David-Neel: Auf der Suche nach dem Licht* [1996], but these too cannot fill in her personal lacunae.)

When Alexandra had first traveled in the Himalayas, suddenly rejuvenated, she thought that could she live to a hundred and write her books, she would never be bored. Now, as she sailed for Europe in 1925, she understood that those books waiting to be written must undertake two impersonal, important projects. First, she would supply an accurate picture of the religious culture of Tibetan Buddhism. Second, she would disregard the Gomchen's warning and provide instructions on how actually to practice it. She would let the seekers and the serious and the merely curious know there were undreamed-of ways of being spiritual in the world.

Arriving back in Europe, she decided not to cohabit with Philippe; they had lived too long apart. She settled instead at Digne in southern France and commenced to write. And wrote. And wrote. Her books belong to that rare category of writings that have effected a change in the world. When she first traveled to Asia, the few people who had heard of Tibet associated it with flying monks and copulating deities. By the time Alexandra died, the superstitions were cleared away, replaced by knowledge of a land where conditions had been harsh but the people generally happy, and its religion was reckoned one of the pinnacles of human culture. Other writers (Sir Charles Bell, W. Y. Evans-Wenz, John Blofeld, the German Lama Govinda, Robert Ekvall, Peter Goullart, Giuseppi Tucci, Rolf Stein, Hugh Richardson, David Snellgrove) contributed to this changed perception, but principally it was Alexandra David-Neel who had put the real Tibet and its religion on the map. She was not a fine stylist; her writings cannot be read for aesthetic pleasure, but they have outlasted many literary books that can be. Even today, here and there, a person after reading her best work, *Magic and Mystery in Tibet*, becomes a Tibetan Buddhist. The Tibet she wrote about is now dead and the Chinese would wish its memory obliterated, but her book erected a monument in which it lives on still.

After her books made her famous, letters postmarked the world over began pouring into Digne, begging her to use her psychic wizardry to cure an illness, or make a business enterprise succeed, or to kill the letterwriter's spouse. She might open her front door to find a supplicant dropping to his knees and kissing her feet, or else a woman pleading to live as a renunciant in a tent in the Great Sage's yard. Like some unearthly spirit Alexandra David-Neel lived on and on, outlasting everyone, and everything fell away but the writing. Finally at a certain moment she scribbled, "I can write no more" and put away her pen. That was eighteen days before she died, a few weeks short of her hundred and first birthday. Some years earlier the famous Jesuit theologian Teilhard de Chardin had visited Digne and reproved her for not believing in miracles. "No," Alexandra had answered, "I make them."

Book

II

WORLDS IN
COLLISION

chapter II

Everyone Was Dear

SO LONG AS THEIR high mountains kept them isolated, the Tibetans' attitude toward Westerners—which was generally indifferent and dismissive—remained an academic matter. But after 1959, an academic matter turned into one of life and death. No longer could anyone like Alexandra David-Neel steal across the border and report back about Tibet's religion to the outside world. The Chinese communists were in fact determined that there would be little religion left to report. During the 1960s, within the country the communists leveled monasteries and forbade the teaching of Buddhism, and outside it the world's power brokers forgot Tibet in favor of China's potential billion-customer-per-item market: Thus was Tibet whited off the global map. The fate of its religion was, under such circumstances, not hard to predict. Most of the globe's once-vast store of languages and faiths are now extinct. As time and time before, the first generation of exiles would struggle to uphold the old traditions;

the second would waver between sentimental relics and modern careers; afterwards, Tibetan Buddhism would wither into a memory and, eventually, not even a memory. The "last ancient civilization," as it was called, was under a death sentence.

The fate of Tibetan Buddhism, such as it was, was left in the hands of the few traumatized lamas who managed to stumble into exile. So ignorant were they of the world that many of them had grown to adulthood never even having heard of America. Perhaps it was just as well that those monks had little interest in foreigners and no interest in proselytizing them. Backward, from another century if not another planet, what could they offer a modern citizen of the West?

Let us imagine a hypothetical situation: The year is 1959, and a lama has just escaped from Tibet. Out of curiosity you arrange to meet him, to see whether Tibetan Buddhism has anything of value to offer you. Well, he might not be able to keep the appointment, never having seen a car, bus, train, or plane before. You send him the money to make the travel arrangements, but having grown up in a monastery, he won't have had much experience handling money. As for any decision the travel requires, in his monastic routines he may never have had to make a decision. Can he counsel you professionally? Unless you're a farmer or small trader, he will never have encountered your occupation. Can he advise you in private matters, considering in the monastery he scarcely encountered families or women? Can he counsel you in worldly affairs, since he has no experience of the politics of the workplace, or any other politics, or the social sciences, or economics, or . . . practically anything else you care to name. With all this going against the poor lama, why even bring up the linguistic barriers? Such were Tibetan Buddhism's ambassadors to the modern world, upon whom rested its last hopes before oblivion.

But Tibetan Buddhism did not fade away in the night, as the Chinese communists (and Western secularists) expected. After 1959 lamas like the one described above were suddenly thrown into the West's dizzying hypermodernity, barely speaking English, not comprehending secular ways, carrying only the robes on their backs and their bizarre faith with them. Seemingly doomed to fail, within a dozen or so years they were successfully teaching Westerners in droves, and in doing so, they rewrote notions of what sacredness and piety are.

One lama in particular—known simply as Lama Yeshe—attracted Westerners by his *joie de vivre*, his emotional warmth, his ability to connect; indeed many people thought they had never seen someone so vibrant. Whatever it was that he was exuding, the young Westerners who met him wanted to acquire it themselves. Strangely enough, Yeshe was happy to teach them. (Teaching Westerners was all but taboo to Tibetans then; Yeshe's sister volunteered to support him, if only he would stop such a shameful activity.)

Lama Yeshe managed to surmount the language barrier and other obstacles, too. He strung together every English word he learned and added body language and pantomime, to talk with his new young friends from the West. Since his English was picked up from hippies in India, out of his mouth came the most improbable sentences: "Dharma is like American bed—everybody can join in. . . . Change misery into blissful chocolate. . . . Now you going to say, 'He crazy, he Himalayan gorilla,' but I say, 'You check it out.' . . . Question-answers?" He called everyone "dear," and indeed he made each of his students feel that he or she was dear to him. He was always saying *thank you*, as though whatever happened gave him some reason to be grateful. Once he was driving in California—his car zigzagging down the road as he took in the scenery, oblivious to uninteresting things like stop signs—when a state trooper pulled him over. As the policeman wrote out the ticket, Lama Yeshe kept repeating, "Thank you, thank you, so kind." (Fortunately, he did not call the trooper *dear*.)

As for the *Tibetan* in Tibetan Buddhism—that cultural Himalayan superstructure that has so perplexed foreigners—Yeshe simply sawed it off. Differences between East and West he thought were a matter of taste, and he demonstrated that even a lama from Tibet can have a taste for the West. Tibetans are nearly addicted to their salty butter tea, but Lama Yeshe preferred Earl Grey. For the incense used in Tibetan religious rituals he substituted bottled spray cologne—so much easier, and, besides, he liked the aroma better. He asked some Italian followers, "Can't you find a way to insert into your rituals, you know, spaghetti?" During the rituals he conducted, he would suggest the participants hold each other's hands, which had never been done in Tibet (and predated the New Age fad of eternally hugging). Hitherto Tibetans had tended to view Caucasians as idiot savants, preternaturally good at, say, constructing engines but otherwise dumb to the subtleties of the spirit. But Yeshe observed that the Europeans and Americans he met had attended school since age five or six, and their education and skills, though different in content, rivaled any rinpoche's.

In Buddhism (and Asian religions in general) the stumbling block for most Westerners is the guru—that mysterious being to whom the seeker must surrender his life. Yeshe dismissed exalted guru worship as unnecessary; if his students wanted an all-wise sage, he referred them to their own inner nature, which differed not a jot from the Buddha's. Instead of an off-putting authority figure, young Westerners discovered in Lama Yeshe a lovable man who was curious about them, who wanted only to help them. One young man (Jonathan Landaw, later a writer on Buddhist subjects) described his first impressions of him:

> The first was that this man—whose name I did not know—would be a completely trustworthy guide along the path to spiritual development. The second impression . . . [was that] this monk was certainly no distant, austere and unreachable being but rather had all the earthly qualities I treasured. This came as a relief to me since I had harbored a suspicion that spiritual evolvement according to Buddhism might entail emotional coldness. This monk's warm and humorous presence refuted this fear immediately and completely.

As ever more Westerners met Lama Yeshe and other lamas like him, a doomed faith of the past came to seem, just possibly, a plausible religion for the future. By the year 2000, Yeshe and his students had alone founded one hundred and thirty centers in twenty-nine countries. Who was this Tibetan man, who grew up never seeing a white person and then suddenly was teaching thousands of them?

BIOGRAPHICAL BACKGROUND: Thubten Yeshe was born in Tol-ung (or "Upper Village") near Lhasa in May 1935, into a family of modest farmers. Practically from infancy Yeshe pestered his parents to let him become a monk—as common in Tibet as an American boy wanting to become a baseball player. Little Yeshe achieved his ambition early, entering a monastery at age five. In ordinary times his whole biography might have reduced to a sentence: "He entered a monastery and prayed for sixty or seventy years." But Tibet soon plunged into unordinary times, and by 1959, after passing his youth peacefully in the monastery, Lama Yeshe realized that if he wanted to keep practicing (and keep living), he had to flee his homeland. One Western disciple later described his resolve to escape as "the first decision of his adult life."

Actually, Lama Yeshe had made an important decision earlier. He refused to obtain his *geshe* degree (which might be likened to a Ph.D. in Tibetan Buddhism). Many years later, when pressed why he had shunned this prestigious degree, he would laugh: "And be *Geshe* Yeshe!" Yeshe told the uncle who offered to finance his studies that the money would be better spent on feeding the poor, and as for himself, he would rather go on a three-year retreat. His unspoken reason at the time had to do with the fact that Tibetan Buddhism—far more than Christianity or Judaism—is taught through a graduated, systematic course of studies, in some ways resembling a college education in the United States. Becoming a *geshe* would have committed Yeshe to a prescribed method of teaching and a formal relationship to his students. Yeshe endorsed this formal approach, for others, but he wanted to teach more spontaneously, feeling his rapport with the particular student and adapting himself to whatever the particular situation demanded. Thus almost accidentally Lama Yeshe prepared himself for the time when, shaken up and spat out of Tibet, he would have to teach in undreamed-of and unconventional situations.

By 1959 the question was not whether Yeshe should become a *geshe*, however, but whether he could remain alive at all. Knowing he had no choice but to flee, he set out on foot over the Himalayas on a route hazardous under the best of conditions. Traveling under the worst of conditions, in winter, without provisions, avoiding known roads (rather like Alexandra David-Neel earlier, but in the opposite direction), made the route of the escaping lamas a trail of tears. Many simply perished, and when, exhausted and debilitated, Yeshe arrived in India, he wondered whether he should have died too. Perhaps he had, and gone to hell. The excruciating heat made him feel he was living inside an oven. The unfamiliar food caused him nausea, and he suffered stomach illness for months on end, as dysentery ravaged the refugee camps. (The wretchedness of these camps is evoked in Dervla Murphy's *Tibetan Foothold* [1966], where despite the mortal misery, the author noted, the Tibetans' "consideration for and politeness to each other positively makes me feel I've moved to another planet.") Monastic discipline had trained the monks in stoicism, and soon in those primitive camps they resurrected their old regimen of classes, studies, debates. Lama Yeshe often arrived late to the morning class, confessing sheepishly to having shamefully overslept. He had overslept (though this he confided to no one) because he stayed up most of the night trying to teach himself English. When the other monks found out, they ridiculed him. If he wanted to learn another language, he should be practical and learn Hindi.

No lamas would need English, since they did not socialize with, much less teach, Westerners. And so it might have remained, had not a rich, spoiled American decided to act upon a whim. The gorgeous Zina Rachevsky, the daughter of a Romanov prince and an American heiress, had been making headlines since she was a teenager by acting on her whims, which often included sex and drugs. Unsatisfied by *la dolce vita*, she decided to get instructions from a wonder-working Himalayan seer such as she had read about in Anagarika Govinda's biography, *The Way of the White Clouds*, which had just been published (and was the first popular presentation of Tibetan Buddhism since Alexandra David-Neel). Zina jetted to Darjeeling in north India, where the Tibetans could not understand her language or what she was asking for, so they pointed her to Lama Yeshe, who knew some phrases in English. That's my man, she thought, and without waiting for an introduction, she burst into his room and demanded, "Teach me Buddhism." It would hardly have astonished Yeshe more had a three-horned demon materialized out of the air and commanded, "Let's do a jig!" One does not teach the precious dharma to Westerners, and as for women, particularly women loaded down with jewelry and makeup, they are a temptation better avoided.

A Tibetan lama takes a vow, however, to put his own wishes last and the well-being of all other sentient creatures first. Lama Yeshe fended Zina off with a small teaching, but to his surprise she returned the next day. And the next and the next. Soon the friends she made joined her for instruction, and Zina decided her lama should have a center of his own. She chose Sri Lanka, a Buddhist country, but when they could not obtain visas, she settled for a partially Buddhist land. She bought the king's astronomer's house at Kopan, on a hill outside Katmandu in Nepal. Soon on Katmandu's street corners one hippie would tell another, "Say, this Tibetan monk's talking at two on Sunday. Speaks English. Sort of." In 1969 Lama Yeshe began giving monthlong courses at Kopan, but even by the third year only fifty-four people attended. After that, however, the multiplication factor came into play. One hundred and twenty students enrolled in the fourth year; two hundred in the fifth. Those students felt that they had found a better way, but once they returned to their old routines back in Europe and America, their newly gained awareness and tranquillity began to slip away. They wrote letters begging Lama Yeshe to come visit and teach them in their homelands. In 1974 he flew to America—a trip that left in its wake a book (*Wisdom Energy*), a Tibetan center (in Nashville, Indiana), and a publishing house (Wisdom Publications). The next year he traveled the world for eight and half months, and like mushrooms sprouting, wherever he stepped a center afterwards sprang up. On his personal altar, amid traditional holy objects, he placed a toy airplane, to symbolize how he could reach and teach so many students. If a toy makes an improbable sacred object, Tibetan centers materializing overnight from Australia to America were more improbable by far.

As improbable as the following riddle: Who is happier, Person A. or Person B.?

A. has	B. has
plenty of money	no money
supportive family	no family
a home	no home
a country.	no country.

Person A. was, of course, Zina Rachevsky, and Person B., Lama Yeshe. She, who had everything, was applying to him, who had nothing, to remedy the deficiencies of her situation. Zina became a Buddhist nun, her imperious manners dropped away, everyone commented on her radiance, and she died, though in significant pain, sitting in the lotus meditative pose. How did Lama Yeshe so turn her life around?

THE DIFFICULTY WITH DESCRIBING what Lama Yeshe taught is he never seemed to teach the same thing twice. To one person (Chris Kolb) he taught straight off the most advanced visualization and breathing exercises; the next (Paula de Wijs) he told to think of everything she had ever done, starting backwards from that day. For each person, a different technique—and each one seemed right for that particular person. Yet the fireworks of his infinite variety were all lit by the same match, or rather by three matches.

(1) Buddhism, as Lama Yeshe taught it, is not a philosophy, it's not metaphysics; it's not even a religion. Buddhism, he reiterated, is a study of

your own mind; it is a way of coming to terms with yourself. Most Westerners who sought him out were at least somewhat dissatisfied with Christianity or Judaism. It was a relief to them that they had not entered another religious temple of *Thou must* and *Thou shalt*, but instead only entered the labyrinth of themselves. One American told Lama Yeshe that his father would disapprove of his becoming a Buddhist, because his father was a hard scientist. Lama Yeshe slapped his hands together (in Tibetan debate style) and exclaimed, "Buddhism is a science! A science of the mind."

(2) Happiness, he taught, comes from within. Possibly most people would agree with that statement, even as they search for a lover, a better job, or a nicer home to import it from outside. "Hippies come to Kopan and sigh at sunset, 'So beautiful!' " "Boooteefuhl," Yeshe pronounced it, and then he would surprise his students: "Lama hates the sunset." His point was that if we become too dependent or attached to outward things, no matter how lovely seeming, they will ultimately pass away and disappoint us. Far from encouraging pessimism, the impermanence of outward things means that we can enjoy nearly every pleasure, so long as we don't become possessive about it. Bliss is not only permitted; it is the preferred state, he taught, because it is nearer to our original nature. The hippies he met, in raging against their parents or society, often warped their blissful original nature by simultaneously pitying themselves. He encouraged them to dress better and everyone to see himself as beautiful.

(3) The world is not exactly the way our senses report: "Out there" is not quite what you think it is. Lama Yeshe taught about what psychologists call *projection*—that we project our emotional preconceptions and then mistake those distortions of people and events for their reality. How can we go beyond distorted appearances and touch ultimate reality? Lama Yeshe's wild recommendation was one no minister, rabbi, or iman in the West would have then likely dared offer: "Identify yourself strongly as a deity." "The purpose of seeing yourself as a deity," he explained, "is to transcend mundane appearances and actions." Most Westerners who

attempt such a visualization will think they are merely playacting, but tantric Buddhism believes every human being is fundamentally divine and pure.

Instead of pretending you are a deity, it is truer to think, Yeshe said, that in everyday circumstances a deity is cleverly passing himself off as you. In tantra, all formulations and appearances are ultimately illusory, including this one, but at least this one—seeing yourself as having the good qualities of a deity will dispel your neuroses and bring you closer to the nature of what is—is closer than the projecting, self-pitying mind can ever come.

How quickly, in three easy steps, Lama Yeshe's teaching progressed from the familiarity of our own minds to a strange, heightened reality a god would recognize sooner than would a mortal. As for what made those teachings so potent, so exhilarating, it was not only what he taught, of course, but how he taught. After all, those lessons were what Tibetan Buddhism had preached all along when Westerners had dismissed it as black magic and superstition. But Lama Yeshe became the first Tibetan determined to make the teachings appealing to those Caucasians once thought to be incapable of spiritual understanding. "I couldn't change the Buddha's teaching," he said, "but I had to find a way to get it across." Admittedly, he began so ignorant of Americans that they might as well have been Martians, but by ceaseless probing, he converted the strange into the cozily familiar:

I daren't have any fixed plan. Each time I talk to people I have to check what background they're coming from. Are they religious, or nonreligious, scientific, nonscientific, philosophical, or just ordinary? Then I try to talk according to their language. It takes a lot of energy.

It did require a lot of energy and a lot of work. To understand a new worldview Yeshe plunged, sometimes in disguise, into nightclubs, beaches, shopping malls, strip joints, gay day parades, etc. (Later he called people who were wasting their time "nightclubbers.") No subject was taboo. After a lecture in Amsterdam, his embarrassed hosts tried to hurry him along as they passed a sex shop, but he insisted on going in and asking what each item was for, while they hemmed and hawed. Incredibly quickly, he became comfortable enough with Westerners that they could be comfortable studying an alien religion with him. At Kopan he observed his students feeling homesick, so he asked them to describe their favorite breakfasts back home. A few days later they awoke to find a tent set up in the yard, with Lama Yeshe dishing up the various breakfasts described— cooked eggs or museli or bread with marmalade or cheese—something of a feat since he hadn't tasted those foods before and the exact ingredients were not available in Katmandu. His students' stomachs (and cultures) were fine, he felt, and could stay just as they were. What needed changing, what is almost impossible to change, was the mind; what needed challenging was all one's assumptions; and how strange for his young European and American pupils that the maestro of change and challenge was this man who only a few years before had no idea how their minds operated and what their assumptions were.

What worked in Lama Yeshe's favor was that the moment seemed propitious for a new kind of religious teacher. The Judeo-Christian tradition had lost its monopoly hold on Westerners' imaginations. From many traditional Christian and Jewish families came sons and daughters for whom its doctrines furnished less consolation and could not shape an explanatory worldview. But the fact that some people cannot believe literally in the Bible or miracles or an omnipotent God does not necessarily mean they do not need or want a religious dimension to their lives. For those who both did and did not want a faith, here was Lama Yeshe sounding a new message—in fact, delivering a religion that could dispense with God and belief too. Can you do the following two things? (1) Breathe in and out? (2) Be kind? Meditation on the breath can alter your connection to your own body and life, and practicing compassion will change your relation to the world. That, in the version of Tibetan Buddhism he taught, just may be enough, or at least enough to begin a new spiritual life.

LAMA YESHE NEVER MEANT his students to accept anything he said on faith, in the abstract. Both his character and his teaching become less abstract in the endless stories his disciples delight to tell about him. The life of Jan Willis, one of Yeshe's first American students, furnishes just such an instructive story.

Today Jan Willis is a professor of Tibetan and Indian religions at Wesleyan College whom *Time* magazine described as "a philosopher with a bold agenda." Back in the 1960s, however, she was one more confused, angry, and idealistic youth. As a young African-American woman having experienced her share of indignity and insult, she drifted into radical politics. In *Dreaming Me* (2001) she tells how she planned to become a Black Panther, until out of the blue she felt a pull in a different direction. The name of that pull was Lama Yeshe.

Wonder-working gurus with their impossible knowledge seemed to Jan Willis to belong to a lost Age of Fable, nothing she ever expected to encounter herself. When traveling in Asia she overheard Lama Yeshe's name spoken, however, and "a sort of warm tingling feeling began at the nape of my neck and then radiated downward and outward to encircle my body. Then," she recalls, "I noticed that the hairs on my skin stood up erect." This was in 1969, when Jan and two friends were on the hippies' version of the earlier Grand Tour. They started off overland across Europe (a trip that began badly in France with a serious auto accident), then on to Mother India, up to Nepal, to Katmandu—a frequent destination then on the seeker's quest. To see this Lama Yeshe whose name generated such electricity in her, she trekked out to Kopan.

And there she met—face-to-face—disappointment. Zina Rachevsky, who treated Lama Yeshe as a personal possession, informed Jan that he was too tired to receive visitors and, no, Zina did not know when he would be available. Dismayed, dejected, Jan began to slink away when a door creaked open and a hand shushed her while beckoning her inside. "Hello!" said a man with a huge grin, whose speech sounded vaguely like English. She heard him say, "I am Lama Yeshe"—what good fortune!—but his next remark dumbfounded her. "Lama is so happy that you have come, especially after . . . you know . . . that bad thing in France." When her astonishment subsided, she promised him, most certainly, she would come again. Waving good-bye to her, he called out, "I had been waiting for you," and Jan wondered if that was something gurus were trained to say.

As she got to know him, Jan was surprised repeatedly at how intuitive Lama Yeshe could be. He would often guess what she was thinking, but the trouble was, much of the time she did not like what she was thinking. Having grown up black during the 1950s, she was bred to feel inferior; but because of her obvious intelligence, her inferiority complex had a compensatory underside of unspoken superiority. In her background black girls were not supposed to be so smart, though, and growing up, whenever she showed her natural intelligence, she was made to feel she was somehow bad or evil.

All the contradictions stewing in her left her ashamed but defiant, angry but helpless. One morning at Kopan, Yeshe emerged from his room carrying his toothbrush and towel, obviously headed to the bathroom, but he stopped, studied Jan, and said, "Living with pride and humility in equal proportion is very difficult, isn't it? Very difficult!" Another time, finding her in a silent rage, he said, "It's good to say to yourself, 'Buddha's mind is angry today.' " This notion that her mind even when furious was somehow the Buddha's mind eased the tension, at least for a few hours. Jan came more and more to appreciate Lama Yeshe, but with her history of hurts, she still did not trust enough to accept him as her guru.

Their teacher-student relationship took a crucial turn the next year, 1970, when Lama Yeshe sent Jan to Dharamsala to study with his own teacher, Geshe Rabten. On her way there she briefly went AWOL, detouring to Benares for a few days of fun, visiting old friends and seeing movies. Upon her arrival in Dharamsala, she learned that Geshe Rabten was in retreat, but since Lama Yeshe had sent her, she judged it permissible to interrupt him. When she did, Geshe Rabten let loose in Tibetan a tirade of angry abuse at her, which the translator finally rendered as "Geshe-la wants to know why you arrived late?" But there were no phone connections then between Nepal and Dharamsala; there was no way Geshe Rabten could know she had dallied along the way. Once she survived his initial tirade, however, she felt in paradise. Geshe Rabten taught her those advanced teachings that demonstrate how clinging to false images of ourselves generates our suffering. She deserved to study with a teacher of Geshe-la's eminence, she believed, because she was such a hardworking and intelligent student. She forgot that she had interrupted his own meditation retreat. She was too caught up in how much she was lessening self-cherishing by studying with this master teacher to be bothered by his possible needs. She was eager, when she returned to Nepal, to show Lama Yeshe exactly how much she had mastered.

But then, at Kopan, the sudden explosion, the inexplicable tirade, happened all over again. Meeting Lama Yeshe again for the first time, she was astonished as he pointed an angry finger at her and let loose a string of angry Tibetan invective that sounded eerily like Geshe Rabten's tirade. Then it dawned upon her what he was doing. She prided herself on the wisdom that she had gained studying with a grand master in Dharamsala, but she had always valued intelligence, wisdom, while undervaluing the compassion that must accompany wisdom to make it worthwhile. Lama Yeshe knew that Jan's pride was the other side of her low self-esteem, and that low self-esteem would not be long in returning. His apparent anger was, in reality, a surprise ambush on this symbiotic complex in which pride disguised itself as humility and humility masked as pride, which had always hampered her. "How painful it must be for that gentle, kind man to feign harsh anger at me," Jan thought, and also, "I knew—from that moment—that I could trust Lama Yeshe to be my teacher and my guide."

Jan and her two friends were the first (and for a while, the only) students in Lama Yeshe's class at Kopan. She returned to the States, but the better part of a decade later was back in Katmandu under quite different auspices. In 1980 she came back to Nepal on a National Endowment for the Humanities fellowship to record the oral histories of prominent Tibetans living there. Lama Yeshe requested her, however, to undertake a different project first—that of translating the stories of the legendary bodhisattvas who had attained enlightenment within a single lifetime. (She agreed; the result was Enlightened Beings [1995].) Lama Yeshe had surprised her in the past, but never so much as when, in the middle of her labors, he asked her, "Don't you want to know what the system these people practiced was like? I mean, don't you want to try it yourself?"

Jan knew that the tests of endurance those saints had suffered were almost superhuman; they were not for the likes of an ordinary person like herself. She answered instantly, "No. Thank you, Lama, but no way!" Her answer perplexed Yeshe. "Why, Daughter, wouldn't you want to try something so wonderful?"

Thinking it over, she realized that she might be passing up the chance of a lifetime—maybe of several lifetimes. Well, why not? The retreat would extend for six weeks in which she would speak to no one, meditate almost the whole day, and perform tantric rituals. As she started making the elaborate preparations necessary, two words of Lama Yeshe haunted her. He asked how many mantras she had already recited, and when she answered, roughly thirty-five thousand, he looked at her in disbelief. "That's all?" His momentary pause made her worry that she was about to run a marathon having done no more than run around the block previously. Yet he remained confident, and his confidence infected her. "I am sure," he promised Jan, "one-hundred-percent sure that you will be able to taste the great bliss. Don't worry, dear. You will."

Although her retreat ended in failure, apparently Jan did briefly experience the great Mahamudra bliss. She demonstrated what it's like, to be an ordinary person on the edge of Enlightenment. Before the retreat could begin, Lama Yeshe had to effect the "mind-to-mind transmission," to work a subtle fundamental shift in her mode of perception. He said almost apologetically to Jan, "Now, I have to do this little thing, and tell you this." He pointed quickly upward, as he leaned forward and whispered, "Mind is like the sky." That was all, but all at once she felt "a vast, blissful calmness. A stillness that was, in its immensity, all of a piece and all peace filled." In her Baptist family, presumably they would have called it grace.

It took her the first few days of the retreat to become accustomed to the absence of talk and conversation, but once Jan did, the silence appeared to heighten her other senses. Especially sight; never before, she felt, had she seen like this. Outside her window, the little blackbirds with yellow beaks perched on the fence, each one stood out as an individual, with his or her own distinctive face, body, and idiosyncrasies, and she saw how each blackbird related to the others. One day, after about two weeks, she vividly saw herself, or she imagined seeing herself—she would have sworn she saw herself—standing on the roof of a nearby house and, what's more, from that roof she could look back and see herself sitting here in her own room. Her normal visual orientation shifted, as though no longer determined solely by eyesight, and her sense of self was no longer bounded by her body. Her sense of being could inhabit anywhere she chose. "It felt as though my mind suddenly became immeasurably vast," she described the sensation. "There was no longer any separation between me and everything else in the universe." The difference between meditation and "ordinary life" vanished, as everything became meditation or rather as everything vivified into a seamless lucidity. My housekeeper must think I've gone nuts, Jan thought, since she was wandering about the house never without an irrepressible smile on her face.

And then the bottom fell out. Her state of elation did not desert her, but her body did. A slight dizziness deepened into nausea, and a few days later the room seemed to be spinning all the time. She could not climb out of bed. Lama Yeshe had gone to Australia, but a telegram she sent to him produced a telegram in return, five words: "Health most important. Stop retreat!" Only years later did Jan discover that she was allergic to the sulfates in liquor, and in accordance with the requirements of a tantric retreat, she had to partake of substances such as alcohol that are normally forbidden. The tablespoon of Nepali *rakshi* swallowed six times a day had worked like rat poison in her system. Someone else might have blamed that Nepali liquor for the failure of the retreat, but like a good Tibetan Jan attributed it to obstacles within herself. (Otherwise, with her heightened awareness, she might have deduced sooner that the *rakshi* was at fault.)

That retreat was one moment in the private tutorial Lama Yeshe gave Jan over the course of many years. For a decade and a half he instructed her in the hardest subject to master—how to have confidence in yourself; he gave her a private seminar in how to come out of self-hiding. She first arrived at Kopan so insecure that she tried to be inconspicuous, and whenever spoken to, she assumed she had done something wrong. Lama Yeshe once made a fist and then spread it out into five fingers and said, "When I say one thing, Jan makes it into five." She apologized, "Is that very wrong?" "No," he answered, "it means you're smart." In the late '70s, after he attended a college class Jan taught, he kept repeating, "I am so proud of you," but indirectly he had been saying the same thing for fifteen years. Somewhere along the way it sank in. When he was already sick, but still wanting to understand the Western mind better, he asked her to teach him European philosophy. She prepared a xeroxed book of readings, "From the Pre-Socratics to Wittgenstein," and they met regularly to discuss it, and this sank in too, that she was now her teacher's teacher. As he lay dying, he kept reading the book, highlighting passages with a yellow marker, and Jan observed, "So it is with the great lamas—they never stop learning." For a young woman who had been yelled at and called evil for being intelligent, Lama Yeshe was the example she had needed.

A decade after Lama Yeshe died, Jan was driving down a highway in Connecticut during an unexpected snowstorm, when her car spun out of control and slammed toward the highway's guardrails—sure instant death. Someone else interviewed for this book lamented that, when thrown and dragged with his foot in the stirrup by a galloping horse, he could not remember his mantra. Under such extreme circumstances, who could? Jan evidently did, for she heard herself scream OM MANI PADME HUM! Just then on the slippery highway her car skidded again, swerving back into the middle lane. During that instant of her brush with death, her one thought was: In all future rebirths may I never be separated from Lama Yeshe. Once safely home, and recovering from the scare, she recalled what had happened, and thought, "Perhaps I am a Buddhist after all."

LAMA YESHE ATTRACTED STUDENTS like Jan Willis in unprecedented numbers, for a good reason: He was doing something unprecedented. Those advanced tantric practices unique to Tibetan Buddhism had always been carefully guarded, passed orally from master to disciple, only after the latter passed through a graduated series of strict initiations. In *The Secret Oral Teachings*, Alexandra David-Neel claimed that tantric practices (such as Jan's Mahamudra retreat) would remain secret even if they were set down in the middle of a highway, because ordinary folks had no interest in them. But Lama Yeshe believed people would not only be interested but also understand them, and so he taught Tibetan tantra to *Westerners* for the first time and on a scale undreamed of. In doing so he showed that Tibetan Buddhism had something to offer besides the good and the true common to all religions.

Some Tibetans denounced Lama Yeshe for selling their religion to tourists at a discount. Western critics offered a different critique: Lamas like Yeshe were derailing religion from its serious purpose. Religion was meant to transport souls from sin to salvation, but Yeshe and his cohorts were merely moving kids from feeling bummed out to feeling groovy, as Tibetan Buddhism joined the New Age feel-good potpourri of the 1970s. If America was in the midst of a "culture of narcissism," as social critics charged, the vow Yeshe asked his students to take seemed to fit in perfectly:

Now, and for the rest of my life, I will enjoy myself as much as possible and try to create a good situation around me by giving to others the best part of my divine qualities and blissful energy. [Italics added]

Great! Do what you please and assume you're pleasing heaven—who wouldn't want to be a Tibetan Buddhist?

But Lama Yeshe believed that if you cannot enjoy yourself, you can hardly practice tantra, which attempts to transmute ordinary sensory experience (almost regardless of what it is) into inward bliss. He believed that if you cannot shed low self-esteem, then you will suffer from whatever happens, instead of with deitylike confidence striding through advantage and adversity equally. A person, to practice tantra, must first master certain preliminaries: (1) *renunciation*, disenchantment with daily life; (2) *bodhicitta*, an awakened, compassionate heart; and (3) *sunnyata*, realization that everything is empty of permanence and independent identity. Americans may have some trouble especially with the first of these, being taught to pursue happiness instead of thinking that such a pursuit will frustrate and disappoint us. But when Lama Yeshe taught tantra, he assumed his Western students would have no trouble doing it. Other Tibetan tantric books available in English—from Lama Govinda's *Foundations of Tibetan Mysticism* (1959) to Geshe Kelsang Gyatso's *Clear Light of Bliss* (1982)—were so jargon ridden and technically complex as to form a circular trap: You couldn't understand them unless you already practiced tantra, but couldn't practice tantra until you read them. Next to such volumes, Lama Yeshe's *Introduction to Tantra* (1987), *The Bliss of Inner Fire* (1998), and *Becoming the Compassion Buddha* (2003) are simplicity and lucidity itself, giving Westerners a tantra they can and probably will want to do. More than "want to": *need to*. Such are the destructive forces now at work on this planet, Yeshe believed, that only the powerful antidotes found in tantra could counter them and provide an individual happiness in an increasingly dark time.

If testimony were needed that such happiness was possible, one needed to look no further than Lama Yeshe himself. He was never depressed, never in a bad mood, always laughing. Young Americans in search of an awe-inspiring guru were relieved to find Lama Yeshe did not inspire awe but something better: He was lovable, as much fun as he was wise. (And this was the man who repeatedly observed, "Cyclic existence is no fun.") He could be as full of merriment and pranks as a clown in Shakespeare. One evening the door to his room was found stuck, and forcing it open, his American attendant panicked to discover Lama Yeshe dead!—his head hanging off the bed, his eyes rolled back. A minute later Yeshe couldn't stop laughing at the success of his practical joke. Another time a thief broke into his room, which caused no end of consternation, until it was discovered the thief was Yeshe in disguise. Really, was this the way a tantric master behaves?

Perhaps. He presented himself as nobody special, unaccomplished, and so lazy, he always needed a two-hour nap after lunch. One day important visitors deprived him of his nap time, however, and Lama Yeshe acted as if he'd been cheated out of a treasure. How absurd—unless he was secretly practicing advanced meditations, and his nap time was when he did them. Such may have been the case, for on another afternoon he casually remarked, "Normally I don't fall asleep. But this time I did, just for a few minutes, and I dreamt that a powerful protector made offerings to me. How strange." So perhaps he was up to something besides a good snooze. He insisted on eating liberal portions of curds, honey, garlic, and meat—a very peculiar diet. But in Pabongka Dechen Nyingpo's *Collection of Notes*, those are the exact foods prescribed to support the body of the tantric meditator as he completes the highly strenuous practices that precede enlightenment.

Jan Willis was convinced that Lama Yeshe had attained extraordinary degrees of insight. Once when they were walking together in Katmandu, she suddenly had the thought, "death." All she said to him was, "In my immediate family?" and he answered, "No, not that close." (Later she learned her grandfather died on that day.) He seemed so attentive to his students that he almost could have been reading their minds. One young man at Kopan—this was after his classes there had swollen from a handful to an overflowing roomful—decided to test out Lama's power of intuition. As Lama Yeshe was giving his talk, the boy visualized a glass of orange juice and mentally offered it to him. Lama Yeshe looked directly at the young man and said, "Very nice, dear, thank you," and continued his teaching. There are hundreds of such stories. The better the people knew him, the more distinct is their sense of a man keyed to a different frequency. Some suspected that he was more than simply a lovable sweet presence, despite his doing everything to conceal what that "more" might be. He said there are practitioners who use everything, their eating, drinking, even their breathing, to benefit others, and many people thought he was speaking out of his own experience. Lama Zopa, his closest protégé, argued that Yeshe even practiced in his sleep, that with his "subtle body" he read the volumes he left open near his bed, for he had had no time to have read everything that he had. No one who did not know him is, of course, likely to accept such claims—nor would Yeshe have wanted anyone to. But even his most casual students believed that, as long as Lama Yeshe was around laughing and joking and spreading reassurance, they were safe, and nothing could go very wrong.

In his mid-thirties Lama Yeshe had been diagnosed with a cardiac malfunction, and the heart specialists had told him if he curtailed all activity, he might live another six months. Lama Yeshe decided not to accept the cardiologists' diagnosis as gospel. "What they don't see is that the human being is something special," he said. "We are beyond the ordinary concept of what people think we are." The cardiologists told him that he must absolutely cease traveling and remain quietly in one place. But he had to travel, Yeshe believed, because only once there could you see what those particular students needed and adapt the Buddhist teachings accordingly. When Lama Yeshe could be there in person, embodying it, the 2,500-year-old dharma became fresh, relevant, malleable to the situation at hand. (The Italian textile manufacturer Pino Coronna, for example, hated Yeshe with a passion for having "stolen" his two sons. When Lama Yeshe visited Italy, Coronna met his sons' teacher at his wife's insistence, and after only an hour with him Coronna decided to fund Yeshe's center in Italy.) But had he heeded the doctors' advice, and had the necessary operations, and stayed in one place, Lama Yeshe might still be alive today.

Yet he outlived the physicians' predictions anyway, as for the next fifteen years he charged forward, a nonstop engine in perpetual motion, traveling, teaching, lecturing, and founding new centers. The airport was practically his home as he flew everywhere to teach and be with his students. None of them suspected that he suffered in this period more than two hundred heart attacks. In early 1984, when the end was unmistakably near, this man who introduced Tibetan Buddhism to the West flew there, to California, to die in his students' care. They exerted themselves to provide him every measure of comfort possible. "It's putting us through a lot of change. Is this why you're doing it?" one student asked him. "Yes, dear," he answered. On March 3, 1984 (the Tibetan New Year), Lama Yeshe died in Cedars-Sinai Hospital in Los Angeles, cocooned in medical bureaucracy and high-tech machinery, embracing his students, laughing and joking to the last moment. "People think death is worse than losing a lover, a mother, a brother," he said. "But death is better than a lover or mother or brother."

AFTER LAMA YESHE DIED, he became referred to as a Living Buddha, a great bodhisattva who had demonstrated how wisdom and compassion can operate in the present age. This posthumous adulation is a far cry from those early days when he was derided as a "*paisa* lama," a crafty monk selling the dharma to rich Americans. Indeed, if his success is any measure, the Tibetans should have merchandised Buddhism long ago. Yeshe and his students have founded one hundred and thirty centers around the world, some hardly more than study groups, but others providing schools and hospices. Right-wing politicians, who want to shift all humanitarian responsibilities onto "volunteer" and "faith-based" organizations, could use Lama Yeshe's Foundation for the Preservation of the Mahayana Tradition (FPMT) as a model (except they haven't heard of it). The FPMT, nonprofit, staffed by individual volunteers, oversees activities from publishing books to feeding three thousand monks at the new Sera monastery in India. The FPMT's "Mongolia Project" has revived Buddhism in that country, producing TV programs about Buddhism—each introduced by a Hollywood star such as Pierce Brosnan, Richard Gere, or Keanu Reeves—that have been watched by half the Mongolian population. (After 1937, when the Soviet occupiers murdered 37,000 Mongolian monks and changed the alphabet to make the old scriptures inaccessible, Buddhism disappeared from that land.) The FPMT now plans to build near Bodhgaya the largest Buddha statue in the world, which will house whole temples inside it. If built, it will dwarf the Statue of Liberty. It may eventually even dwarf the legend of Yeshe, the little lama who fled Tibet never having met a Westerner, knowing no European language, and who then . . .

LAMA YESHE'S STORY, from a Tibetan viewpoint, does not end with his death. A year after he died, a worldwide search was initiated to discover his reincarnation. One student had a premonition that the mother's name would be Maria (or its closest Tibetan equivalent); another saw the name Paco in a mirror. Coincidentally, at Lama Yeshe's center south of Granada, a couple named Paco and Maria had given birth to a son in February of 1985. When Lama Yeshe's chief disciple, Zopa Rinpoche, visited this center (though keeping his mission secret), he was showed a home video made when Lama Yeshe was last there. Remarks in the video that nobody had paid attention to at the time now seemed significant. "This is a lovely place, I'd like to spend a long time here," Lama Yeshe had said. He had added to Maria: "You'd make a wonderful mother." A traditional method of testing potential infant reincarnations is to place before them the old lama's personal objects, mixed in with others exactly like them. The Spanish baby, named Osel, immediately grabbed, as though they were the best toys in the world, the ritual bell, the vajra (a ritual implement), and the mala (prayer beads) that had belonged to Lama Yeshe.

After his official recognition, little Osel continued to demonstrate—at least to those amenable to the possibility—uncanny affinities with Lama Yeshe. When baby Osel met the young reincarnation of Lama Yeshe's old teacher, his tiny body shook with excitement, and, despite never having seen a prostration, he prostrated before the other child. Suzanna, an old student of Yeshe's, had last seen her beloved lama when he was so sick and frail that she started to cry. To reassure her Lama Yeshe had feebly lifted his arms in the air, clicked his fingers, and attempted a little dance. Now when she visited Osel, the little boy ignored her until someone said, "Don't you remember Suzanna?" At that point Osel raised his arms, tried to click his fingers, and jigged wobbly. A journalist, Vicki Mackenzie, has accumulated a dozen such anecdotes in *The Boy Lama* (1988). Others such as Mick Brown in *The Spiritual Tourist* (1998) have continued to track Osel through his present training at a monastery in south India, but Mackenzie's account cannot be superseded for one good reason: The "recollections" of his earlier incarnation apparently occur during the child's first years, after which they fade as the boy becomes ensconced in his own life-story.

And Osel's life story will not resemble his predecessor's, if for no other reason than because Lama Yeshe forged a new situation for Buddhism in Europe and America. There is no longer need for pioneering figures to break down the barriers as he did. An Australian disciple, Adele Hulse, is currently writing Lama Yeshe's biography—a decadelong project that has already accumulated fifteen hundred pages of interviews. One story she will surely tell concerns Lama Yeshe's finally being able to revisit Tibet in the early 1980s, and finding there a priceless Buddha statue smashed by the Chinese communists and corroding at the bottom of a river. When Lama Yeshe related this incident, he shocked everyone by laughing so hard he nearly fell off his chair. What was so funny? Perhaps how the communists had demonstrated the fundamental Buddhist lesson of impermanence. Hilarious, too, to try to destroy Buddhism by beating up a piece of metal. Lama Yeshe's biography, if reduced to a sentence, might run: He picked up that broken, corroding statue of the Buddha, restored it, and brought it to the West.

chapter III

Playboy of the Gods

LAMA YESHE COULD TRANSPORT the wounded figure of Tibetan Buddhism only so far. He did master new worlds, but not completely. He never fully mastered a Western language. In his one-of-a-kind English when he spoke of a "warm peeling," for example, his students felt the warmth of his feelings before they deciphered the actual words. Like his English, his whole mode of being testified to a transitional figure, made in Tibet but responsive to the West. Uncorrupted, uncompromised, untroubled by spiritual doubt, it could be said that Lama Yeshe was in the West but not really of it. He commuted to America and Europe, and died in California, but he never actually experienced what it was to make a home, a life, in a modern Euro-Americanized country.

There was another lama who did, however, inhabit America, and he carried Tibetan Buddhism into the heart of its culture. He identified with America, spoke its slang, and used Made-in-USA references when teaching. He dismissed other lamas who lacked his popular appeal as "those ethnic Tibetans." Unlike Lama Yeshe's, his tale involved both good and evil, a tale in which he was both exemplar and outrage. This other Tibetan demonstrates what happens when one extricates the dharma from its traditional setting and relocates it in unheard-of and compromised realities.

Only a few years after Zina Rachevsky ferreted Lama Yeshe out of his hut in India, Chögyam Trungpa began living and teaching in America. In the story of Tibetan Buddhism in the West, 1970 is an almost prehistoric date. Had you ransacked America, you would have uncovered scant interest or materials (except for Alexandra David-Neel's books) about Tibetan Buddhism. By that decade's end, however, the religion was firmly entrenched. It was a human whirlwind who wrought this change, but at first glance Trungpa looked so unimpressive he was often mistaken for a little Chinese man in a business suit.

It all happened so quickly. In little more than a decade, Trungpa founded nearly a hundred Tibetan Buddhist centers. His books were selling hundreds of thousands of copies. He gave thousands of lectures, attended by such numbers that all together they would populate a middle-sized city. Some in his audience went on to become his students, doing practices (e.g., the hundred thousand prostrations) once dismissed as fables from the East. He established the first, and only, accredited Buddhist university in the United States. Well-known writers and artists flocked around him, likes bees to a pungent new honey.

His contrast to Lama Yeshe could hardly have been more startling. Lama Yeshe's vision was essentially ahistorical: The essence of Tibetan Buddhism was timeless and placeless, not confined to Tibet or even to Buddhism. This ancient religion, Lama Yeshe believed, if presented skillfully, could make itself happily at home in the modern world. Trungpa thought such a happy vision ludicrous: Modernity is too different, and in it true spirituality may disintegrate into inconsequentiality. One cannot stand outside modernity, he held, with a pure and monkish idea of religion, and hope to affect anything. He handed back his lama's robes, so that no outward sign would distinguish him and no monastic safety net would cushion him from what he called "the dance of life." He would sound the pure Tibetan Vajrayana but in a new and different medium—like, say, a classical theme played on a jazz trombone.

Yet what is peculiar is that even a well-stocked library contains almost nothing written about Trungpa personally. No one accuses him of being a fraud, but the little so far in print paints him as something of a rogue. His many devoted and intelligent students could rebut the insinuations made against him or at least put them into context of his greater achievement, but—this is especially peculiar—for the two decades since his early death, they have shied away from doing so.

"Peculiarity" is the leitmotif of his biography, running from his birth to his death. In old Tibet a few infants were selected by signs and by omens—Trungpa was one such child—to be raised, from infancy on, in perhaps the most rigorous religious education ever devised. The goal of that education was to create persons as close as possible to living Buddhas: perfect in happiness, understanding, and compassion. Here, then, is a plot-idea about innocence and experience that Henry James might have relished: Shanghai someone of such understanding from that rustic world and plop him down in the mad traffic of contemporary America. Who could prophesy what would come of it? Unless, that is, Nietzsche had already predicted it: "Someone today with true understanding would be like a god," Nietzsche wrote, "but a god trapped in the stomach of a beast."

FOR ANYONE INVOLVED WITH Buddhism or spiritual matters in the 1970s, to have met Chögyam Trungpa was probably easier than not to have. He seemed to pop up everywhere.

"Hey, this Tibetan guru is speaking here tonight. Wanna go?"

The young woman, a college student, thought the offer over and then answered, "Hell, no!" For good measure she added, "That's the last thing I'd want to do." In her mind she pictured an obscenely (and obscene) fat charlatan, spouting an Asiatic mumbo jumbo that was supposed to be the word of God. Or suppose he did make sense, so much the worse—then you'd have to become his devotee, and your life would never be your own again. "What's he like, anyway?"

"They say he plays Monopoly and drinks Colt 45."

Oh. That wasn't too mystical or weird. The year was 1972; the city was Los Angeles; and Chögyam Trungpa was speaking that night near UCLA. The two young women arrived early to get good seats, watching the auditorium fill to capacity as folks waited to hear a wise man from the East. And waited. And waited. Trungpa habitually arrived a good hour or two tardy for his talks. When he finally showed up that evening, an almost visible shock rippled through the audience. On each of his arms hung a nymphet in a miniskirt, and he clapped a bottle of Scotch down on the lectern. Our young woman in the first row could not stop laughing: Poof, she thought, just like that, he's exploded everybody's image of a holy man. (If that wasn't his goal, she reasoned, he would have told his nymphets to wait offstage and camouflaged the booze.)

Once Trungpa began speaking, the audience's expectation of an Oriental Wizard of Oz further evaporated. His talk eschewed magic and mystery in Tibet and instead he used familiar situations recognizable from their jobs or from popular entertainments. Certain difficult Buddhist concepts (e.g., "emptiness" or "nonduality") had proved all but impossible to present adequately to Westerners, yet most of that audience didn't even realize he was presenting them as he found equivalents in English slang. Nor did he repeat the standard Tibetan precept to "treat all sentient beings as though they had once been your mother." Trungpa knew many Americans hated their mothers.

In rendering ancient Tibetan Buddhism into ordinary English and modern psychology, Trungpa may have performed as dexterous a feat as exists in the history of translation. Half a thousand years it had taken to transplant Buddhism from India into the old warrior society of Tibet. Chögyam Trungpa was using all his ingenuity to retransmit it to America that very evening. Over the course of many such talks, many such evenings—and regardless of the controversies elsewhere in his life—his success in doing so puts ordinary dreams of triumph to shame.

LET US RETURN FOR a moment to his beginnings. As a boy Trungpa often dreamed of trucks and airplanes. That sounds hardly unusual, but he had never seen, not even in a picture, a plane or truck. He described these unheard-of contraptions to his teacher, who dismissed them: "Oh, it's just nonsense!" Almost everything a contemporary American knows would have seemed just that—nonsense, fantasy—to an old Tibetan. Everything we take for granted, from the moment when the alarm clock goes off and we jump into the shower, to cooking breakfast on the stove or microwave as the phone rings, until the last thing at night when we turn off the computer or TV, would have seemed a magical trick to that boy growing up in remote Tibet.

Yet his peculiar upbringing in Tibet did prepare him for the unexpected. When Chögyam Trungpa was born in February of 1939, a huge rainbow arched over his birthplace (near a tiny village called Geje). His mother's relatives all reported having the same dream, that a lama had entered their nomad's tent that night. Not long thereafter a search began to find the reincarnation of a deceased high lama, the Tenth Trungpa. The great Sixteenth Karmapa had a vision of a village that sounded like Ge-de, and the baby's parents' names were . . . and here the Karmapa spelled out in his vision Chögyam's mother and father's names. When after months of trial and error the search party arrived in Geje, the small boy unerringly picked out objects once belonging to the Tenth Trungpa, as though they were being returned to him.

As the new Eleventh Trungpa, before he was six years old, Chögyam was studying from five in the morning till eight at night. By age eight he had gone on monthlong meditation retreats. By age twelve he had accomplished the preliminary practices, the ngondro, with its hundred thousand prostrations, hundred thousand mantra recitations, etc., which are said to make body and mind supple. His teachers were legendary figures in Tibet, Jamgon Kongtrul and Dilgo Khyentse—rather like a physics student having for his freshman instructors Albert Einstein and Niels Bohr. Jamgon Kongtrul had a premonition that darkness would soon devour his country, and Tibetan Buddhism's survival rested on a few youth such as Trungpa. "You are like a flower in bud which must be properly looked after," Jamgon Kontrul told him. Chögyam Trungpa was looked after: A thousand years of Tibetan learning were compressed into his education, like treasure secreted away before the enemy's arrival.

In young Chögyam's boyhood what was solidly there one moment might utterly vanish the next. When he was recognized as the Eleventh Trungpa, he acquired a new name and a new identity. His parents and home disappeared when he was taken to be raised in a monastery. Trungpa later wrote a prose poem "Nameless Child" to describe this childhood with all the usual elements of childhood missing:

> Because he has no father, the child has no family line. He has never tasted milk because he has no mother. He has no one to play with because he has no brother or sister. . . . Since there is no point of reference, he has never found a self.

If that describes Trungpa's missing childhood, the larger world around him, indeed everything familiar and comfortable, would soon become a missing item as well. The elements that usually make up one's sense of self—such as country, class, culture, a shared first language—were whisked out from under him as the Chinese began their conquest of Tibet.

Chögyam Trungpa supplied one of the first accounts, Born in Tibet (1966), of the peaceful kingdom crushed under the invaders' boot. Its early pages depicting his unusual education yield to tales of his hiding in the mountains after the Chinese occupied Tibet and then of his dramatic attempt to escape. He meandered the trackless Himalayas over one icy peak after another, month after month, uncertain of his direction, as his food ran scarce. It can seem almost miraculous, given the near-suicidal odds, that so many lofty eminences of Tibetan Buddhism (the Dalai Lama, the Sixteenth Karmapa, Dilgo Khyentse, Dudjom Rinpoche, etc.) survived the harrowing trek into exile, to give their religion a second chance abroad. Among those ragged majesties was Chögyam Trungpa, stumbling into India more dead than alive in late 1959.

The Chinese invasion of Tibet did not merely destroy Trungpa's past; it also destroyed his future. Everything he was trained to do was erased from the blackboard. The Dalai Lama appointed him spiritual director of the Young Lamas' School in Dalhousie, and he held that extremely modest position until 1963, when he received a scholarship to Oxford. There Trungpa became a *Guiness Book of World Records* unto himself. He was the first Tibetan to become an English citizen, the first Tibetan to compose a book directly in English, the first to start a Tibetan Meditation Center in the British Isles, and a few years later the first to start one in America. All those firsts indicate that the old rules no longer applied and even he could not say in advance what the new ones would be.

Lama Yeshe continued to keep his monastic vows, as though he had never left Tibet. Chögyam Trungpa, however, entered into a no-holds-barred encounter with the West. As a child he had desired to learn foreign languages (and had to settle for learning Tibetan dialects like Amdo). Now in England his quick mastery of the language was an astonishment. Allen Ginsberg later praised Trungpa's ability to talk every sort of spoken English from "redneck, hippie, chamber of commerce, good citizen [to] Oxfordian aesthete slang." At Oxford Trungpa mastered more than the English language, however. If degrees were given in the "good life," Western version, Trungpa would have earned his Ph.D. overnight. During his escape from Tibet, when no water had been available Trungpa went thirsty rather than drink Tibetan beer (*chang*) or fermented spirits. In the West he may never have refused a drink again. He was rarely out of control, but his sports car certainly was that evening in 1968 when he crashed it into a joke shop, full of comic novelties. The consequences were hardly humorous, though, having left him paralyzed on his left side for life.

Trungpa drew from his auto accident a valuable lesson, though not exactly the most obvious one. He decided to return his lama's robes, wishing no longer to hide behind a monk's appearance or anything that put him at a different angle of experience from those around him. He surrendered his monastic vows but not, he declared, the intention behind them: "More then ever I felt myself given over to serving the cause of Buddhism." He promptly celebrated this dismantling of barriers—between lama and layman, between Tibetan and Westerner—by marrying a sixteen-year-old upper-class English girl named Diana Pybus. His Tibetan colleagues were outraged that Trungpa had betrayed not only his religion but also his country at the hour of her greatest need. Trungpa believed, to the contrary, that those colleagues were engaged in a more subtle betrayal, clinging to outward Tibetan forms (but not necessarily to the inner Buddhist essence) in circumstances where they no longer applied. Samye Ling, the Tibetan center he cofounded in Scotland, should be, he argued, simply a meditation center. However, Trungpa was outnumbered and abandoned; he had lost his country, and now he forfeited the regard of his fellow Tibetan exiles. In those dark days of 1969 he decided—to the relief of all concerned—to move to America. One of his colleagues predicted, "If anything, his outrageous behavior, his affront to conventions, may make him more charming to the Americans."

The prophecy proved more accurate than anyone could have guessed.

JANUARY 1970—THE START of a new decade. For Chögyam Trungpa it marked his entrance into yet another new world. In leaving England, he left behind much that he valued. From their experience of empire in Asia, Englishmen of the better sort knew the protocols of respect due a gentleman from the East. Like Britain, Tibet possessed a historical civilization with its pomp and ceremonies, and Trungpa relished the formalities and the courtesies of English public life. (In America he would instruct his students how to speak proper Oxonian.) But if Englishmen understood how to treat Orientals, they also knew how to pigeonhole them. Numerous Englishpersons expressed an interest in Trungpa but only as a fascinating curiosity—in the spirit of "Let's go see the exotic lama at Oxford!" Few, very few, indeed, thought he might have something worthwhile to teach them.

Americans by contrast acted as though Trungpa had the alchemist's stone or the formula for eternal youth tucked away somewhere in his baggage. During the early 1970s in America the mystical East was more in fashion than fashion was. Trungpa disappointed some spiritual seekers because he hardly looked (or acted) the part of a guru. He wore business suits, he eschewed health foods in favor of steaks, and he smoked and drank. That he was such a modernized, Americanized guru worked overall in his favor, though. In no time, it seemed, crowds attended his every movement and young people hung on his every word, willing to change their lives according to what those words were.

In an ancient fable, wherever the Buddha stepped lotus flowers grew. Wherever Trungpa set foot in America, Buddhist centers sprang up. In 1970 some of his students from Scotland purchased land in Vermont to establish Tail of the Tiger, the first Tibetan center in the United States. That summer Trungpa taught at the University of Colorado, and two centers began in Boulder. Swiftly there followed centers in Los Angeles, Boston, San Francisco, New York, and Toronto, as well as meditation lodges, a fledgling college named Naropa, an experimental therapeutic community in Connecticut, preschools, even a theatrical group. By 1973 a nationwide organization, Varjradhatu, was set up to oversee all these organizations and activities, which behind their diversity reflected a single fact: Chögyam Trungpa had learned the secret of teaching Americans.

Before 1970 the only form of Buddhism with any general appeal here was Zen, and especially popular was the *roshi* or master, Shunryu Suzuki (1905–71), who founded the Zen Center in San Francisco. His talks, published under the title *Zen Mind, Beginner's Mind* (1970), sold more than a million copies. Trungpa and Suzuki were bound to detest each other. In addition to the enormous difference between flowery Tibetan and spartan Zen Buddhism, a generational difference separated the two men. Furthermore, Suzuki kept the traditional vows and precepts, while Trungpa broke them all. When they met in 1970, however, the rapport was instant and profound. Soon the younger man was calling Suzuki "Father," and the older man calling Trungpa his "son." They shared the experience of both being cut adrift from their Asian homelands and cast into America—and liking it.

Suzuki originally came to this country to provide middle-class Japanese-Americans some instruction, but he stayed on and started teaching ordinary Americans, because (he said) "Buddhism needed some fresh opportunity, some place where people's minds weren't made up about Buddhism." That Americans were ignorant of Buddhist histories and hierarchies might well work out to be an advantage. It could have been Trungpa talking: For both of them the United States was Buddhism's brave new world.

When Suzuki invited Trungpa to lecture at San Francisco's Zen Center, he cautioned his students, "Someone is coming tonight. After he comes, maybe no one will be left here at the Zen Center but me." Trungpa arrived, having to be carried in on a stretcher, as he called out to Suzuki, "I am so druuuunk!" Yet that night, David Chadwick recalled in *Crooked Cucumber*, Trungpa "delivered a crystal-clear talk, which some felt had a quality of not only being about the dharma but being itself the dharma." Suzuki joked to the students that, if this was drunkenness, they should drink more. (Suzuki never criticized Trungpa's excesses, but worried only that he would not live a very long life.)

What did Trungpa learn from Suzuki? Trungpa's mind housed the equivalent of a library about Tibetan Buddhism to pass on to his students, but there was Suzuki teaching mainly one thing: meditation. "Where there is practice [i.e., meditation]," Suzuki said, "there is enlightenment." How simple! Trungpa thought. But in Tibetan Buddhism meditation is a somewhat advanced practice, begun after one has mastered considerable instruction and discipline first. With Suzuki's example before him, Trungpa had his American students bypass the potentially bewildering preliminary studies and dive straight into meditation immediately. Trungpa treated all the young men and women coming to him as though each was already capable of emulating the great masters of Tibet. Every hippie who came to Trungpa, simply by coming to him, took on some aspect of a noble monk. Most of them relished the elevation, even if they were not sure exactly what was happening.

Trungpa did suffuse his students with his high estimation of their potentiality, but unlike Lama Yeshe, he did not invariably treat them tenderly or sweetly. In *Cutting through Spiritual Materialism* (1973) Trungpa said it was a guru's duty to insult his students (meaning, affront their distorted egotism), and in this duty he did not fail. Some inner radar of his seemed to detect where a person's hidden vanity lay, and he would home straight in on that sensitive spot. Consider the time when the American called Bhagavan Das—made famous in Ram Dass's best-selling *Be Here Now*, where Das is portrayed wearing blond dreadlocks and walking barefoot all over India—came to pay Trungpa a visit. That night everyone drank until they passed out, and the next morning Das woke to find his long blond dreadlocks had been cut off while he slept by Trungpa. The night before Bhagavan Das had preached that material objects do not matter, and Trungpa thus demonstrated that they did matter to Das. Fortunately for Trungpa this was the 1970s, when many people imagined that being confronted would remake them for the better.

Trungpa could have taught the traditional dharma in the traditional way, and in doing so increased his students' comfort and ease in themselves. But he preferred "to wake them up," as he called it. His approach could mean dispensing with nicety and politeness, as his encounter with the poet Allen Ginsberg illustrates. The two of them first met in New York City in 1970 quite accidentally, when they scrambled to get into the same taxi. Ginsberg and Trungpa next bumped into each other on the other side of the continent, in a bar in Berkeley, California.

Sitting at the bar, Ginsberg complained to Trungpa how endless tour-ing, endless planes to catch, endless lectures to give had left him exhausted. Trungpa volunteered a different interpretation: "You're exhausted," he told Ginsberg, "because you don't like your poetry." Talk about hitting a person where it hurts. "What do you know about poetry?" Ginsberg shot back at that—that obnoxious Mr. Know-it-all. Taking another sip of his Bloody Mary, Trungpa continued as though Ginsberg had not spoken: "Why do you need to depend on a piece of paper when you recite your poetry? Don't you trust your own mind? Why don't you do like the great poets, like Milarepa—improvise spontaneously on the spot?"

The Bloody Marys were evidently fueling Trungpa's criticism, which now switched to Ginsberg's appearance. "Why do you wear a beard?" he asked him. "You're attached to your beard, aren't you? I want to see your face." Ginsberg excused himself. He darted into a nearby pharmacy, pur-chased some scissors, and snip, snip, off came half of his beard. Pleased with his spontaneity, Ginsberg returned to the bar, where Trungpa looked up from his drink and noted perfunctorily, "You didn't shave it off. All you did was cut off two inches." Trungpa was already late for a lecture he was to deliver, but he proposed having a few more drinks while Ginsberg shaved the damned thing off. Ginsberg found himself in the unusual posi-tion of being the socially responsible person: If Trungpa would go give the lecture now, he would shave during the lecture.

Midway through the talk a clean-shaven Allen Ginsberg emerged from the men's room, and Trungpa shouted from the stage, "He took off his mask!" That evening Ginsberg mounted that stage and recited poetry—not the old-fashioned poetry you find in books—but poetry he made up on the spot, full of awful rhymes like "moon" and "June" and "dear" and "beer." "It was the first time I ever got onstage without a text and had to improvise," Ginsberg recalled. "And it was really awkward and unfin-ished, but it was . . . so liberating when I realized I didn't have to worry if I lost a poem anymore, because I was the poet, I could just make it up." He also discovered that he liked sporting about *sans* beard. With the beard, he was a recognized, labeled media personality; without it he could be anybody, or nobody, whoever he pleased. Upon reflection, Ginsberg was thunderstruck that a mere couple of hours' contact with Trungpa had altered radically both the way he looked and the way he wrote. Then and there Ginsberg decided to ask Trungpa to be his teacher and, please, insult him some more.

Whenever he encountered Trungpa, Ginsberg thought, how fresh and unexpected he (Ginsberg) became, even to himself. Is that what having a guru was like—to be in a state of continuous productive upheaval? Ginsberg called the quickened sense of being he felt around Trungpa (this was the early '70s, after all) "love": "The reason I wound up with Trungpa was because I loved him." In 1970 and 1971 many others were also falling in love—or fascination, or hope—with this recent arrival to America.

WHAT TUNE WAS TRUNGPA playing on his enchanted flute that so beguiled his audiences in the 1970s? Unlike other Tibetan lamas in exile, who tossed off the customary pearls of Tibetan Buddhism before western students, Trungpa realized that what a teacher might teach today was a real problem. All the beautiful religious truths of all the sacred traditions had already been repeated over and over *ad nauseum*.

Yet Tibetan Buddhism did possess certain insights, about the nature of human existence, about the relation of life to death, which were hardly common currency in America. The difficulty, the great doubt, was whether they could ever be rendered to a contemporary audience in the West. Trungpa had suddenly to speak in a language invented by daily journalists, Dale Carnegie, and Hollywood scriptwriters. Could he render Tibetan mysticism not only into novel English but into secular sentiments? That would be something new in the world. He intended to try: Trungpa introduced his key work *Shambhala* (1984), with the words "This book is a manual for people who have lost the principles of sacredness."

Item number one in that "manual" was Trungpa's insistence that the principle of sacredness may be, actually, quite a good principle to lose.

Back in the '70s, almost everyone attending Trungpa's talks had already toured the spiritual bazaar, donned and discarded one self-help and quasi-religious fad after another. Trungpa opposed this quest for salvation; he criticized Americans for using "spiritual techniques" to become even more egotistically preocuppied with themselves. Saying mantras or wearing robes or even religion itself, he added, was not going to save you. Which raises the question What then will?

In Henry James's *The Ambassadors* the character Strethers repeatedly tells himself, "Only let go," and in various ways "only let go" was what Trungpa told his students. Only let go of your search for salvation, and you may discover that letting go was what you were searching for. When Trungpa climbed onstage with his nymphs and Scotch, he cut through his audience's preconceived ideas of spirituality; he quite literally cut through Bhagavan Das's, when he cut off his dreadlocks. Once when Trungpa lectured in Vermont, Ram Dass (or Richard Alpert—not to be confused with Bhagavan Das) came and sat on the stage below him, as though indicating that he was just beneath Trungpa in spiritual attainment. Trungpa said nothing but throughout the lecture dropped the ashes from his cigarette into Ram Dass's hair. At another retreat Trungpa's senior students, at his prompting, rushed into a serious discussion with peashooters and turned the room into a hullabaloo of pillow forts and play fights. Is that the way serious-minded Buddhists behave? Perhaps. For nobody in the room was now daydreaming or bored or lost in intellectual argument any longer, but all were, well, cutting through spiritual materialism.

Item number two in Trungpa's manual concerns what happens when you stop striving after the way you think things should be. If you surrender your sense of limitations and your need to redeem them, you may find yourself, he suggested, already living in an uncontrived, happier condition. Needless to say, a good American therapist would not agree. Freudian psychology holds that beneath the layers of cultural accretion is still a stratum of troubled personal identity, composed of identifiable complexes and leftover childhood neuroses. In Tibetan Buddhism, however, pare down a personality far enough and you reach, beyond child-hood's wrong beginnings, into pure luminous being, no different from what the Buddha experienced upon enlightenment. Trungpa could hardly tell his initial American audiences that they were all secretly Buddhas, for they would either dismiss him as a mystic or their egos would inflate like balloons. Trungpa's challenge was to smuggle in this "prepsycholog-ical," religious way of looking at things under the cover of ordinary Amer-ican talk.

He thus talked about buddha-nature without appearing to, by allud-ing instead to a person's basic goodness. In Trungpa-speak, "basic good-ness" does not mean, despite its sound, niceness and decency. One disciple recalls telling Trungpa that she was basically a nice person, and he winced, as though he had just bitten into something truly nasty. He wasn't interested in "niceness." Nor was he a psychotherapist who would either support or correct people's vested notions of themselves. When his stu-dents expressed their convictions with great earnestness, he would some-times look out the window and yawn.

Trungpa thus attempted his end run around psychotherapy. Psychia-try and psychoanalysis, he knew, can be powerful tools for dealing with personal problems, but sometimes one cannot even know what the prob-lem is. By contrast, awakening one's basic goodness (a/k/a buddha-nature) may make some problems dissipate or recede to inconsequence without any analysis at all. You may be already all right, if only you will allow yourself to be. His task was to jolt people into realizing this latent potency, this healing (or actually already healed) aspect within them-selves. "Cheer up," Trungpa would exhort audiences at his talks. "Cheer up right now!"

Item number three in Trungpa's manual is for those who have cheered up. If your own moody self-obstacles don't get in the way, you won't need religious principles, for then everything will appear sacred. Once you experience your own basic goodness then everything, and not just what you previously liked, may begin to seem good; whatever you encounter may now interest you. In *Chögyam Trungpa: Sa vie et son oeuvre* (2002) the French writer Fabrice Midal catalogued Trungpa's own interests, and their range is staggering. His enthusiasm for the arts might be expected, since they appeal to the same imaginative faculty that religion does. But in addition to art, Trungpa considered that daily life, cooking, speaking, the way you drank your tea, the way you shopped for clothes, all can be—for the person who has "cheered up"—an excellent way to practice Buddhism. A few critics objected that the arts, as Trungpa envisioned them; did not really produce art. The goal of the "spontaneous poetry" that he encouraged Ginsberg to write was not great poetry but an intenser awareness in the poet (or poet-manqué). The "arts" Trungpa himself practiced—spontaneous poetry, calligraphy, ikebana flower arrangement, the zen of archery, etc.—were like the cooking and elocution he taught, activities that demand single-minded concentration and avoid complexities of thought. That greater art made from irony, contradiction, and thought doubling back on itself—Shakespeare's plays, James's novels, Yeats's poetry, Cezanne's painting—lies outside Trungpa's canon. But such art may come at too high a price, he thought, since complex reasoning and second thoughts so often trap people within their own psyches and cut them off from their spontaneous goodness.

The challenge was How could Trungpa coax people into realizing their elusive "basic goodness"? Trungpa was no longer a monk, and he dismissed religion, yet he did what Tibetan lamas have always done: He encouraged his students to meditate. (Meditation is so empty of content that it's hard to turn it into spiritual materialism or appropriate it for egotistical purposes.) Meditation completes Trungpa's "manual for people who have lost the principles of sacredness," which, if the truth be told, was a manual for reintroducing those principles, albeit incognito or in disguise. Trungpa's principle of "letting go" resembles *sunnyata* (or emptiness); his "basic goodness" is the Buddhist principle of compassion; and appreciating or accepting whatever happens begins the Tibetan practice of "nonduality." Thus through a roundabout back entrance Trungpa led his students into something rather like Tibetan Buddhism, without the name.

Harvey Cox, the Harvard theologian and author of the bestseller *The Secular City* (1965), took to the road in the early 1970s in search of "an authentic contemporary form of spirituality." All such roads then led to Trungpa's Naropa Institute in Colorado. (In the early 1970s, Naropa metamorphosed from a mere idea—that of combining meditation with academic study—into a college almost overnight, thanks to Trungpa's ability to combine the visionary and fund-raising. Today, Naropa is the only fully accredited Buddhist university in the United States.) Cox went to Boulder to scoff, but he stayed to sit. Skeptical about the fad of meditation and half intending to expose it, Cox experimented with meditation himself. He was astonished:

> From the very outset, from the first hour-long meditation, I sensed that something unusual was happening to me. My level of internal chatter went down. I did not invest situations with so many false hopes and fantasies. I walked away from the sitting feeling unruffled and clear-headed. I could teach with more precision and listen to people more attentively. [etc.]

Besides meditation, what Trungpa taught was himself or through himself, Cox surmised, so you almost had to be there. Some teachers write so well, you need never encounter them personally, while others depend upon eye contact, a gesture, or a knowing look to give their message substance. Trungpa was neither of these types of teacher—neither a book, nor an exemplar—Cox believed, but one whose value emerged fully only in the teacher-student or master-apprentice relationship. In that relationship Trungpa could be offensive, or be tenderly kind, as he keyed himself to the needs (if not the wishes) of the particular student. Being with him, his students said, could feel so ordinary—rather like being in the weather—but an uncanny sense of something more kept stealing in, when one wasn't looking.

He seemed less a saint than a provocateur, whose genius was to make every encounter exciting, fun. "If it doesn't have a sense of humor," Trungpa would say, "it's not Buddhism." His own humor could sink to childish levels: He might stand behind a door and when someone entered jump out and yell Boo! Once after his lecture, a woman announced she was a vegetarian and demanded to know how Tibetan lamas could eat murdered meat. Instead of pointing out that Tibet did not grow enough edible crops, Trungpa paused, and finally said in a tiny voice, "Well, you are what you eat." The audience burst out laughing, though no one knew for sure what he meant. It was typical of Trungpa not to solve people's puzzles but to return them to them, which oddly kept them returning to him. The introduction of Tibetan Buddhism into America became, in his hands, not a matter of soul-anguish or dour proselytizing but playful as a theater piece.

THE YEAR 1974 SAW Trungpa change his manner of teaching. That year His Holiness the Sixteenth Karmapa first visited the United States. It was the Karmapa who, some thirty-odd years before, had had the vision that led to the infant Trungpa's recognition. In Tibet the Karmapa was treated as a king of kings and considered little short of divine; afterwards, in exile, he lived like a poor peasant at first, and he enjoyed that equally, joking with Indians in the bazaar. In hosting his visit, Trungpa might heal the rupture that had estranged him from the Tibetan community ever since his marriage. The Karmapa's visit thus represented the homecoming to the Tibet that Trungpa could never go home to in person.

Trungpa announced to his students that His Holiness the Karmapa would honor them with a visit in Boulder. Their response was: Groovy. "Let's show him a great time," one student suggested. "We can take him out for steak and then to a disco."

Second student: "He can sleep on the water bed."

Third student: "Do we have to vacuum the floor?"

Boulder back in the '70s was a groovy little city. Car bumper stickers proclaimed, "Visualize Using Your Turn Signal," and Boulderites voted marijuana their favorite cure for a hangover. Trungpa suffered a revulsion: Such casualness was not the proper response to a prospective visit from His Holiness. Imagine a Catholic, ecstatic about the Pope's imminent visit, who suddenly hears someone next to him say, "As long as we don't have to clean the toilet." Trungpa felt a similar disgust at his students' reaction to the arrival of the holy of holies.

Trungpa's first American students were in the main hippies, and secretly he didn't much care for hippies (whereas a "Tibetan hippie" is what Lama Yeshe sometimes called himself). A poster of that era showed a longhaired youth meditating naked in the woods, and its caption read, "Milarepa Lives!" Trungpa considered the poster near-blasphemy. Milarepa was Tibet's great ascetic yogi (circa 1025–1135), but his asceticism entailed more than shedding his underwear and gazing vacant-eyed at his navel. Milarepa belonged to a venerated and formal tradition of learning. It was time, Trungpa decided, for these students to learn veneration and formality. For the Karmapa's visit they borrowed good china and silver and polished that silver to its brightest sheen. Many of the young men bought their first suits, and the young women learned that the height of fashion was not the tie-dyed dress.

Theirs would be no brief flirtation with respectability. Prior to the Karmapa's visit, Trungpa would go to give his talks wearing whatever he happened to be wearing, perhaps khaki pants and a plaid shirt, and following his talk he might stop at Arbie's to grab a quick bite. Subsequent to the Karmapa's visit, be began wearing suits at his talks, and he expected his audience to dress respectably too, to honor what was being taught. Those audiences were hippies fleeing their own traditions, but it was time they acknowledged they had landed, in fact, in another tradition. Trungpa took the declining hippie patient into his clinic and sent him forth a robust bourgeois. One student of his reminisced about the "makeover":

Everybody [in the early '70s] was ready to do anything. Anything!
We got into this, and it seemed fantastically radical and profound.
Fifteen or twenty years later, we all look like Presbyterians. . . .
There's a kind of normalcy, which is very much the direction
Trungpa Rinpoche pushed us in.

The videotapes of his early talks show a wild-eyed audience, mini-
mally clothed and maximally hirsute; the late '70s ones, sedate folks who
might have ambled over from a Rotary Club or PTA meeting. Trungpa
repeatedly addressed his audience as "ladies and gentlemen," which may
sound quaint, but he was reminding these refugees from respectability
that they had become the "ladies and gentlemen" of a great tradition.
Trungpa did for the counterculture what Bill Clinton later did for the
Democratic Party: he escorted it from the excitable, idealistic margins and
relocated it in the supposedly durable center, which had hitherto been
deemed too conservative for habitation.

Trungpa had at first lived informally with his students, but he now set
up a kind of court around himself. How do you, in fact, organize a large
group, so that many people can relate to a central figure? At first he copied
the predominant model on offer in America—the corporate organization—with its divisions and departments and hierarchy of officers, but he
came to dislike that model as too impersonal, too mechanical. He hit
upon an inspiration, albeit almost a millennium out of date: A medieval
court would be nobler, a reminder to his students of their heroic capabilities. Other American Buddhists poked fun at Trungpa's pretensions, but
Trungpa liked fun. Sometimes when he traveled in America and Canada,
he went incognito—as the Prince of Bhutan. Doubtless a joke, since few
Americans would know where on earth Bhutan was, if it was. But as Freud
said, our jokes unconsciously reveal ourselves . . . in this case, revealed that
Trungpa was redonning the ceremonial regalia of the spiritual prince he'd
once been in Tibet. The students traveling with him grew a trifle weary
every evening of having to dress up in tails and long dresses and white

gloves, in a charade of royalty. Tie-dyed dresses and tattered jeans had come a long way.

Harvey Cox, returning to Naropa after the Karmapa's visit, remarked on the new regime there. He was greeted upon his arrival with polite courtesy: "How long can you stay with us this summer?" Previously there had been no you/us, Buddhist/non-Buddhist distinction. As a Christian, Cox was relieved that Trungpa was now emphasizing his Buddhism because, before, it had so blurred into generic spirituality that how could one know he was not a Buddhist.

After the Karmapa's visit, Trungpa started instructing his students in the ngondro, the hundred thousand prostrations, mantra recitations, visualizations, mandala offerings, etc. Up and down, up and down, they performed the prostrations, fearing that their knee joints might calcify and their muscles petrify. But the longer they persevered, the more supple their bodies became and some claimed even their acrid sweat doing these exercises turned sweet tasting. Such advanced techniques should be imparted, he believed, only in the close supervision of the teacher-student relationship. His talks (and the books made from them) therefore remained general for a general audience. Whoever wished to delve deeper, and do the hard work, could come study with him, and thousands did. Trungpa thus created two "tracks" of Buddhism in America—one public and quasi-secular, the other private and religious—and by the early 1980s both appeared to be alive and thriving.

OR SO IT APPEARED. Skeptical outsiders began to express reservations. Could this be the same Chögyam Trungpa about whom the devotee relates an inspirational success story and the hostile critic reports misconduct leading up to tragedy?

Both sides agree that Trungpa hardly comported himself according to *The Lives of the Saints*. There was the little matter of, well, sex. An Oriental pasha might have envied Trungpa as he selected the female devotee who would enjoy his favors that evening. In certain periods the Boulder center had a sign-up list, to which women added their names who wanted to sleep with him, and Trungpa would scroll down the list, so that each night a new beauty materialized in his bed. There was nothing sly about it: Trungpa believed that sex, defanged of possessiveness, was as natural as in the Garden of Eden. He never assumed that a cloistered, desexualized atmosphere was the best context for spreading the dharma—or even if it was, it was hardly the atmosphere prevailing in 1970s America. The inspiring teacher Trungpa thus gained a second reputation: Give a free-association test to an American Buddhist, and the first association upon hearing Trungpa's name may not be dharma or enlightenment but fucking.

And the second word association might be booze. Erotic activity, even for the enthusiast, uses up only a few hours on most days, but Trungpa appeared able to drink all the time. Eventually the beer bloated his body and had to go; the whiskey corroded his innards and had to go; and so he settled upon the gentle Japanese liquor, saki. Ginsberg had seen hooch lay waste to Jack Kerouac, and he attempted to rescue Trungpa from the same fate. Trungpa remained unfazed, saying that Ginsberg's confusing him and Kerouac was more muddled than any drunkenness. In an essay "Alcohol As Medicine or Poison," Trungpa proposed there is a right and wrong way to drink: "Conscious drinking—remaining aware of one's state of mind—transmutes the effect of alcohol." To his young admirers their teacher, fueled by such mindful drinking, winged into the furthest reaches of mind and thought, where man had scarcely trod before. Others disagreed. When the poet Robert Bly was giving a reading in Boulder, an inebriated Trungpa stumbled onstage and started banging a gong. Bly could barely contain his fury, demanding: "Your drunken behavior—is it just you, or is this a traditional manner, or what?" Trungpa answered, "I come from a long line of eccentric Buddhists." As his students emulated him—perhaps they were drinking in the wrong way—Trungpa's Boulder center became the only Buddhist sangha in the world to have its own chapter of Alcoholics Anonymous.

Trungpa saw little benefit in being bound by ordinary constraints.

"I'll do anything to wake people up," he repeatedly said. In fact, he expanded the Catalog of Anything. One of his attendants daydreamed continuously, so Trungpa willfully tripped going down the stairs to startle him into being more alert. The attendant apologized profusely, but soon his daydreaming resumed. The next time Trungpa threw himself past his dozy attendant down the stairs he wound up in the hospital. Another time Trungpa had his driver drive his Mercedes into the water on the beach, from which sea burial it had to be laboriously extracted. Some marveled: See the complete freedom of the guru! Others countered, What do you expect of an uninhibited five-year-old? (Still others like Allen Ginsberg thought an adult five-year-old the best guru imaginable.) Trungpa was certainly an *enfant terrible*, or genius, at shocking people out of their complacency. Perhaps he was successful nineteen times out of twenty at rousing his students from their comfortable self-deceptions. "Guru" may be the one profession, however, where a 95 percent success rate equals failure.

Ginsberg enjoyed having his status quo turned upside down. But others like the poet W. S. Merwin wanted to learn about Buddhism, without stepping onto a roller coaster zooming off the rails. In 1975 Merwin and his Hawaiian girlfriend, Dana Naone, applied, late, to participate in Trungpa's three-month retreat in Snowmass, Colorado. Merwin had done none of the preliminary courses, however, and he was unfamiliar with Trungpa's "crazy wisdom" manner of teaching. Three out of four applicants for the seminary in Snowmass were refused, but a famous writer in attendance added luster, and so Trungpa accepted Merwin's late application regardless.

That Snowmass retreat coincided with Halloween, and Trungpa, as the master mixer of the sacred and the profane, decided a Halloween party might be just the ticket. Instead of donning masquerades, the guests would have their normal egotistical masks stripped off (and, Trungpa intimated, the stripping might not stop there). As the revels accelerated, Trungpa realized that Merwin and Naone were missing from the spirit-

bacchanalia. When they refused to be coaxed from their room, Trungpa ordered his guards to break down their door. Merwin, a pacifist, panicked and greeted the intruders waving a broken bottle. After they were forced downstairs, Trungpa yelled at Naone, "You might be playing slave to this white man, but you and I know where it's at. We're both Oriental." Then he demanded, "Are you afraid to show your pubic hair?" At Trungpa's command, Merwin and Naone were forceably undressed, as Naone screamed at Trungpa "Fascist," "Bastard," "Hitler," and (if those weren't damning enough) "Cop." They were then allowed to slouch back to their room, while a seemingly drunk Trungpa ordered everybody else to undress.

As orgies go, the one in Snowmass hardly compares with the Sodom and Gomorrah of a Saturday-night frat party. Surprisingly, Merwin and Naone decided to remain for the duration of the retreat, reasoning that, despite his excess, they could learn from Trungpa things then not taught anywhere else in America. But the gossip mills were churning, and rumors of the debauchery filtered into various poetry circles, where denunciations of Trungpa became the order of the day. Ginsberg judged this righteous indignation pure hypocrisy: "[William] Burroughs commits murder, Gregory Corso borrows money from everybody and shoots up drugs for twenty years but he's 'divine Gregory' but poor old Trungpa, who's been suffering since he was two years old to teach the dharma, isn't allowed to wave his frankfurter!"

The brouhaha appeared to be dying out, when *Harper's* magazine ran an article, "Spiritual Obedience," which gave the incident national coverage. The writer of the piece, Peter Marin, professed horror not at the shenanigans but that later neither Trungpa nor his disciples would admit to his having done anything wrong. Some students, so Marin reported, converted the debacle into a teaching or morality play in which the unclad Merwin and Naone were the naked Adam and Eve (and by inference Trungpa must be God expelling them from Eden). Then in November 1978, the Reverend Jim Jones led the infamous mass suicide of his

People's Temple group in Guyana, and some critics barely familiar with Trungpa worried that in Boulder, at Naropa, another Jonestown cult was in the making. Boulder's local newspaper, the *Daily Camera*, editorialized about Trungpa's guards, his limousines, and his drinking, "To avoid being called a cult, it might help not to act like one." One man's guru is another man's fascist, which is what poets like Bly and Kenneth Rexroth now took to calling Trungpa. Rexroth pronounced, "Chögyam Trungpa has unquestionably done more harm to Buddhism in the United States than any man living."

A de-facto harem at one's beck and call, a bar pouring drinks nonstop, and a following to humor one's every whim may seem a formula for any man's downfall. But Trungpa didn't fall down, not then anyway. Tibetan Buddhism views reality as a kind of magic show, and perhaps Trungpa was a magician, with a sleight of hand making vanish the consequences of his excesses. He was so inspiring a teacher that his students lived in the inspiration; so fascinating that criticism gave way to wonder. In the early '80s he surprised his followers by announcing that they needed to relocate their headquarters, and after scouring and rejecting half the globe (Bermuda, New Zealand, etc.), he astounded them further by choosing a geographical "nowhere"—Nova Scotia. Shortly after moving to Nova Scotia himself in late 1986, he performed the ultimate magic trick, the final vanishing act.

At the time of his death he was only forty-seven, a body worn out by alcohol: Yet he had accomplished more than most people would, given ten lifetimes. He had been a controversial figure, but the thousands attending his funeral attested to his larger triumph. The day of his funeral was dreary and rainy, and many mourners were frazzled from having driven overnight to get there in time. But as Dilgo Khyentse stepped out of his car, the sky suddenly cleared, the bluest blue, and a rainbow encircled the sun; then two distinct clouds materialized in the sky, and there arched between them another rainbow—a *ciel et lumière* show such as supposedly light the way as great lamas enter the *bardo*. Trungpa's bones were pulverized and mixed with jewel dust, then siphoned into gold statues, to grace more than one hundred centers affiliated with him. Construction began on a mammoth stupa in his honor, which $2.7 million dollars and fourteen years later was completed, with the media and thousands of still-devoted followers attending the ten-day consecration ceremony to pay tribute to his memory. Yes, a triumph . . . had it only ended there.

JUST AS DEATH DID not quite end Lama Yeshe's story, it is not the last word in Trungpa's either. A decade before he died, in 1976, Trungpa had anointed a "dharma heir" to succeed him—one Osel Tendzin, né Thomas Rich—a former street kid from New Jersey whom Trungpa found amusing. Trungpa put a high premium on being amused. More important, by appointing a Westerner as his dharma heir, Trungpa demonstrated that Tibetan Buddhism could become as American as apple pie—or as street kids from Jersey.

As Trungpa's successor Thomas Rich would become the head of a whole ancient Tibetan lineage. As befitted such a dharma prince, he was indulged and cosseted, surrounded by attendants and chauffeured about in limousines. In advanced Tibetan practices a person visualizes himself as having the unlimited potentiality of a deity, which without the proper training can result in a psychological inflation. Possessed of the position and prerogatives of a demigod on earth, Rich grew puffed up. When a venerated old lama visited Naropa, he wanted to give Trungpa's designated successor a special teaching. Rich/Tendzin hastened to the rendezvous excited, expecting to learn occult powers, masteries that would put nothing beyond him. The old lama's teachings were disappointingly simple, though, consisting only of: "You must always be kind."

Possibly Tendzin should have scrutinized that lesson more closely. A year after Trungpa died, a shock jolted the Buddhist communities in America. Not only did Osel Tendzin have AIDS, but he had infected several partners without telling them. Tendzin called a meeting to confront the growing scandal, but since he billed the meeting as a "teaching," everyone had to pay thirty-five dollars to hear his explanation. Trungpa had reassured him, so Tendzin claimed, that as long as he (Tendzin) performed the Buddhist purification practices he would not infect his partners with AIDS. Everyone in that audience sat there stunned, scarcely knowing what to believe.

In *The Double Mirror* (1994) Stephen Butterfield, a former student of Trungpa's, said he was "not so sure that Trungpa would have been incapable of giving the advice Tendzin attributed to him, even while knowing full well that it was wrong." Alexandra David-Neel had reported Tibetan yogis condoning, for the sake of enlightenment, deadly practices, and besides, Butterfield argued, in those last years Trungpa's brains were pickled in alcohol. Everyone else concurs, however, that Trungpa would not have advised anyone to disregard natural laws, and that Rich (who died of AIDS in 1990) was lying to save his own skin. In fact, back in 1979 when Trungpa first observed his dharma heir veering arrogantly out of control, he had summoned Rich to his house. Trungpa then picked up an enormous calligraphy brush and hurled it so furiously that black sumi ink splattered everyone there (clothes went to the laundry; walls had to be repainted), as he screamed NO: "From now onward, it's NO! That is the Big No, as opposed to the regular no. You cannot destroy life. . . . You have to respect everybody. . . . You can't act on your desires alone." Afterwards, Thomas Rich became a reformed fallen angel . . . for a while.

Yet Trungpa cannot escape blame entirely. He had, after all, chosen as his heir someone potentially capable of wreaking such harms. As the scandal spread, Trungpa's critics felt vindicated: What else would you expect of a defrocked lama who turned Buddhism into psychobabble and told American narcissists to think even more about themselves? Even his most devoted followers could no longer think, as they had during his lifetime, that their teacher never made a mistake. For some the Rich/Trungpa scandal uttered the last word about Buddhism's capacity to adapt to the West, and it was an ugly word.

BUT PROBABLY THERE IS no last word about someone so complex as Chögyam Trungpa. People who met him during the 1970s either (a) became his students or (b) were outraged by him. He was outrageous. He would sometimes meet a woman by immediately placing his hand on her vulva and saying, "Hi!" From this distance, however, a third reaction to him is possible—curiosity: What was it all about? What was he up to?

Pundits labeled the 1980s the "Me Decade," but the 1970s might be called the "God Decade." The era was rife with religious dabbling and spiritual experimentation, and what built up Trungpa's reputation during those years caused it to unravel somewhat afterwards. His books were assembled from talks, and the impromptu period-hip rhetoric that made them appealing then now makes them read, on the cold page, dated and disjointed. The same was true of his conduct. Trungpa's drinking and womanizing made him seem in the "liberated" 1970s *one of us.* "Drinking with him, and then discovering the incredible extent of his discipline and practice," recalled one student, "convinced me Buddhism was not just for people sitting on mountaintops." But as the hedonistic openness of the '70s yielded to the "political correctness" of subsequent decades, Trungpa has come to seem *one of them*—someone whom you'd think twice before entrusting with the education of your soul.

Critics censure Trungpa for his heedless example, especially in matters of sex. Yet regarding his "satyriasis," Trungpa was not a typical Don Juan. Although half crippled, he followed a grueling schedule with no privacy or days off, and women were comfort, his consolation. Sometimes when the perfumed hour of rendezvous arrived, and the lights dimmed, he only asked of his prospective lover, "Please hold me, Sweetheart." Consequently, unlike conventional Don Juans, his promiscuity did not leave in its wake a bitter succession of resentful ex-conquests. A conference of Buddhist women that met in Boulder is revealing in this regard. Some participants, breaking from the official agenda, began tearfully to tell of their sexual exploitation by Zen roshis and other Buddhist teachers. The air in the room grew tense, as everyone waited for someone to denounce Trungpa. Yet none of his former paramours, it turned out, felt ill-used by him. Some women defended Trungpa, saying that his physical intimacy was an extension of his emotional intimacy. The others postulated that Trungpa was operating on some honorable but different principle, even if they weren't sure what that principle was.

That principle, to give it a name, was William Blake's "The road of excess leads to the palace of wisdom." Trungpa was excessive sexually and in drinking, certainly, but he was excessive in everything: in counseling his students, in the number of talks he gave, in the variety of art projects he instigated, in building up his organization. To have behaved with temperate caution in the erotic sphere would have been, he thought, to give sex more than its due. *Excess*, in fact, may not be the right word but a negative label applied retroactively to behavior that at the time people thought of as rather positive—as breaking dead prohibitions and extending life into an exciting new fullness. His "outrageousness" was an (almost) acceptable "language" of that era, and by speaking it he reached people even Lama Yeshe could not.

Trungpa, in any case, had no desire to be a poster boy for the conventional good. He did not believe Buddhism's mission was altering things or changing behavior, but rather bringing more awareness to whatever one did. "He was not attempting to teach us right and wrong," his disciple Pema Chodron said, but how "to relax into the insecurity, into groundlessness. He taught me how to live, so I am grateful." Pema Chodron is an American Buddhist nun who for twenty-five years has abstained from sex and alcohol, yet she defends Trungpa: "As far as I'm concerned, if you're going to call things right and wrong you can never even talk about fulfilling your bodhisattva vows."

Instead of preaching about right and wrong, Trungpa thus tumbled down the staircase; rather than teach morality, he drove his Mercedes into the wet sand. He handed his companions a wacky dilemma to be present to and to solve. This is the situation, he seemed to imply; give it all your awareness, figure it out. People chase around and around in their own thoughts, Trungpa said, which gets them nowhere. If for once they can be shocked out of their mental habits, their circus of internal distractions stunned into silence, then they may discover a core of rightness and kindness and happiness that has been there all along. They will then be naturally kind, naturally alert, precise in their dealing with situations, and accurate in their relations with others. Meditation will get you out of distractions and obsessions temporarily, while you do it. Trungpa's outlandishness was meant to jolt people out of distracted states permanently, for which he was labeled, then, and even more since, an untrustworthy and immoral teacher.

But morality was not a big problem, Trungpa thought; he could handle morality. When Boulder's Protestant ministers objected to a scandalous man like Trungpa teaching youth, he sent Harvey Cox of Harvard to reassure them. After the Halloween scandal, when all its participants sank into an embarrassed silence, Trungpa couldn't understand why nobody was talking about it. (Discussion might have even made sense of the scandal. Seeing Merwin out of step with the rest, Trungpa could have asked him to leave, but decided it was kinder to shock him out of his aloofness.) So long as nothing was deceitful or hidden, he thought, everything would come right in the end. Toward the end of his life Trungpa acknowledged he may have made a fatal mistake in America, but that mistake fell in an area other than morals.

HIS GREAT FAILURE IN AMERICA, Trungpa came finally to think, was that he had undervalued the importance of psychology. When he first arrived in this country, he listened carefully to young Americans talking among themselves, and he recognized that they used psychological frames of reference. When they described their experiences in subjective, personal terms, Trungpa took it to be a cultural phenomenon, a fad—like the way, say, they decorated their rooms. With his intuitiveness and linguistic mimicry, he adapted to the fad with ease, and he became the panjandrum who translated Tibetan metaphysics into good psycho-logical lingo. He knew, for example, that "living in samsara" was not the same as a "neurosis," but if he used psychological terms, his students got it right away. And perhaps only he remained unconvinced by what he said. For Trungpa did not really subscribe to the Freudian psychological under-standing of character and personality.

Many Americans at that time insisted that individuals needed to do the psychotherapeutic work on themselves first—work through their per-sonal handicaps left over from family and childhood—and only after-wards would they have the inner clearance to attempt spiritual work. Trungpa thought that progression from psychotherapy to spirituality was pure humbug. Sadness, aloneness, depression he did not consider internal maladies in need of a psychiatrist. They were part of the human experi-ence of being alive, and if you did not treat them as a problem, especially an insurmountable problem, they would cease to be one. The "Cheer up!" with which he exhorted audiences made it seem easy: You can activate the potentiality for happiness within yourself simply by choosing to, by sid-ing with something beyond mood, deep and true within yourself. As it says in the *Hevajra Tantra*:

> Sentient beings are just Buddhas,
> But they are defiled by adventitious stains.
> When stains are removed, they are Buddhas.

Trungpa, it will be recalled, did not really have a childhood but, in effect, a long meditation period instead. And so he minimized the early traumas still causing havoc in seemingly composed adults. By discounting the importance of the individual psyche, Trungpa optimistically assumed that creating a hybrid Western Buddhism would face no large obstacles. He also could be cavalier in choosing his dharma heir: So what if Thomas Rich was scarred by his upbringing, when realizing his basic goodness would heal those scars. Only late in the day did he realize a psychological orientation belonged to America as much as does technology or vast geographical distances or mixed immigrant populations, and to plant the dharma in America required planting it in personal neuroses and post-adolescent hangups. In any American contest between a person's psychological history and his innate goodness, Trungpa finally saw, the odds were that personal history will win out. After ten years teaching in America, he told a friend that Freud was more relevant than he had realized.

Trungpa contemplated the possibility that he had failed. Americans could take to Buddhism, certainly; they would devour it and digest it, and then regurgitate it as psychobabbling New Age pablum. And what was he doing in his adopted country? Trungpa mused possibly that he was the most American of all Americans, of those people who had populated a continent by constantly uprooting themselves and resettling, uprooting and resettling. It seemed that he had experienced this restless rootlessness himself since year one, since before he could remember, when he lost one identity and became the Eleventh Trungpa. He had kept planting the dharma and then having to uproot it, in one country after another, on one continent after another, first in Tibet and then not in Tibet, then in India and then not in India, in England and not in England, and now in America, which may not be his final settling place after all. The weariness of generations overtook him. By the early 1980s his speech became slurred, long pauses interrupted his talks, he sniffled constantly—he was a man visibly sick. The alcohol was killing him, yet he refused to stop drinking. Life at all costs had never been Trungpa's criterion. He had accomplished so much, and he did not care for its prolongation in the indignity of a rehab program. He summoned his inner resources, though, to make one last effort and to replant the dharma again, this time in a safe country where it could withstand the rough winds of change to come.

In *Thunder and Ocean* (1996) the Canadian journalist David Swick shows that the province of Nova Scotia where Trungpa transferred his organizational headquarters, despite its McDonald's restaurants and American-sounding speech, was then genuinely another country. Relocating there,

Trungpa was not hunting new worlds to conquer but a way out, out and into a less modern and more traditional manner of life. Trungpa was not thinking small: He was envisioning the next thousand years, and he now deemed a safe, protected environment necessary for entrenching Buddhism in the Western Hemisphere.

Possibly he felt by then the need for such an environment himself: The oldfangled pace of Nova Scotia might prove restful, a couch on which his body, which was visibly wearing out, could recuperate. A month after moving to Halifax, however, he suffered a heart attack, and for seven months he hung on in a "semi-coma," though seemingly aware and at peace. On April 4, 1987, four days shy of the Buddha's birthday, he died, age forty-seven. The master was dead, and a silence descended, with many wondering whether the whole wondrous magical show was over.

Subsequently traumatized by the Thomas Rich scandal, Trungpa's Buddhist organization ceased its rapid expansion, some members acting as if they had a secret or wrong to hide. Yet if Trungpa was "wrong" about anything fundamental, it was—not about psychology—but misjudging the extent and durability of his own work. He had founded nearly a hundred centers, he had attracted thousands of students, and his writings had introduced Westerners to Tibetan Buddhism by the hundreds of thousands. Despite certain reservations about his conduct, Helen Tworkov, the editor of the Buddhist magazine *Tricycle*, judged that "Trungpa was the most effective [religious] teacher, the greatest comet, ever to pass through America." Even mainstream Christian churches and Jewish synagogues were emulating the Buddhist-style meditation Trungpa taught, teaching practices like mindfulness, and employing Buddhistlike approaches to direct experience. During the Merwin controversy, Allen Ginsberg had joked that Pandora's Box "has been opened by the arrival in America of one of the masters of the secrets of the Tibetan Book of the Dead.' . . . We might get taken over and eaten by the Tibetan monsters." It was meant as a joke, but was the joke coming true?

A DRAMATIST MIGHT HAVE invented Chögyam Trungpa and Lama Yeshe as a study in contrasts. One of them lived untouched by controversy, while controversy was the very water in which the other swam. One never touched alcohol or women, and the other never stopped touching them. One went around, strikingly, in traditional lama's robes, while the other looked more striking for having donned a business suit. Yet, as the furor of that period recedes, those two men now seem strangely akin—two unlikely brothers. At nearly the same moment they both fled Tibet, to save their faith (and their lives), and traveled to the unknown, and both insisted on all calling the unfamiliar Home. Each brought with him from Tibet—it was about all he brought—religious precedents and dogmas, yet instead of preaching them each man taught spontaneously out of himself, to meet whatever the new situations demanded. They died at nearly the same age, and during their abbreviated life spans each accomplished prodigious missions despite grave physical handicaps (a fatal heart condition in one, partial paralysis in the other). Before their deaths they had sowed Tibetan Buddhism in America and Europe on a scale undreamed of previously. Subsequently nobody has replicated their achievements, nor needed to: Later Tibetan lamas arriving here found the soil by them already prepared.

Book III

DAKINIS DESCENDING A STAIRCASE

chapter IV

•

A Tibetan Hermit,
Made in England

WHEN CHÖGYAM TRUNGPA HAD first arrived in England, he pleaded with a new acquaintance: "You may find this difficult to believe, but back in Tibet I was quite a high lama. I never thought it would come to this, but, please, can I teach you meditation? I must have one disciple!" As Trungpa taught her meditation and Buddhist scripture, occasionally she felt his hand inching up under her skirt. This was the early '60s, when stiletto heels were the fashion. Trungpa wore sandals, and as her spiked heel ground into his foot (no words were exchanged), he would return to his teaching, from which she felt she received inordinate benefit.

Trungpa wooed her by explaining that though he had taken religious vows, his uncontrollable love for her had swept everything before it, like a river in flood. The young woman, Diane Perry, dismissed his love as a load of baloney; moreover, she wasn't going to be responsible for a monk's breaking his vows. Had she known the truth, that Trungpa had known women carnally since he was thirteen and had a son, she would have jumped into bed with him, no hesitation. What a lost opportunity, Diane reminisced, to have practiced sexual tantra with a master.

Their friendship survived Trungpa's frustrated mashing because, while England was a pond stocked with erotic possibilities, Diane Perry appeared his one chance to have an actual follower. Few British in the early '60s could have told you exactly what Buddhism was—something to do with a potbellied statue? As for the Tibetan version, the very few books in English on the subject, such as Dr L. A. Waddell's *The Buddhism of Tibet, or Lamaism* (1895), dismissed it as (in Waddell's phrase) "a sinister growth of poly-demonish superstition," hardly connected to true Buddhism at all. Whenever Diane and her mother invited Trungpa to visit— this man who a decade later would be inundated with disciples— he invariably proposed the upcoming weekend, for he had nowhere else to go. That a bright girl like Diane was drawn to Buddhism many of her friends considered an immature error of judgment on her part.

Some folks make their first big mistake before they are born. Some children believe they got imprisoned in the wrong gender; some adults (e.g., Henry James in old age) change their nationality, to repair having been born in the wrong country. Diane Perry suffered both these misgivings, feeling that she was in the wrong sex in the wrong place. As a child, she overheard someone remark that girls' bodies change at a certain age, and she thought, "Oh, good. I can then go back to being a boy." (By the time her "change" came, however, she went from wanting to be a tomboy to simply wanting boys.) And though working-class English born and bred, she always felt a longing, almost a homesickness for Asia. (In her teens she started working to squirrel away the fare for a tramp steamer that would one day take her East.) To those miscalibrations of gender and geography was added another blunder—she couldn't shake the feeling that she was also born into the wrong religion.

Christianity meant nothing to her, but nobody told her there might be an alternative. To her the Christian personal God seemed no more convincing than a man-made idol. She grew up in postwar, sepia-tinted London with its rationing of food and shortages, but the absence she felt the most was of any faith in which she might believe. From a Buddhist perspective, Diane Perry's birth occurred in a time and land of darkness, 1943 England, where one could grow up, as she did, without even hearing the Buddha's name. Actually Diane heard it—once. She and her mother were watching a BBC TV documentary about Thailand, its landscape dotted with repetitive statues, which her mother hazarded to identify: "That's the Buddha. He's some kind of Oriental god." "No, not a god," Diane thought. "He lived and has a story, like Jesus." Her intuition was right, of course, though was soon forgotten, with no one then to tell her what that story might be.

And so begins an incongruous tale. A working-class Cockney girl was never expected to live, as Diane later would, for years on a solitary mountaintop at the other end of the world. Yet Diane Perry's *Guiness Book of World Records* achievement—twenty years on a Himalayan mountain—would erase the boundary between East and West; as much as Lama Yeshe, she redrew or annihilated the hitherto fixed categories of cultural geography. Diane Perry's life story recounts episodes similar to Chögyam Trungpa's *Born in Tibet*, only hers were Born in the West. For her to have become his student in the 1960s was oddity enough; but in the 1970s and '80s, she in a sense *became* Chögyam Trungpa. The place he had vacated in the Himalayas, she stepped into, and the career and adventures he might have undertaken, had history not intervened, she lived out in her person. Tibetan Buddhism? Western spirituality? As she inhabited that solitary mountaintop in the clouds, the two blended and became one.

SOME CRITICS DISMISS BUDDHISM in the West by focusing on its popularity in Hollywood: A religion created to relieve suffering becomes the hobby of the most spoiled, indulged people in the world. By contrast, Diane Perry's upbringing was firmly rooted in the traditional Buddhist ground of life's travails. Her father died when she was two, and her mother took over his tiny fishmonger's shop in London's rough East End, barely making ends meet. Her mother's one luxury was to hold a séance in their small flat every Wednesday evening. "I grew up with tables flying around the apartment," Diane joked. Those séances were her pre-Buddhist education: They immersed her in talk of death as a positive experience, of the continuation of consciousness, of the possibility of other dimensions of being—things that most Western Buddhists, try as they might, have trouble swallowing. To her such spiritualist hypotheses, like "facts" picked up in childhood, seemed as obvious as sunshine or rain.

But even the séance attenders didn't know what to make of Diane. Such a strange child. One night as she and her mother were riding on a crowded bus, Diane said with sudden conviction, "Every person on this bus is going to get sick and die." Her mother reassured her, "There's a lot of suffering in life, but there are good things, too." Of course, Diane thought, but those good things end in sickness and death. And the bus, all lit up and animated, felt to her like a boating party, oblivious of the fatal cataract ahead. But when Diane expressed such thoughts, the adults called her gloomy, so she quit voicing them aloud.

She baffled her mother by repeatedly asking, "How do we become perfect?" There are manuals to help explain sex to children, but none to answer questions like that. Her mother, and later the minister, could only respond, "Be very good, and be very kind." They don't know, she thought, convinced as she was that, deep down, we are already secretly perfect. Spinoza had written, "Ultimately, Reality and Perfection must be reckoned the same." But Spinoza was a metaphysician from another age, while Diane was an otherwise sensible English girl who merely had some weird ideas. Had she grown up in a Buddhist country, though, her ideas would have sounded far less strange. Suffering (sickness-aging-death) is the first Noble Truth of the Buddha; the first truth of Tibetan Buddhism is that beneath that suffering, we are already innately perfect. Diane's offbeat notions unknowingly pulled her in a certain direction, toward a land she had no name for.

. . . unless that *terra incognita* was Asia. From childhood she had been an Orientalist. Her childhood drawings had Asian themes, reproducing images such as Japanese women in kimonos; when Chinese restaurants opened in London's West End, she begged to go there, to see Eastern faces. After she started dating, she never wanted to go out with pale English boys, only Asians.

If the Orient had solved her dating problem, might it do the same for her religious one? Christianity, as noted, left her unpersuaded, and the Christian God, she recalls, reminded her of "a sort of superior Santa Claus." When her schoolteacher led the class in singing the hymn "All Things Wise and Wonderful, the Lord God Made Them All," Diane wondered, "All right, but then who made all things stupid and ugly?" She queried her Jewish sister-in-law about Judaism; she read the Koran—but there was still the same old obstacle, still St. Nick in the Clouds. In her late teens she turned to Sartre and Camus, then all the vogue, but could not quite accept their claim that existential despair was the final say-so.

The university would surely unlock the doors of philosophy and understanding—why else attend?—but she lacked money for college. Instead she took a job at the local library, with its monastic hush and knowledge neatly arranged in rows. One library patron returned a book with a title so intriguing Diane immediately checked it out. In *The Mind Unshaken* an English journalist recounts his stint in Thailand, in the course of which he supplies a brief overview of that country's religion. Diane was dumbstruck. Elated. Here before her eyes, in black and white on a page, was everything she believed—and not the nostrums of a crackpot either—but the teachings of a world religion. And no God anywhere in sight in it, thank god. Thailand's religion, Buddhism, presented she thought "a perfect path," step by step, already all laid out. By the time she had finished half the book, she announced to her mother that she was a Buddhist.

"That's nice, dear," her mother said. "Finish the book, and you can tell me about it."

When Diane did tell her, instead of raising objections, her mother announced she was a Buddhist, too. Her mother, Lee Perry, fishmonger, was a good choice of parent for England's first teenage Buddhist girl. Earlier, when Diane as a toddler got badly burned, Lee Perry had instinctively prayed, "She is too young. Let me feel the pain for her." The doctors marveled that a small child could be so brave, but in truth Diane felt nothing. Much later she realized that her mother had somehow done *tonglin*, the Tibetan practice of assuming another's pain. The small sums of money Lee Perry would send her made Diane's long years in India financially possible, though that support meant she did not get to see her daughter. At the end of her life, Lee Perry's dying wish was to be Diane's mother again in her next lifetime, for another parent might fail to recognize that she had special needs.

Having declared she was a Buddhist, Diane scavenged the scant literature available to learn what a Buddhist actually *does*. In everything that she read desire entangles the poor vulnerable mortal in coils of suffering and to extricate yourself from suffering, you have to extinguish desire. Dutifully she discarded her boyfriends, stopped wearing makeup, and asked her mother to donate all her pretty clothes to charity. In their place she decided to wear Buddhist monastic robes, except that she had no idea what such robes looked like. Maybe like a Greek tunic? She cut and stitched together a yellow tunic and fastened it around her waist with a belt. After six months a thought struck her: She couldn't be the only Buddhist in England. She searched the phone book under Bs. At the first Buddhist Society meeting she attended—gracious! the other women were not wearing Greek tunics, but fashions, cosmetics, and high heels. She regretted having forfeited all her pretty dresses, and in response her mother handed her a key. Years later when Diane read about Buddhist "Skillful

Means" in dealing with others, she recalled how when she wanted to dispose of her dresses, her mother had not protested but simply locked them away in an armoire.

Diane had turned to the phone book because she had no mentor, no older, wiser voice to counsel her. She did have a kind of "inner voice," though, whose whispers of intuition sometimes surprised her. Possibly many people have such intuitions, and Diane was unique only in heeding hers. Yet as her inner voice now urged her in the direction of Tibetan Buddhism, she was hardly pleased. Her foraging bookstores for books on Buddhism had netted a scant haul, but one odd volume contained a brief chapter about "Lamaism." The chapter dutifully listed the four major Tibetan traditions: Nyingmapa, Gelugpa, Kagyupa, and Sakyupa. What a mouthful of syllables: *NyingmapaGelugpaKagyupaSakyupa*. But her inner voice whispered to her: "You're a Kagyupa."

Diane: "What's a Kagyupa?"
Inner Voice: "It doesn't matter. You're a Kagyupa."

"Oh no, wouldn't you know," she thought, "just when everything was going along so nicely." Diane trusted her voice enough, though, to become the only young woman in England bent on penetrating that farrago of superstitions called Tibetan Buddhism.

So little to go on. She unearthed a translation (by Evans-Wenz) of *The Life of Milarepa*, who in the twelfth century had founded the Kagyu sect. The tale's mythological embroidery would put off any sensible Englishman, but from her own childhood, from the séances and from "out-of-body" experiences when she was sick, Diane knew there was more than one way to read such symbols. Milarepa had passed his youth as a black magician, perpetrating unspeakable deeds, but then he atoned and did penitential labors and became a great yogi. So karma doesn't imply the passivity of fate, she realized, but it means that by what we do now we determine our future. Reading *The Life of Milarepa* she thought, "We can become responsi-

ble for our lives instead of being helpless victims. Isn't this good news?"
And she also thought: I guess I'm a Kagyupa after all.

Yet still she liked boys and liked tight dresses and liked to dance, even
while she dreamed of becoming a Tibetan nun. (At this point she wasn't
sure, though, if there were Buddhist nuns, or only monks.) When friends
from her two worlds, the partygoers and the Buddhists, happened to
meet, they seemed to be talking about two different Dianes. She worried
that some schizophrenic division split her down the middle, with a friv-
olous side and a spiritual side, and she wasn't sure which she sided with.
Her inner voice settled the matter: "Don't worry. You are young, enjoy
yourself. When it comes time to renounce, this way you'll have something
to renounce." So she relaxed and she did enjoy herself, though often the
thought would recur that she should go to India and find her guru, as it
says to do in all the texts. She learned of a Mrs. Frieda Bedi, an Englishwoman in India who ran both a school for young lamas and a small
Kagyupa nunnery (so there were nuns!) in Dalhousie. Excited, she fired
off a letter to this Mrs. Bedi in India, offering to come help, while confessing that she had no skills that could possibly be of help. Mrs. Bedi
wrote back, "Just come."

Easier said than done. It took working a whole year to save up fare for
the passage. And then there she was, in 1964, in India! Anyone else might
have confused it with Hell. Dalhousie accommodated the influx of Tibetan
refugees as best it could, but "living conditions" there—grossly inadequate food, shelter, and medical treatment—might have been described
equally as dying conditions. Diane's tiny, freezing room leaked so badly
that, when it rained, she had to sleep under the bed with the rats. She
taught English at the Young Lamas Home School (among her pupils was
Lama Zopa, later Lama Yeshe's chief disciple). Yet wretched as the physical
arrangements were, she would not have traded them for a town house in
Mayfair. As one of the few Westerners there, she enjoyed an easy daily intimacy with the living legends of Tibet. To meet the Dalai Lama, she borrowed a Tibetan princess's dress, which elicited from him the

compliment, "You look like an elegant lady from Lhasa." The Dalai Lama next made a comment that caused the translator to pause, "I am puzzled. His Holiness has addressed you as Nun, and he greeted you as only one old hermit would greet another." Diane would indeed become a nun, as well as a hermit, but she had no inkling of that then. She surprised herself by answering the Dali Lama's compliment, "I am not from Lhasa. I am from Kham"—though in fact she knew nothing about the Kham region of Tibet. A week later, however, on her twenty-first birthday, she met someone from Kham, and he was to change her life utterly.

That summer month after month everyone in Dalhousie awaited the arrival of the esteemed Khamtrul Rinpoche. The first time Diane heard the name of this revered Tibetan figure, she felt something like electricity going through her body, and she was convinced that he was her teacher. On June 30, her birthday, the phone rang, and after answering it, Frieda Bedi turned to Diane. "Your best birthday present is at the bus station." When Khamtrul Rinpoche arrived and entered the room, nervousness overtook Diane: She did not even look up but stared stupidly at his brown shoes. Mrs. Bedi was explaining who Diane was, when, still not daring to glance up, she whispered, "Tell him I want to take Refuge." "Oh yes," Mrs. Bedi added, "and she would like to take Refuge with you." "Taking Refuge" formally commits a person to the Buddhist path, and no lama would give Refuge to a stranger—particularly a stranger who has yet to look at him—without examining his or her preparedness. But Khamtrul Rinpoche answered, "Of course." Hearing his assent, Diane finally looked up and . . . it was so much like seeing an old friend that she nearly said, Good to see you again. She eerily felt she was staring at the deepest part of herself, but somehow transposed onto this other person's countenance. Within a week she had confided to Khamtrul Rinpoche her desire to become a nun—which demands a long period of probation—but again he answered matter-of-factly, "Of course."

Upon her ordination Khamtrul Rinpoche gave her a Tibetan name: Tenzin Palmo. Since under that name her fame has spread throughout the

Buddhist world, and increasingly beyond, it is as Tenzin Palmo she will move through the remainder of this chapter. For the next five years she served Khamtrul Rinpoche as his secretary—five years of great good fortune that brought her daily in contact with her teacher. She felt that to observe Khamtrul Rinpoche day after day was to probe what the essence of being human means and to watch what happens when it is brought to fruition. After five years with Khamtrul Rinpoche, observing his just-right response to every conceivable situation, she was convinced: We all have buddha-nature, and this is what it is like.

Yet they were also five miserably lonely years. The only nun among eighty monks, she could not share lodgings, or eat, or practice rituals with another soul. Worse, far worse: She might have buddha-nature, but in those surroundings there were no provisions for a nun's education, for furthering her understanding of what that nature was. She felt like someone who had traveled to the most beautiful lake in the world, in which she alone was not permitted to swim. Khamtrul Rinpoche explained that, in all previous lifetimes, she had been a man, but now she had taken a woman's form and he was limited in what he could do. (His remark reminded her of how once she had believed she was actually a boy and that her girl's body was some sort of mistake.) More recently Tenzin Palmo has come to think that, at this juncture in history, a woman can do more good and undo more injustices than a man, but back at Khamtrul Rinpoche's monastery she lamented her female body, which denied her access to Buddhist instruction, the very thing she hungered for most.

In 1970 Khamtrul Rinpoche proposed a remedy, and she did not need to think twice before accepting it. He recommended that she undertake a prolonged retreat—the Tibetan Buddhist equivalent of a postdoctoral degree. And Khamtrul Rinpoche knew the perfect place: a tiny Buddhist nunnery in a valley so off the beaten track no one was sure how to spell its name. (Everyone who has interviewed Tenzin Palmo has come up with a different orthographic possibility. Vicki Mackenzie in *Cave in the Snow* spelled it "Lahoul"; Malcolm Tillis in *Turning East*, "Lahaul"; and Martine Bachelor in *Walking on Lotus Flowers*, "Lahul.") A twenty-seven-year-old Englishwoman venturing to remote Lahoul might well have dreaded the isolation, the unhealthy deprivation of human society. Tenzin Palmo fretted about the opposite. When she arrived in Lahoul, an old nun informed her she would need twenty plates and twenty cups, for they often ate their meals and performed chores together, rotating from house to house in the nunnery compound, in a kind of circulating sewing bee. When the nuns shoveled their flat roofs clean of snow, the shouting back and forth rang from rooftop to rooftop. Tenzin Palmo was officially on retreat, but the retreat took place in the middle of this hubbub, which she could neither be part of nor shut out. The Lahoulis were lovely, but she had not traveled to the ends of the earth to join a sorority party. Frustrated, determined to enact a true retreat in the spirit of the legendary hermit-sages, she devised a solution. What Tenzin Palmo did next no other Western woman had ever attempted, nor likely will again.

Her proposal was modest, to build a small retreat cabin aways apart. She prayed to the dakinis (Tibetan spirits or energy-forces, considered to be feminine in character) that if they found her a propitious place, she would practice there wholeheartedly. The next day she confided her plan to another nun, who objected, "How can you build a cabin? You don't have any money. You should find a cave instead."

Tenzin Palmo: "Haven't we been through this before? If there is a cave, there is no water. If there is water, there are people around."

Other nun: "That's true. But last night I dreamed about an old nun around here who used to meditate in a cave, supposedly not far away, supposedly there was water. . . . You should ask her."

The old nun was now eighty but a mountain goat of a woman who had no trouble climbing to a cave about two hours distant, with Tenzin Palmo and a party of monks and nuns trailing behind her. Well, not exactly a cave, more an overhang near the edge of a cliff, but Tenzin Palmo decided that it could be sealed off and that it was perfect. The others decided, on the contrary, she could not possibly live there. "It will be too cold in winter," they argued. "No person can live here and live."

Tenzin Palmo rebutted, "Caves are naturally insulated, warmer in winter than a house."

The others: "You would not be safe from robbers."

Tenzin Palmo: "There are no robbers in Lahoul. Lahouli women walk around wearing all their jewelry."

Others: "If a soldier climbed here, he could rape you."

Tenzin Palmo: "By the time a soldier straggled up here, he'd be too exhausted for anything but a cup of tea."

Others: "But what about snakes? What about snakes!"

"Oh but I like snakes," Tenzin Palmo answered, at which point they conceded defeat. Later, she thought: But there are no snakes in Lahoul. She had heard her friends say *drul*, the Tibetan word for snakes, but what they had actually said was *trul*, or ghosts. And they had concluded that if she liked ghosts and befriended roaming spirits, she was beyond fear and let her dwell where she will.

She hired a workman to brick up the sides and front of the overhang, thus constructing a tidy cave reminiscent of Alexandra's cabin-cave in Lachen, though even smaller. Extend your arms over your head—from fingers to feet, that was about the length of it. Only partially extend your arms overhead, that was about the width of it. Attached to it abutted a small side room, the size of a large closet, to store the provisions— kerosene, rice, lentils, tea—that she hired a man to carry up there, which had to keep her in store for the six months when heavy snows made entrance and exit impossible. Altogether she squandered approximately thirty dollars outfitting her turtle shell in the sky. How long could she, could anyone, inhabit that six-by-ten-foot world, as the interminable winter snows cordoned it off into its own miniature planet? Only a month would amount to a failure; six months would be considered respectable; a year would begin to test (and according to her Lahouli friends, exceed) the limits of endurance. When Tenzin Palmo entered her cave, she was thirty-three; when she exited it, unwillingly as it turned out, she was forty-five-years old. A dozen years had passed, as in a dream.

What happened during those long years in the tiny cave? Nothing. Nothing happened. Actionless, motionless, time stood still as day and night alternated repetitively and weeks and months slid by unmarked on the slate of the sky. For a dozen years she lived a story without a story line, whose "event" was its eventlessness. The only "news" here was the mind turning in on itself day after day, while elsewhere governments and nations rose and fell.

Tenzin Palmo was not simply dwelling in a cave: She was inhabiting one of humankind's oldest dreams. The critic Northrop Frye has written that Mountain and Cave are two archetypes which have tantalized the human imagination time out of mind. Shelley in his poetry fantasized an Ancient Jew who attained sagacity on a mountaintop where his only neighbors were the passing clouds. William Butler Yeats perused old Indian lore to locate a real equivalent of Shelley's fictitious sage. In his best-selling Into the Wild, John Krakauer reported about an American youth who, in lieu of a cave, holed up in an abandoned bus in the woods to obtain enlightenment, and unprepared for the brutal winter, died in it. This archetype that beguiled Shelley and Yeats and so bewitched holy seekers became Tenzin Palmo's actual daily fare, and she was prepared to endure, to live it out to its final meaning.

Tenzin Palmo thus entered the tunnel of no escape and no distraction. She couldn't telephone a friend, turn on the TV, smoke a cigarette, dash to the corner store, or in winter even go for a walk. Gone were the hundred little diversions and distractions that keep one from coming to terms with that objectionable companion, oneself. Since her goal was not to "bliss out" but rather to train the mind, her daily schedule was as regimented as any clock-punching office worker's, if not more so. One of her few possessions, a loud alarm clock, would sound shortly before 3 A.M.

3–6 A.M. First meditation period of the day

6–8 A.M. Tea and attending to necessities

8–11 A.M. Second meditation period

11–12 A.M. Lunch, her one meal of the day, invariably rice and lentils, dried vegetables, and for desert half a dried apple.

1–3 P.M. Painting Buddhas and bodhisattva or copying texts (her written Tibetan was by now more legible than most Lahoulis')

3–6 P.M. Third meditation

6–8 P.M. Tea ("I'm English, you know.")

8–11 P.M. Fourth meditation

And then to bed, except there was no bed. She tried to sleep, or half sleep, in a sitting position, so as not to dissipate lucidity: sleeping sitting up, she said, was good for her mind but bad for her back. When vertical sleep became too achy, she would curl up on her meditation box. Tenzin Palmo's meditation platform, approximately 1½ by 3 by 4 feet, where she meditated during the day and half the night and then rested a few hours, was her version of a shipwrecked sailor's raft—a raft to sail the ocean of suffering and dock in ultimate safe harbor. Solitary meditators often suffer a nervous disorder called in Tibetan lung, which she was given medicinal pills to combat, but she never felt the need to take them. Sometimes she would step outside, surveying her pristine dominion, wave upon wave of valleys and mountains, and ask, "If you could be anywhere in the world, where would you be?" Her inner voice would answer: Here. "If you could be doing anything you chose, what would it be?" This.

At times she inhabited a world as enchanted as anything Shelley or Yeats fantasized. Her cave was high up (13,200 feet), if not entirely above tree line certainly above the line where the predictable happened. Once a deranged shepherd boy strayed near her cave, keeping his distance but intent on doing her harm. When she smiled at him, he scowled back. She discovered her water supply tampered with, the next day the window to her cave broken. How vulnerable she was, with nobody else around. Tenzin Palmo prayed to the dakinis, and the next day she found the boy had repaired her water supply and had begun leaving flowers at her door. Praying to the dakinis was standard operating procedure in Lahoul, the Tibetan name of which is *Kasha Khandro Ling*, or "Land of the Living Dakinis." One year a terrible drought dessicated the region, and some monks arrived, explaining they'd come to placate the spirits of the place. No sooner did they perform their rituals than the rains began to pour. And pour and pour, until the contents of her leaky cave were soaked as though having been tumbled in a washing machine. Two soggy weeks later, the monks returned, prostrated, prayed, and right on cue the rains stopped. One nomadic visitor informed Tenzin Palmo that her cave had been home to a yeti, but her being there had scared him away (and sometimes she did find large, unidentifiable paw tracks). Tenzin Palmo lived an existence such as usually only children read about in books, where the boundaries between inner and outer, dreaming and waking, oneself and the world, quietly dissolve.

She even enjoyed the wolves, who climbed on the roof of her cave and howled, her lunatic nightly serenade. But at times all enjoyment faded and left only ordeal and endurance. The temperature could sink below even the memory of zero degrees; and she lit her stove but once a day, to cook the noonday meal. One year the man hired to bring her supplies failed to arrive, while her provisions dwindled away. "What did you do then?" she was later asked, and she answered plausibly, "I grew very thin." She halved her daily portions, and then halved the half and after that halved the half of the half, until she was living on a few calories per diem and melted snow. When the man finally showed up, she did not express anger or even demand to know what had detained him, assuming he had his reasons.

Possibly the practical Lahoulis were right, that no one can live so high up, so isolated, and that for her to attempt to do so transgressed human bounds. During the brutal winter of 1979 a blizzard raged inexorably day after day, completely burying her cave and her in it, fatally depriving her (she thought) of oxygen. For years she had meditated on impermanence and mortality, and now—put to the test—she appeared to fear death less than some people do a visit from their mother-in-law. In that cave, soon to be her tomb, she took out her Tibetan "precious pills" that one swallows before dying to purify the mind-stream. (Their recipe: herbs, gems, ground-up relics, which after being prepared are prayed over by lamas and consecrated at religious ceremonies. So impossibly tightly are the pills bound in silk, she later joked, one could have a heart attack trying to unwrap them.) Dying entails torment, Tibetans believe, but also an opportunity, the chance to liberate consciousness from its corporal prison and direct it into a better rebirth. As the ceaseless snows buried her cave Tenzin Palmo performed the appropriate meditations. When those meditations reached the point where one envisions his guru, gratitude to Khamtrul Rinpoche overwhelmed her. Just at that moment she heard his voice within her: "Dig out!"

Dig out? Was such an escape possible? She pried open the door to her cave: on the other side a solid wall of frozen snow. Using a shovel, then a pan lid, and finally her hands she burrowed a tunnel through the packed snow. Blackness was in front of her and blackness behind, she was in a grave, or womb, and still she burrowed. Finally after an hour she propelled herself into open space, into intoxicating air and giddy light. But still the snow was coming down furiously, so she crawled back, as the tunnel collapsed behind her, to bury her in her cave once more. (Her premonitions of suffocating proved unwarranted, though, since caves do "breathe.") The third time she tunneled out, the blizzard had stopped, and she beheld a blinding white universe, monolithic, featureless. A helicopter whirred overhead, scanning for survivors from an avalanche that had buried whole villages (while her cave had actually afforded the safest refuge possible).

It really is too much, she thought. People are right, you cannot live in a cave. She was on the verge of feeling sorry for herself, when she recalled the Buddha's teachings: This life—what our ordinary perceptions register and our normal moods reflect—is by its very nature intertwined with sickness, decay, and suffering. Why then demand, on the gross physical level, to be happy? She recalled the time that her eye had become infected, and the pain was so excruciating that if she moved or lay down, it shot into new octaves of agony. For weeks in the cave she sat and simply watched the pain, finding it "like a symphony, with the drums, the trumpets, the strings, all those very different types of pain playing on the eye." Trying to resist or ignore the pain exhausted her, but if she went with it, rode it, the pain became bearable. From her mixture of suffering and Buddhist insight, Tenzin Palmo came to understand the difference between momentary felicity and ultimate well-being. After she realized that physical suffering was inevitable, that it always was and always will be, neither its presence nor absence much fazed her again. Ironically, she achieved a kind of permanent happiness by surrendering expectations of happiness. She had reached safety within herself.

After nine years in the cave, interrupted by her forays to obtain supplies or to see Khamtrul Rinpoche, she determined to brave the final step. As though that decade on a mountain ledge with its occasional breaks had been too lax and gregarious, she vowed to seal herself off in unbroken solitude—a retreat within a retreat, as it were—for three years, three months, and three days. Let that time fly by, for to her the time did quickly pass (the last year of the retreat felt hardly longer than a month). Outside the cave a notice on a makeshift fence warned in three languages, IN RETREAT—DO NOT ENTER (which the porter who brought her provisions heeded, leaving her supplies without ever seeing her). Mere months short of her retreat's completion, however, a man barged into her cave, yelling and knocking things over. It was an Indian policeman shouting that her visa had expired and for her to report to the magistrate tomorrow and leave India within ten days. Ordinarily after such isolation one needs weeks gradually to adjust to society, but the next day Tenzin Palmo descended from her pinnacle. As she trudged down the mountain, she harbored no ill feelings, knowing the policeman and the magistrate were only doing their duty. The farther down the mountain she descended, the more people gathered to meet her, bursting with curiosity. What other-worldly insights had she experienced? Had she obtained enlightenment? those crowded around asked. They awaited the revelation.

"Well, one thing I can tell you." Tenzin Palmo said. "I was never bored."

That's it? Twelve years beyond the beyond, and all she has to report back is: *Not bored?* Yet her lack of boredom—like her looking death in the face during the snow avalanche and her calmly tolerating excruciating eye pain—is its own testimony. She was no Samuel Beckett character inhabiting abstract nonspace, muttering languidly to herself. Whom she resembles is Alexandra David-Neel meeting adversity blithely, but while Alexandra's fields of adventure were the tablelands of high Asia, hers were the remote corners of her mind.

What did Tenzin Palmo learn during those years in the cave? Tenzin Palmo has given talks collected in *Reflections on a Mountain Lake: Teachings on Practical Buddhism* (2002), which attempt to deliver the understanding she gained during those dozen years. Her theme is the transformation of the mind into an instrument more user-friendly; in effect she has written a manual, "How to Be the Master of Your Own Thoughts."

Generally thoughts and images pop into our minds unbidden, which is fine when we happen to be happy but not when we are anxious or angry or depressed. Tenzin Palmo shows her readers how to avoid being at the mercy of their haphazard thoughts—how to be free of (un-)free associations. When we meditate, she says, a part of our mind withdraws from the ceaseless stream of relentless memories, daydreams, fears, and fantasies, and simply observes them. As the observing mind gains steadiness, even morbid thoughts or disturbing feelings become like overnight guests in our house who do it no permanent damage. This manumission from the tyranny of reflex thought is, she suggests, the one freedom available to anyone. That freedom is what Tenzin Palmo mastered in the cave.

In *Reflections on a Mountain Lake* a reader learns what distinguishes Tibetan from other varieties of Buddhism. Tenzin Palmo writes that in Hinayana or Theravadin Buddhism, as practiced in Sri Lanka and Thailand, desire and attachment are considered the culprits, leading us indirectly into suffering. But in Mahayana Buddhism, practiced in Japan and precommunist China, the villain is less our cravings than our ignorance: We mistake for real what is not (e.g., our distorted self-image) and dismiss as unreal (i.e., our inherent buddha-nature) what actually exists. As for the Buddhism of Tibet—the Vajrayana—it is philosophically close to Mahayana Buddhism, but when you come actually to practice it, it becomes a distinct path unto itself.

Mahayanists believe in patiently nurturing one's embryonic buddha-nature, principally through ethical conduct, until gradually, after many and many a lifetime, a person will be reborn as a Buddha. Vajrayana, or Tibetan Buddhism, holds to the contrary that if we already have buddha-nature, surely it's more sensible and effective to begin to use that nature now. Tenzin Palmo describes the path visualization practices whose purpose is to animate one's dormant buddha-quality. Everyone visualizes all the time anyway, recalling last night's TV program or dreading tomorrow's doctor's appointment. Unlike such visualized daydreaming, the visualization practices Tenzin Palmo prescribes—such as seeing yourself as a deity—are meant to activate something existing but not yet realized. Glimpses of one's buddha-quality during visualizations (or in everyday life) are like exercises that strengthen and build up one's truest, inmost nature. Such practices are not pretend-fantasies, she argues, but gateways to our true being:

> . . . they are an extremely skillful conduit back to very profound
> realms of our psyche which we cannot access by means of logical,
> linear thinking. There are very subtle levels of our psychological

makeup we can access only through enlightened imagery. These meditations . . . open up profound levels of the mind very quickly.

Besides visualizations, Tenzin Palmo describes meditational practices that can manipulate one's inner energy and redirect even anger and heated passion to good effect. This is another distinguishing characteristic of Vajrayana, that it utilizes the energy in neutral and negative situations that other traditions reject—in fury and sensual gratification and fear; the demonic as well as the angelic; in even sleeping and dreaming—and refines them and uses them as fossil fuel for the passage. Tenzin Palmo obviously spent a large number of her approximately six million minutes in the cave activating or transmuting her internal energies into consciousness. With this result: that the woman who exited that cave after twelve years resembled (according to those who later heard her talks) a Buddha perhaps more than she did a Cockney girl who grew up in London's East End.

What is such a person like who has passed twelve solitary years in a cave (and the cave of oneself)? Her friends and acquaintances describe Tenzin Palmo as someone who, whatever she does, gives the impression there is nothing else in the world she would rather be doing. "I don't know if I am particularly warm toward others," she has said, "but I feel whomever I am with is at that time the most important person in the world." One friend observed that, though it may be biologically inborn to put oneself first, she lives out Blake's aphorism "The most sublime act is to set another before you." She does not even appear to arrange experience into "me" versus "them" as she goes out to greet whomever or whatever in whichever shape it comes. Her most often remarked-upon quality is her steady clarity, uncluttered by preoccupations and preconceptions of "worthwhile" versus "trivial." Her mind seems to operate level with experience, not darting ahead in imagined projects, or lagging behind in dreamy regrets. This type of concentration might well be learned over the course of long years in a cave, when today, the future, and past days all look rather identical.

Friends of Tenzin Palmo have commented that, were they about to suffocate in a cave, they would panic and not, as she did, quietly meditate. If their crucial supplies failed to arrive, they would react furiously, not calmly subration the few lentils left. Her apprenticeship in equanimity was conducted in a cave, but it has carried on afterwards, and carried her smoothly through changing countries and conditions. Despite a preference for solitude, when giving talks Tenzin Palmo shows herself at home in groups and obviously wants to be there. When on speaking tours, undertaken to raise money for teaching Buddhism to underpriviledged Asian women, she inquires each morning where the schedule has her posted that day, and then matter-of-factly flies or drives to that particular city. (Gradually an organization has built up that supports Tenzin Palmo in her work and which facilitates the practical arrangements of her tours.) Arriving, she asks what topic she is to lecture on, and then, without notes or preparation, speaks lucidly for the time required. People at those talks describe her as earthly yet "spacious," self-effacing yet vividly personal— not at all what one expects of a hermit from a cave. Without referring to herself, Tenzin Palmo says that human personality is itself not what one expects. "The Buddha's great understanding," she continues,

> was to realize that the further we go [into ourselves] the more
> open and empty the quality of our consciousness becomes. Instead
> of finding some solid little entity, which is "I," we get back to the
> vast spacious mind which is interconnected with all living beings.

As petty as this sounds, most people would probably abhor such equanimity as Tenzin Palmo exhibits, in themselves or their loved ones. Vicki Mackenzie, a journalist who extensively interviewed Tenzin Palmo, feels hurt that she cannot occupy a more important niche in her subject's affections. "You know in your heart that if she [Tenzin Palmo] never saw you again she really would not miss you. And her lack of emotional need is disconcerting," Mackenzie says, because one "likes to be flattered, wants to be wanted. From her, however, you'll never get it." "I don't think it's a bad thing," Tenzin Palmo responds. "It doesn't mean that one doesn't feel love and compassion," but some people "get upset if you are not attached to them . . . because we confuse love and attachment."

A world populated solely with Tenzin Palmos would be a kind world without wars, homicides, competition, and tantrums. It would also likely be a world without *Hamlet*, the great Renaissance portraits, Boswell's *Life of Johnson*, and Dickens and Faulkner. Carl Jung declared, even were it possible, he would refuse Enlightenment: he desired to know the self's antics, all the fretful dramas of individual personality, and to live them out to their last cry of meaning. Yet Tenzin Palmo's model of "unselfish detachment" may suit an overcrowded, resources-strained planet better than Jung's cultivation of individuality. Since the eighteenth century, heightened individualism has spent itself in emotional fuss and financial profligacy. The eccentric eighteenth-century aristocrats and the nineteenth-century high bourgeoisie and the twentieth-century millionaires required acres of architecture and servants and goods, which are now too rationed to support such histrionic personal displays. By contrast, Tenzin Palmo lived in India on less than fifteen dollars a month. If everybody ate as much, or rather as little, as she did and occupied no more spacious quarters, the human population would possess an *overabundance* of food and housing. If nobody excited more emotional disturbance than she does, animosities, jealousies, and broken hearts would vanish. Her religion likewise came in a tidy manageable package, requiring no proselytizing, no mass demonstrations, no fanatical dogma. Buddhism may appeal to Americans today who want the satisfactions of faith but do not have much extra room (for community or tradition) in their private lives. With its compact emphasis on individual meditation, Buddhism may fit the overpopulated twenty-first century because, as with Tenzin Palmo in her six-by-ten-foot cave, it can accommodate itself and take up less space.

After a cave, what's your next career move? Tenzin Palmo no longer had any agenda to guide her. Unlike that teenager who rued giving away her party dresses, by now she really had dispensed with desire. And without desire, how do you choose or do anything? Rumors of her had been quietly spreading by word of mouth, and invitations now poured in from many places suggesting she come live there. Italy, where nothing quite worked, where telephoning was an uncertain proposition, and the bureaucracy ensnared everything in red tape, made her feel comfortable; it was rather like being in India again. She settled (for the time being) in Assisi, the birthplace of Saint Francis, with its monasteries and nunneries cuddling the surrounding hills. (When Lama Yeshe earlier visited there, he exclaimed upon seeing Saint Francis's cave, "See! . . . See! Western yogis meditate in caves, too.") Tenzin Palmo, a nun herself, felt at home amid the monastic settings.

In her cave she had sometimes forgotten to meditate, idly fantasizing about starting a Buddhist nunnery in India, imagining even details of the robes the nuns would wear. Khamtrul Rinpoche had indeed proposed that she found a nunnery, but she had dismissed his suggestion as wild, beyond her meager abilities. In 1992, with the handsome monasteries of Italy to inspire her, she thought she might return to India and try. Like a madwoman or innocent, she took on all the obstacles involved, including a world tour to raise funds, and then tackled the Indian bureaucracy where approval for proposals such as hers can lie suspended in infinite limbo. Despite all the obstacles, by 2000, she had secured land and was living in Himachal Pradesh (near Khamtrul Rinpoche's old monastery), and the first young women began their novitiate there. When Tenzin Palmo had first ventured to Asia, it shocked her that the Buddhism she practiced in London bore little resemblance to its actuality in Sri Lanka or Thailand: There nuns, inferior womankind, had to walk or crawl backwards when leaving a monk's presence. Despite all the kindness to her at Khamtrul Rinpoches's monastery, Tenzin Palmo had suffered bitterly, excluded from the rituals and denied full access to the teachings. In inaugurating her nunnery, Tenzin Palmo was helping end twenty-five hundred years of women's second-class citizenship in Buddhism.

In the year 2003 Tenzin Palmo celebrated her sixtieth birthday, and should she prove to be anything like those legendary Tibetan practitioners who flowered in old age, there's no prophesying what her final act will be. One can predict, though, that her likes will not be seen again. No one will retreat into a remote cave, because soon the earth will have no remote caves; all the once out-of-the-way outposts will have been settled, militarized, or touristed. No one will train under a guru like Khamtrul Rinpoche, because those Tibet-educated high lamas will soon be extinct. Tenzin Palmo's work will be carried on by the young women who go forth from her nunnery, but native born to Asian Buddhism, they do not really resemble her. As England's first teenage Buddhist girl who found the way herself, Tenzin Palmo in fact appears to resemble nobody: She has no true antecedents and no descendants either.

Yet a scholarly gentleman in Lahoul, perusing his books, believed he identified Tenzin Palmo's spiritual next-of-kin: Alexandra David-Neel. Both women were magnetically attracted to Tibetan Buddhism, as each broke every precedent to pursue her dream of it. Of the two, David-Neel explored a vast geographical terrain and braved a thousand more adventures. Even so, the Lahouli scholar concluded, Tenzin Palmo was the one who went further, the one who delved deeper. She did not march over snowy passes or converse with hermit-wizards or don gold-inlaid robes to bless the natives. Instead Tenzin Palmo sat in a cave for twelve years and watched the coming and going of thought and mastered how the mind works: which was precisely what the Buddha advised one to do.

Before founding the nunnery, Tenzin Palmo had consulted the Dalai Lama to ask whether she should attempt such an undertaking. She could anticipate what he would say: *Yes, of course. After eighteen years of retreat, it's time to do something practical and help others.* But in fact he did not say that. This man who spends all his days in practical ways helping others surprised her. "Starting a nunnery? Excellent," he said. "But try not to spend more than a year or two on it. Then return to your retreat."

Tenzin Palmo's retreat on that snowy mountain precipice did not transpire in "historical time," among historical events, but it accomplished something in history nonetheless. During those years as she meditated in her cave, across the border to the north the Chinese communists were dynamiting monasteries and burning sacred texts, in order to eradicate that country's religion. But Tenzin Palmo faithfully enacted the prescriptions and guidelines in those texts, and Tibet as a spiritual entity was reborn in her.

chapter V

•

Interlude:
An American in Tibet

TENZIN PALMO LIVED IN HER cave no differently (except for the stove and alarm clock) from an old Buddhist hermit; earlier, the Thirteenth Dalai Lama intimated that the foreign woman, Madame Alexandra, was in effect a Tibetan despite or underneath her Western appearance. But what a Tibetan sees as a reincarnation, most Europeans or Americans will dismiss as a flukelike coincidence or at most a metaphor. The metaphor of such tales as that of Lama Yeshe's Spanish reincarnation is that once-alien Tibetan Buddhism now makes itself quite at home in Western containers or bodies. In this regard the strangest story of all concerns an American man, and it can hardly pass unmentioned in a book about Tibetan Buddhism in the West.

In the late 1930s Theos Bernard (1908–1947) was a promising, well-credentialed young man with both a Ph.D. and a law degree from Columbia University, when he joined that small fraternity of madcap dreamers (over the centuries only a few hundred strong) who would explore forbidden Tibet. He became the latest of those doomed-to-failure adventurers who determined to brave the impossible in high Asia. (He came by this urge almost by inheritance, from parents who admired all things Oriental and an uncle who helped introduce hatha yoga into the United States.) In some photos Bernard looks like a forerunner of the hippies; in others he resembles George Bernard Shaw doing his gleeful impersonation of the Devil. But no devil, at least not a Western one, had enjoyed much luck then in trespassing into the impenetrable kingdom.

Bernard did manage to reach the Indian side of the Tibetan border—that was the easy part—where the other Western hands in the region mocked him and his cockamamie ambition. They told him the legend of an ancient ageless pilgrim who had been trying to enter Tibet for 1,700 years and been turned back for 1,700 years. "And good luck to you, Mr. Bernard."

He did have good luck, unprecedented luck. The British authorities in India, wary of other nations' influence, routinely expelled non-English travelers sniffing around the Tibetan border. But Bernard skillfully inveigled from them the permission to enter Tibet—with the proviso that the Tibetan government also consented to his request (which, as they well knew, it never would). But then Bernard did something ingenious, not writing the Tibetan government for permission, but instead hiring a Tibetan to travel to Lhasa and press his case in person on the grounds that he (Bernard) wished to learn about Buddhism sufficiently to promulgate it in America. He nervously waited for the response from the regent of Tibet, who he realized that despite his ingenious maneuver would still refuse him admission. Then he would need to decide whether to emulate David-Neel and dare the thousand rigors of some mountainous back entrance, or, more sensibly, to call it quits. At long last the telegram did arrive. "Bernard of America," it began and proceeded to welcome him with open arms: "Your much Religionship may visit Lhasa as your desire. Wire if you need dwelling here." A second telegram from the Kashag, or Tibetan Cabinet, followed, which Bernard expected to withdraw the offer. Instead it read:

AS YOU PROBABLY KNOW TIBET BEING A PURELY RELIGIOUS COUNTRY THERE IS A GREAT RESTRICTION OF FOREIGNERS ENTERING THE COUNTRY BUT UNDERSTANDING THAT YOU HAVE A GREAT RESPECT FOR OUR RELIGION AND HAVE HOPES OF SPREADING THE RELIGION IN AMERICA ON YOUR RETURN, WE HAVE DECIDED AS A SPECIAL CASE TO ALLOW YOU TO COME TO LHASA BY THE MAIN ROAD.

Never, not once, had such an exception been extended. But the exceptions and only-once's were only beginning. Arriving in Tibet, Bernard learned the Tibetan language in record time, and the Tibetan religious education that demands decades to master he completed in a year and a half. The Tibetans had an explanation for why this feat was possible, but even to Bernard the explanation hardly sounded like sober reasoning. Theos Bernard, they said, was a reincarnation and not just any reincarnation but of the great Padmasambhava, Guru Rinpoche, who had first introduced Buddhism into Tibet. A Tibetan oracle explained that, availing himself of Bernard's body, Padmasambhava had chosen to be reborn in the West to learn its secrets, and now fate (or karma) was returning him to his homeland. "This was how they interpreted my action in leaving America and coming to them," Bernard later reported. "So it was not a mystery to them how I came always to do the right thing when passing through these various esoteric initiations, and why it was possible for me to possess such a deep comprehension of all their teachings."

Since Bernard was Padmasambhava's reincarnation, one of the most esteemed lamas in all Tibet, Tr'i Rinpoche, came out of his retreat to initiate him. During the initiation Tr'i's warm hands on his head felt to Bernard as though his skull were being fitted with a spiritual cap. "No one spoke; words were, indeed, superfluous here. When the ceremony was over I had the feeling that I had been talking with him [Tr'i Rinpoche] for a lifetime," Bernard reported. After the initiation Tr'i Rinpoche returned to his monastery some four days' journey east of Llasa but claimed he could read Bernard's thoughts and thus direct his further education from afar. There is an apocryphal legend that Padmasambhava had prophesied that in the machine age ("when horses run of wheels") Tibetan Buddhism would relocate to the West, and evidently, to avoid any mix-ups, Padmasambhava had undertaken the relocation job himself, borrowing Theos Bernard's body to do it.

Theos Bernard's story seems made for drama, as good as any adventure novel. Conrad and Kipling both spun tales of Englishmen who became demigods in Asia, but Bernard's adventure is nonfiction, and in addition, his tale offers a further dramatic possibility. An American, now recognized as a Tibetan holy figure, returns to his homeland to preach a strange religion his country has never heard of. Will the waves part before him, and legions of followers flock around?

In Bernard's story, however, after the unprecedented prologue, nothing noteworthy happens. He returned to America and wrote a book (curiously having two different titles, *Penthouse of the Gods* or *Land of a Thousand Buddhas*), which caused no stir at all. Evidently he lacked Alexandra David-Neel's skill to attract attention. Bernard also lacked something else Alexandra enjoyed—a long life span. To collect rare Buddhist manuscripts, he was making his way again to Tibet in 1947, during the Partition of India, when angry Hindus attacked his Muslim muleteers, shot him, and threw his body into the river. So we are left to speculate: What if Bernard had lived and returned again to America and begun his new career as the Padmasambhava of the West?

But if we jump ahead fifty years, we can perhaps fill in that speculation, or at least we encounter an analogous situation. For then another American, this time a woman, became recognized as a legendary Tibetan reincarnation. Unlike Bernard, she determined to fulfill her responsibilities, to do what any high reincarnation does, only in the good old U. S. of A. After Alexandra David-Neel became famous she refused to act as a guru, but this woman would play that part. Though born thousands of miles from Tibet, she would become the voice of its religion. The result turned out to be as surprising as anything Kipling or Conrad ever conjured.

chapter VI

•

The Reincarnation with
the Beautiful Fingernails

SOME PEOPLE MAY FIND Tenzin Palmo's story, even with all
its unprecedented twists, surprising only in being unsurprising. She was
reared on séances, after all, which was bound to propel her into some offbeat spirituality that wouldn't be the Church of England. She read some
Buddhist books, she met some lamas: Really, her whole career was a series
of dominoes falling in place. Anyone who believes that religion is not a
legitimate sphere of its own (unlike, say, economics or politics) would
have no trouble dismissing her spiritual vocation as a case of more or less
harmless brainwashing.

Skeptics who believe that spirituality does nothing—that there are no
epiphanies or "divine" intrusions into human affairs—will have more
trouble explaining away a woman named Alyce Louise Zeoli. This Alyce
Zeoli (in many ways the opposite of Tenzin Palmo) could be the test case
of whether a religion, instead of being a socially produced bias, can rise

up spontaneously in a person's thoughts and feelings. Her American childhood was devoid not only of Buddhism but of religious faith. As she entered adolescence there would be no dharma texts, no encounters with Tibetan monks. If she was to discover Buddhist insights anywhere, they would have to be buried inside herself. Yet when she grew to woman-hood, she invented her own religion, and though at first she had no inkling of it, that religion was, or corresponded to, Tibetan Buddhism.

ALYCE ZEOLI, born in Brooklyn, New York, in 1949, lacked the inherited wealth (Zina Rachevksy), the education (Robert Thurman), or the career (Richard Gere)to allow her to experiment and eventually by hit-or-miss to chance upon Buddhism. Her upbringing had more in com-mon with Tenzin Palmo's, with its economic hardship and narrowing of possibilities. But Tenzin Palmo merely had too little of the so-called "good things" of life, while Alyce had too many of the bad things.

Her mother was a drunkard, and her father was, well, it scarcely mat-ters since he exited the scene before she could remember him. From her stepfather, though, she learned some quite esoteric lessons: how burning cigarettes sting the body and how quickly bruises on the skin change in size and color. To escape family abuse, she would steal into her room and pray, "Don't let me be like them! Don't let me be like them!" She fanta-sized that Dr. Ben Casey on TV was her real father, and one day, Dr. Casey would come rescue her. But she was trapped just like the rest of her fam-ily. Instead of a magical Dr. Casey, the police came knocking on her house door, numerous times, and finally they advised her to leave her parents' violent home. She accomplished that leave-taking the way girls of her lim-ited resources then often did, by marrying the first boy who came along and having a baby. As the 1960s became the trippy '70s, she and her lit-tle family became part of a new lost American generation—no plans, no projects, no reasons for hope.

Growing up, she had lacked the séances and other experiences that had pointed Tenzin Palmo indirectly to Buddhism. On a trip to Coney

Island when she was about ten, a palm reader did tell her she had been a Tibetan in a previous lifetime. But since Tibet to her evoked images of old men sitting on smelly rugs, the palm reader seemed to be denying her a fortune or future. In high school she liked the way statues of the Buddha looked and gave cheap reproductions to her friends, but attached no importance to doing so. If she had any ambition at all, it was to sing backup in a Motown girl group. But as she came of age (circa her eighteenth year), all sorts of weirdness started happening. Often she might dream something, and the next thing she knew, a few days later, something like the dream actually transpired. For example, she dreamed of a witch who placed a circle on her forehead and said, "Now you have to commence." Three days later a friend was having her astrological chart done and invited Alyce along for the ride. When the astrologer opened the door, there was the witch or anyway the old woman, looking as she had in the dream. Alyce thought her secretly beautiful. The astrologer insisted on doing her chart (which is in fact circular) for free, but having done it, she refused to divulge anything. "My dear," the old astrologer told Alyce, "your whole life is laid out. You don't need any advice from anybody."

Shortly thereafter she dreamed that the farmhouse where she was then living got drenched in a sudden thunderstorm as the sky turned an eerie green. Three days after that, Alyce stood on the front porch watching a downpour exactly like the one in the dream, the sky that very shade of ominous green. Why, she wondered, was this happening to her? In her dream a voice had sounded from the storm, "When you see this, it is time to begin your meditation."

The year was 1968, Alyce was nineteen years old, and Eastern spiritual practices like meditation were coming into vogue. But she had no idea how to meditate. It did not occur to her to find a teacher or get a book on the subject; instead she trusted that whatever source those dreams came from would guide her. She simply lay down on her bed and closed her eyes. Any manual would have warned not to meditate lying down (snoring may replace meditation), and in fact her unconventional ideas for meditation usually came to her while she was dreaming.

One dream told her to meditate on everything she could wish for. What a pleasant assignment, Alyce thought upon waking. All right: She and her husband would be blissfully happy; her baby would grow up and become a doctor; she would have other children, each one a fabulous success in life; and then . . . And then: death. It was the finale to every fantasy, where every wish ultimately led. She clutched her baby son and pledged that at least she would protect him, no matter what. But if he became seriously ill, there was nothing she could do. Health and suffering, good and bad, life and death, they seemed so intertwined—a cul-de-sac with no way out.

Another dream suggested a meditation that seemed morbid to begin with. But upon waking, she set about to do it—to reflect in turn upon each part of the body. What are its purposes and its pleasures? And what would it be like if you lost that body part? Alyce began with her toes, toes that are good for walking, running, dancing. But those activities do not define the meaning of life, and if absolutely need be, could be given up. So she envisioned offering them up—and as she worked her way from toes to crown, she offered her other body parts, imagined cutting them off and giving them to God. It was a taxing, gruesome meditation, but at the end she felt a heady sense of liberation, freed from too slavish an identification with her body. In addition to such meditations, vows and resolutions came to her from she knew not where. She felt there was a faucet in her, the water was already in there, and she merely had to turn the faucet on. One strange but lovely sounding vow that sprang into her head she began to repeat over and over: "I commit myself to benefiting all beings. My life has no meaning other than to benefit all beings."

Alyce would not learn, not for a long time, that her vow was also a Tibetan Buddhist vow, or that her meditations were classic Buddhist meditations. Americans at that time were traveling to India and Nepal to learn the dharma from exiled Tibetan masters, but Alyce was in effect completing a course in Buddhism in her bedroom, having for her teacher not Lama Yeshe but her own dreams. Her first meditation illustrates the first truth of Buddhism that life is suffering, not because it is undesirable, but because everything changes and eventually we must lose what we value most. Her second meditation demonstrates the Buddhist remedy for that suffering, which is not to stop caring for what we love, but to have a less attached or self-referential love of it. In old Tibet a lama, after renouncing daily-life attachments, would train for years before attempting a practice like chöd, which Alyce did a version of when she imagined severing her limbs and sacrificing them to the deity. Alyce had never heard of Buddhist renunciation, but she too had the feeling that she was leaving behind ordinary life as ordered by personal inclinations. "I have left the party" is how she thought of it at the time. "I never said anything to anyone about it," she recalled, "but oddly, after that, people started coming to me." And thus by immaculate self-conception an American guru was born.

THE ABOVE ACCOUNT FROM her students and early admiring articles reads like an Eastern biography that abstracts an idealized person and not like a Western one, which dives straight for the gossip. Alyce's life afforded plenty of gossip. By the time she moved to the Washington area in her early thirties, she was already married to husband number three. She was also more involved with "New Age" spirituality than she now likes to recall. Living in North Carolina in the early '70s, she had gravitated to the Light Center, a New Age congregation, and taken up channeling and giving psychic readings. In those psychic readings, she would skip the monetary windfalls and new romances her clients were aching to hear prophesied and discuss instead their spiritual missions. She made an exception for a graduate student named Michael Burroughs, seeing in his future the ultimate romantic rendezvous: "You are about to be involved in a terrific relationship," she told him. "Boy, I wish I were going to have a relationship like that—and the woman's name is Catherine."

Michael, a charming southerner with a Tennessee drawl, four years her junior, possessed the driving ambition absent from her life and, working on his second master's degree, he had a kind of knowledge that her occasional night class had not given her. By the time he become her third husband (in 1983), she had changed her name—to Catherine.

When the Burroughses moved to Washington, D.C., for Michael to study comparative religion at American University, no one would have envied their lot. Michael played the organ at various churches, and Catherine clerked in a men's clothing store. But at night they turned into pioneers on a new spiritual frontier. Nearly everyone who met Alyce/Catherine during a psychic reading was mesmerized and eager for further contact. One person dropped out of school to study with her; another moved to Washington from another state. She no longer sounded so New Age-y, and the people who gathered around her, unsatisfied by self-centered personal-growth workshops, appreciated her larger vision of a vaster life lived in attunement with the universe. The basement of her rented house in suburban Maryland doubled as a meeting place for such spiritual seekers. Traipsing up and down those basement stairs, her regulars felt happy, lucky to have such a warm, funny friend who also happened to be an inspiring teacher.

In that basement Eden Catherine had to invent terms for unspoken insights that arose during her meditations. She talked about "union consciousness," a level of awareness so deep that it connected all beings. Above all she stressed that each person must become a "vehicle" programmed solely for helping other beings. The group held prayer circles for the sick, and beginning in April 1985 Catherine organized a twenty-four-prayer vigil for planetary welfare (which continues to this day). It was no picnic when you had a job, getting up at, say, 12:30 A.M. and driving groggily to Catherine's house in Maryland, praying your two-hour shift in her basement, and driving home to catch a couple of winks more sleep before getting up for work again. But most of her students, alienated during the Vietnam War, and more alienated by the politics of the Reagan era, felt almost as though they were occupying a front-row seat at some new order of creation. Her little basement group seems in retrospect sweet, idealistic, innocent: they had no agenda, in the beginning not even a name for themselves. Had "fate" left them alone to develop unhampered? Who can say? for one night there came a knock on her door that changed everything.

CATHERINE HAD EARLIER STUNNED her little group by announcing that Michael had received a teaching offer in North Carolina, which their strained finances forced them to accept. Consternation ensued. She could not desert them, they protested; they would pay her to stay and teach them. But she refused money for what, after all, had come to her as a gift. A compromise was reached, as the group scrambled to remake itself into a nonprofit organization complete with a board of directors, a name (The Centre for Discovery and New Life), a logo, and a minimal salary for its director, Catherine Burroughs.

The man who came knocking on the Center for New Light's door that night in 1984 was a rug salesman making his rounds. When not selling rugs, though, he was a lama, and sale of the Tibetan carpets helped support his monastery in south India, where the young monks desperately needed food, clothing, and books. Catherine's group had no clue what Tibetan Buddhists were (were they related to the Hare Krishnas?). But she had been teaching about relieving suffering in whatever form you encounter it. Her group began financially sponsoring twenty-five young monks; soon thereafter they were sponsoring seventy.

The following year (1985) the rug lama returned with exciting news: The head of the monastery, Penor Rinpoche, was coming to teach in America. Would they host him during his visit to Washington? Sure, why not. Toss a mattress on the floor. Barbeque some franks in the backyard— make an occasion of it. *Rinpoche* is a venerated title in Tibetan Buddhism, but Catherine's group thought that Rinpoche was the man's last name. When they went to the airport to pick up Mr. Rinpoche, they couldn't find him amid the pandemonium of Chinese prostrating before some figure. (Tibetan Buddhism had many followers in precommunist China, some of whom, now in exile, had flocked to the airport that day.) When Catherine finally did glimpse him—though she considered herself one tough bird from Brooklyn—she could not stop crying. She felt uncannily the way Diane Perry had when she met Khamtrul Rinpoche, that this unknown man was somehow connected to the very essence of who she was.

Over the next days it became clear that Mr. Rinpoche was no mister but a spiritual prince who in Tibet had supervised a thousand monasteries. So holy was Penor Rinpoche that people collected the earth he walked on as a relic. Seeing what a true spiritual teacher was, Catherine worried that her makeshift teaching was a mistake, perhaps a sin. She had had no instruction and no one had given her authorization. She explained to Penor Rinpoche that she taught only because, first, she saw people suffering and, second, she knew from her own experience that her meditations could help.

Penor Rinpoche questioned her closely about what it was precisely that she taught. She described her homemade meditation in which she visualized the body as pure white light, and she explained her clumsy vocabulary of "no-thing-ness," a vibrational zero, at the heart of everything. Only at the end of his visit did Penor Rinpoche surprise her group by announcing that these were Tibetan teachings. The "zero point" was the Tibetan *sunnyata*, which beneath all its human manifestations is empty of tangible content, luminous, and compassionate. In fact, Penor Rinpoche intimated, her whole group were probably Buddhists without realizing it. He did not ask them to do anything differently, however.

The bombshell came the next year. When Penor Rinpoche next met Catherine, he explained how it was that she knew things she had never been taught. In a previous life, he said, she had been a *bodhisattva*, a being who had so completely mastered the practices that she would never forget them through all future lifetimes. Penor Rinpoche had long dreamed of locating the reincarnation of Ahkon Lhamo, the legendary woman who had founded his own particular lineage in 1665. Catherine, he revealed, was nobody less than Ahkon Lhamo reborn.

And so Catherine Burroughs, née Alyce Zeoli, underwent another name change as she became *Jetsunma* (an honorary title) Ahkon Norbu Lamo, the first Western woman recognized as a high Buddhist reincarnation. Overnight she became a media celebrity, or perhaps media curiosity, as the *International Herald Tribune* ran its front-page story "Meet Tibetan Saint" and the *Washington Post* headlined theirs "The Unexpected Incarnation." Television crews from Germany and Japan descended. Warner Brothers explored the possibility of making a major film, paying half a million dollars to have a script written about her life and strange metamorphosis. Whatever else, Catherine/Jetsunma's group would never confuse the Buddhists with the Hare Krishnas again.

As if all that were not enough, Penor Rinpoche advised Jetsunma's group to acquire a big white house with columns in front, like the one he had seen in a dream, in order to accommodate the ever-more people who would seek Jetsunma out. After much searching, the group found such a southern-style mansion in the countryside near Poolsville, Maryland—a Tara (the plantation in *Gone with the Wind*) for a Tara (the Tibetan goddess). They rechristened it with a Tibetan name so long—Kunzang Odsal Palyul Changchub Choling—that it is known by its initials, KPC.

Of the thousands of people who visited KPC out of curiosity, around a hundred and fifty stayed on to become the core group, the faithful. They took her *Bodhisattva's* Vow to make their every thought, word, and deed of benefit to others. Those who remained at KPC felt blessed to have America's first official reincarnation for their teacher. Even the Tibetans who visited KPC were impressed. Hearing Jetsunma's Sunday talks, one lama exclaimed, "But those texts haven't been translated from Tibetan yet!" Other Tibetans noted her ability to attract so many students, and not just "hippies" as the other centers did, and to get them down to serious work.

By the early '90s, her students were no longer simply learning meditation and listening to dharma talks but becoming nuns and monks, taking the vows and donning the robes. By the mid '90s, KPC was the largest Tibetan religious center in the United States. It was a Horatio Alger success story, with a twist: A downtrodden Brooklyn girl becomes not a business success, not a rich entrepreneur, but a divinity (almost). Had Warner Brothers made its movie then, it could have had a simple happy ending, and the audience gone home to untroubled dreams.

ANYONE WHO VOWS TO make her every deed, word, and thought of benefit to others surely merits a little praise. As if on cue, the glowing articles began appearing. The Australian journalist Vicki Mackenzie, who wrote about Lama Yeshe and Tenzin Palmo, now published a book about "Tibetan" reincarnations in America (*Reborn in the West*, 1996), which included an uncritical account of Jetsunma. A *Washington Post* reporter, Martha Sherrill, wrote an article for *Elle* equally full of commendation.

When Martha Sherrill had written her enthusiastic piece for *Elle*, she knew nothing about Buddhism. But she had enjoyed bouncing on the bed with Jetsunma and exchanging gossip, like two schoolgirls. In her late thirties, Martha stood six feet tall, as strikingly attractive as she was obviously intelligent. She appeared to have won life's lottery, having a fine job, fine husband, and fine little baby. And she had a fundamental decency that hardly fits the clichéd stereotype of the hard-boiled journalist. Publishers and colleagues were telling her it was time she wrote a book, and she thought: Well, why not one about that wacky guru and her happy-go-lucky students in Poolsville. When she told the folks at KPC of her intention, they were elated. Here was someone obviously sympathetic who would direct the attention of the world to Jetsunma. Martha already had a catchy title for the book—*The Buddha from Brooklyn*.

The Buddha from Brooklyn (2000) begins by describing the restaurant where Jetsunma and Martha ate dinner and the vintage of the wine they ordered and the wardrobe Jetsunma wore. Only gradually does it become apparent that these journalistic scenes are not leading into the sympathetic biography that everyone, including Martha herself, once assumed she would write. As the book's publication date approached, the person who handled KPC's public relations asked Martha what to expect from it. She sadly, dutifully synopsized the book, after which the P. R. man asked how they could get copies to sell in the KPC bookstore. "No, no," Martha repeated, "I think you're missing the point."

In writing Jetsunma's biography Martha sighed for the good old days when she had covered Hillary Clinton for the Post. Hillary was a piece of cake compared to trying to interview Jetsunma, who often did not keep the appointments once made. (Tenzin Palmo, who failed to get an appointment with Jetsunma to discuss women and Buddhism, noted how much easier it was to see the Dalai Lama.) Not that Jetsunma was devoutly holed up in meditation retreat, as Tibetan masters are wont to be. No, Martha reported, she was watching Star Trek on television. Or shopping at the mall. Or engaged in intimate pastimes with her husband, whoever her particular husband at that particular moment was.

Michael Burroughs had known Alyce/Catherine/Jetsunma when she was a moody and sometimes troubled woman, and he still observed the same bouts of depression in her, the same days of fogginess, the same struggle with obesity. But now that she was an exalted superior being in the eyes of the KPC, those black humors could not derive from her neuroses—but rather from his bad karma! Michael, whose drive had helped make KPC the successful center it was, increasingly became the scapegoat for whatever went wrong. Eventually Jetsunma divorced Michael, with an uncharitable lack of grace. Her divorce party sported as a decorative centerpiece an effigy of Michael in the form of a cloth mummy, with a banana for a penis. KPC members stabbed the effigy over and over with knives and forks. Only the bright yellow banana remained whole, and then Jetsunma smashed it to eternal impotence. Perhaps the catharsis was needed, but a bit nasty coming from a person of infinite compassion.

After her divorce, Jetsunma went through a number of affairs with newcomers (of both sexes) at KPC. After the romances ended, her ex-lovers would usually redouble their efforts at KPC, as though enticing them into their newfound Buddhist vocation had informed her cupid's plan all along. When she ended her liaison with a likable younger man named Sangye, Jetsunma informed him that "the best way to keep the blessing intact is [for him] to become celibate and never involved with ordinary women again." Sangye wondered why he was to give up sexual intimacy and the prospect of having a family when Jetsunma, who was not a nun, wasn't eschewing such pleasures. After Sangye, Jetsunma at age forty-three married a young devotee twenty years her junior. Jetsunma ingeniously explained their age difference by claiming her handsome new husband had been detained an extra twenty years in the *bardo* (transitional state) between his previous death and his present birth. Jetsunma's messy love life is hardly noteworthy for the 1990s, but a few devotees at KPC began to have doubts. Was this really the way a *bodhisattva* behaves? If lamas really desired a spiritual consort, Tenzin Palmo observed, they would chase after older, wiser women and not young beautiful ones. Or, in Jetsunma's instance, a boy toy.

Martha Sherrill reported more troubles in Poolsville than simply a few sexual shenanigans. Purchase of the big white house there meant that, besides advancing the dharma, KPC had to secure the filthy lucre to pay for the mortgage. KPC's financial situation went from bad to worse, however, when Jetsunma—the teacher who would not touch money—began receiving a salary in the low six figures that amounted to half the center's budget. Money was obviously on Jetsunma's mind. She founded Lady-works, a cosmetics company that marketed a hair-styling cap that could be put in the microwave and then worn under a turban—something no *bodhisattva* had thought to do before. When Ladyworks began edging toward bankruptcy, merit for future lives could be earned by cash contributions to the faltering company. Like Scarlett O'Hara, Jetsunma was not going to be poor again.

When a list of abuses at KPC was read to Penor Rinpoche in India, he said to inform Jetsunma that, though head of the entire order, his sole possessions were the clothes on his back. Inform her, too, that in Tibet and

India the teacher supported the students, not the other way around. He said to tell her that—and also not to wear such garish fingernail polish.

Had Jetsunma crossed some forbidden boundary? Being called by one's students a "living Buddha," peers one's own age prostrating before you, might push anyone into supposing that ordinary human limits no longer apply. The old Tibetan masters like Lama Yeshe were almost comical in downplaying their achievements, claiming to be beginners, ignoramuses, bunglers. But they had been trained since age four or five in a modest deportment and outlook, while Jetsunma had catapulted overnight from a Brooklyn misfit into a semi-divine guru. Small wonder if, despite her best efforts, her exaltation sometimes went to her head.

In her closing chapters Martha Sherrill tracks down those students who felt that their lives were ruined by Jetsunma. In one chapter a young nun is slapped by Jetsunma for flirting with a monk, and that nun, stripped of her robes and ostracized, has the Maryland State Police arrest Jetsunma on charges of battery. (The nun agreed to drop charges after Penor Rinpoche in India wrote a letter of censure reproving Jetsunma's actions.) As the book went to press, Martha felt she had to warn Jetsunma what was coming. "For some reason, I'm not worried," Jetsunma responded. "I'm sure I'm going to like it." In that, as in so much else, Martha says, the lady was wrong again.

THOSE STUDENTS WHO FLED JETSUNMA, disenchanted by her liking the dharma but loving money and position more, were highly intelligent and excellent in character. Their repudiation of her is the most telling condemnation of a guru possible. But the disciples who remained (and they were numerically more), who believed that Jetsunma did only one thing and that was radiate compassion, were also of impeccable character and high intelligence. Their testimonies to her are the greatest validation of a teacher conceivable. Which is the real Jetsumna?

After *The Buddha from Brooklyn* was published, Martha was besieged by one question, asked over and over: "Is Jetsunma the 'Real Thing'?" Curiously, she could answer every question, except this one. "That would only lead into debating whether Penor Rinpoche is the 'real thing,' which would lead into whether the Dalai Lama is the 'real thing,'" Martha would answer evasively, sensing that the question was somehow suspect, tricky. And that's exactly what it was: a trick question.

The trick is that it is an American question but it can only be answered with a Tibetan response. "Is dat de Real Ting?" a Damon Runyan character might demand of some racehorse, moll, or safecracker. The American question is whether the object in question is the genuine article, the top of its line. But the line that Jetsunma could be the top of does not exist in America. Asking if Jetsunma is the Real Thing, in effect, asks whether or not she has "buddha-hood," which is a peculiar question for most Americans to ask. Likewise a skeptic might inquire whether Jacob in the Bible really wrestled with an angel, but the answer scarcely matters, for the skeptic doesn't believe in angels anyway.

From a Tibetan viewpoint, though, the answer is unequivocally yes. From a Tibetan standpoint, Jetsunma along with everyone else has buddha-nature, quite unlike in Christian theology where each person is an original sinner with a fallen soul. Buddhism's good news is that everybody is the Real Thing, that beneath their chaotic upbringing and bad habits all people already possess qualities shining and limitless. It is this cheering message that, beyond all the fads and hoopla, accounts for much of Tibetan Buddhism's popularity in the West.

From a Buddhist perspective, the more troublesome question is whether Jetsunma has *realized* her buddha-nature, or gained sufficient mastery, to qualify her to teach. Again the answer is yes. One can dismiss Jetsunma, Martha herself wrote, but only "if you'd never heard her speak or teach in person." In her audiences have sat Ph.D.'s who claim never to have heard a Ph.D. speak more intelligently; public officials who never heard a public speaker talk more eloquently. "This is truth, this is wisdom," newcomers to her Sunday talks at KPC have often said to themselves, and half wondered whether the woman they were listening to was simply an ordinary person.

What Jetsunma teaches is, unoriginally, Tibetan Buddhism. Unoriginal in what she teaches, Jetsunma has revised Tibetan teachings, though, to remove anything too alien in their presentation. For example, parallel to the Ten Commandments (at least in number) are Tibetan Buddhism's Ten Negative Actions, and of these, we might be curious to know what a Tibetan means by "sexual misconduct." Many traditional Tibetan texts can be reticent, often merely saying, "Everyone knows what sexual misconduct is." (In case you don't: causing monks or nuns to break their vows; adultery; sex on holy days or at holy sites; sex in the mouth or anus.) Jetsunma makes "sexual misconduct" relevant by redefining it as anything erotic that harms another or something that hinders one's intention to help others. By this definition, sexual misdeeds can take place in lawfully wedded marriages, and infidelity occur without a sexual act at all. Similarly, when Jetsunma teaches about compassion (which is her main teaching), she shows movies about AIDS or films about animals tested in labs, kittens injected with flea spray and monkeys battered in studies of brain trauma, to soften hearts by getting them to identify with all creatures that suffer.

Expounding the Buddhist possibilities, Jetsunma flares forth brilliantly, but afterwards comes, her ex-students charge, her calamitous muddle with money and power at KPC. Thousands of miles away in the Himalayas, Tenzin Palmo happened to chance upon a copy of *The Buddha from Brooklyn* and concluded: Jetsunma is definitely the real thing, a tulku or high reincarnation. And her follies are the way such a being would behave, Tenzin Palmo adds, if he or she lacked the proper training. For Tenzin Palmo reborn tulkus are not so important—time and space, city and country, are full of them—but it is their education and training that make the difference. Minus the training, a tulku is not the shining pearl of Buddhism, but merely something hidden within a rough-shelled oyster in the mud.

After her "recognition," like a commoner suddenly made queen, Jetsunma at first had little clue as to how to act her role. She went around asking, How do such beings behave? The faxes from Penor Rinpoche in India, responding to her pressing questions, were too infrequent to be of much help. Nor could tradition guide her. In ages past when monks had traveled to non-Buddhist lands, they had founded monasteries, not centers for laypeople. And here she was, trying to do what not even the Buddha had attempted—to preach, without having undergone years in the wilderness; to teach, without the long ascetic education to ripen and mature her.

Jetsunma had not applied for this job, though, and even at her most questionable she appears less villain than victim. She counts among her happiest days those earlier ones in the Maryland suburb when she could clown around with her peers, when she wasn't some infallible female pope on a plane removed from and higher up than the rest of humanity. After her enthronement, a visiting rinpoche had laughed and said to her, "You're in jail now." She could never have a friend or lover or husband who, in delicious familiarity, was simply her equal. She could never relax, lighthearted, carefree, for whatever innocent action she did raised doubts—often her own—that a realized reincarnation would put her time to better use. Even her children prostrated before her. After her great visions and her teachings about compassion, what was Jetsunma to do? The goddess found herself thrown back into Alyce Zeoli's body, and if she behaved controversially, what else was she to do?

In her writings Alexandra David-Neel supplied an understanding of what a guru is that makes sense of all the contradictions that surround Jetsunma. Tibetans did respect their gurus greatly, Alexandra said, but they hardly expected them to be perfect beings. The very ideal of a perfect or perfectible self was a phantom of Western philosophy but contradictory to Buddhism. The Western tradition posits an essential personality or character that suffers growth and decay intact, while Tibetans believe, on the contrary, that such a constant solid self is a fiction, patched together from qualities that coalesce and disperse depending on conditions. Alexandra compared a Tibetan devotee before his guru to someone watching a crowd pass, waiting to glimpse the holy man in its midst. The devotee put up with his teacher's crowd of rough qualities to get the kernel of wisdom lodged somewhere in them. Thus Penor Rinpoche might deplore Jetsunma's profligacy or fingernail polish but remain convinced that her students could receive valuable instruction from her nonetheless.

The chief difference between modern Westerners and Asians, Alexandra elaborated, is that Asians deem faith a good, a precious commodity in itself, almost regardless of what inspires it. In one Tibetan folktale a devout old woman threatens suicide when her son fails to bring her back from his travels a relic of the Buddha. The son scoops up a dog's tooth, wraps it in silk, and presents it as the Buddha's tooth. So fervently does his mother worship it that the tooth begins to glow and produce miracles. In another tale an ascetic seeks a vision of the Buddha to no avail, when one day he compassionately licks a mangy dog's wounds clean with his own tongue. The animal turns into the Buddha, whom the ascetic triumphantly carries into town on his shoulders, where the people wonder what he is doing with that mangy mongrel on his back.

Jetsunma is certainly better than a canine molar or a maggoty mongrel. The Tibetans say, See your teacher as the Buddha, and you get the benefits of a buddha; see him as a human being, and you get the benefits of a human being. One student at KPC offered a curious insight: "A *personal* relationship with Jetsunma obscures having a *real* relationship with her." Those who abandoned ship, fatigued by all the egotism and questionable finances in Poolsville, left behind a flawed, arrogant woman who deserved being left behind. Those who stayed felt they were lucky to be living in the shadow of the Buddha or of one in resemblance close enough.

IT IS LIKELY THAT there will never be a consensus about Jetsunma. Her sphere of operation does not permit an answer of scientific certainty. In recent years, for example, Jetsunma has been sick an inordinate amount of the time. Those sympathetic to her explain that her illnesses are a form of *tonglin*—her taking on the travails of those around her; those who are hostile say that people who live in stress and disharmony of course get sick more often. Another matter in contention: In late 1998 Jetsunma moved to Sedona, Arizona, the New Age capital of America, and in Sedona she has collected an amazing menagerie—rescued dogs, wounded exotic birds, even iguanas—and spends much of her time tending lovingly to them, even preparing them treats at Christmas. Those sympathetic to her see in this her extending loving-kindness to all living creatures; those hostile criticize the little old cat-lady who has forgotten her human priorities.

Amid those claims of spiritual exaltation and countercharges of moral squalor, perhaps only one remarkable fact about Jetsunma stands out above the controversy. Its noteworthiness goes back to the time before her recognition and enthronement, back to the very beginning: She voiced Buddhism without having been taught it, and she taught the principles of Buddhism without having heard of them. Thus Penor Rinpoche's delight upon meeting her, for here was a great reincarnation, a *tulku*, appearing unannounced a continent and an ocean away.

In the past Americans and Europeans have discovered key aspects of Buddhism on their own, without realizing it. A walk through earlier Western history would uncover numerous Buddha-like figures who expressed Buddhist-like thoughts, but no one knew enough about Buddhism then to remark on the curious affinities. The Greek philosopher Heraclitus, for example, holding that everything in the universe was in constant flux, aptly summarized the Buddhist concept of impermanence. In the Middle Ages several Christian sects—e.g., the Cathars, with their belief in innate human perfection—espoused ideas damned as heretical that are however orthodox in Buddhism. During the Renaissance Ben Jonson's mourning his son's death sounds more like the Four Noble Truths about suffering and its remedy than the Four Gospels: Instead of imagining his son in heaven, Jonson vowed that henceforth "what he loves [he] may never like too much." In the Victorian era the essayist Charles Lamb achieved some composure after the ultimate horror—his beloved sister murdered their mother—not by evoking Christ's mercy but, he said, by "managing my mind," by a sunnyata-like mental dexterity that could detach itself from judgment.

But no one on record ever voiced a homemade Buddhism, or engendered its vows and practices, as thoroughly as Jetsunma did. She in effect repeated the journey Theos Bernard made a half century earlier, but she covered the equivalent distance entirely within herself. Bernard endured the weary ship voyage, toiled across India, cabled the Tibetan government, while any sailing, toiling, or cabling Jetsunma did was within her own mind. At the very beginning of her journey she found within herself what Bernard discovered only at the heights of the Himalayas. Seen in this light, Jetsunma may provide support for what Gautama Siddhartha and those following him insisted upon: that Buddhism, when all is said and done, is a "science" of the mind that anyone might verify on one's own. Jetsunma's strange achievement was, almost accidentally, with a homemade chemistry set in a basement laboratory, to re-create that great Buddhist experiment in suburban America.

Book IV

BUDDHA:
THE SCREEN
TEST

chapter VII

●

Coming Attractions

A CLEVER REPORTER IN Hollywood once stopped strangers on the street and asked, "How's your film script coming?" Supposedly, nine out of ten people so accosted recoiled, "How did *you* know about it?" The story sounds apocryphal, save that at any given moment Hollywood is drowning in flood levels of unproduced scripts. The April 1997 issue of *Harper's* magazine reported that "scripts about Tibet were circulating around the city like particles in an atomic accelerator." The following two scenes might have come from such a script, except that (a) the scenes are slightly too far-fetched, and (b) God would have been the scriptwriter, since they actually happened.

Scene I. There is something he wants to ask, the Dalai Lama says; something he is curious to learn. The emotions an actor expresses while acting, are they real emotions?

Richard Gere, an actor friend of the Dalai Lama's, mulls this over. Yes, he answers, "it's better when you really feel the emotions, when they come spontaneously and fully. They're real and you believe they're real."

The Dalai Lama looks Gere in the eye and then laughs, as though he's just heard the best joke in the world. What's so funny? Gere wonders. Then slowly he understands the humor—that actors intentionally do what others accidentally do, when they substitute their moods for external reality. Someone may feel that she is in love, say, or that things are hopeless, and then that love or hopelessness appears to exist *out there*, as part of a situation she has little control over. Actors do this on cue, and so do ordinary people, only they unconsciously cue themselves. The Dalai Lama continues laughing at Gere's description of real emotions in imaginary worlds.

Hollywood is called the "Dream Factory"—its product of manufacture, technological syntheses of facts and imagination. At the Academy Awards in 1993 Richard Gere presented the Oscar for Best Art Direction. As he stepped toward the podium—in the symbolic heart of Hollywood—he recalled the basic Buddhist precept that our thoughts mold reality. Hundreds of millions of people were tuned in to the Academy Awards. Suppose every single one of their thought-vibrations were harnessed to the same purpose at the same instant? Gere asked everybody all over the world to concentrate, to think the thought of Tibet's regaining its freedom. The audience in the theater sat there as stunned as if a fanatic from a war zone had interrupted a fashion show. Yet Gere's presentation was easily the most memorable of the evening and, in a sense, the most in keeping with the imaginative principle of the movies. Fantasy and reality—it had just become a little harder to distinguish which was which.

Scene II. The Buddha weds Hollywood—that was the idea behind the film script. In 1996 an idealist presented to entertainment-industry deal makers his proposal to make a film bio of the Awakened One, which would transform moviegoers' lives everywhere. (The Idealist's name, being little known, is irrelevant; his personal millions are more pertinent to the story.) Some years previously the Idealist had summoned to a hotel room in Oxford the director Bernardo Bertolucci, the playwright Robert Bolt, the Orientalist Richard Gombrich, and other luminaries to launch his Buddha project. Nothing came of it. Next he flew the director Mira Nair first class to London every other week and put her up at the Dorchester, to plan Buddha the Movie. Nothing came of it. "If you have a story, see me," Samuel Goldwyn once quipped; "If you have a message, go to Western Union." The Idealist did have a message, which fifteen years and fifteen million dollars of his own money had not succeeded in converting into a film. Bertolucci broke away and filmed *Little Buddha*. (Nasty lawsuit followed.) By the time the Idealist arrived in Hollywood in 1996, his checkbook was so depleted that his new scriptwriter flew in using frequent-flyer miles and stayed with a relative.

The Idealist drove through an Edward Hopper–like desolation, an abandoned area in Los Angeles, to find Steven Seagal, who was using this industrial wasteland as a location for his latest action movie. Seagal was by all reports a Buddhist, and if only he would agree to play the evil Mara, the Buddha's tempter, his movie might get bankrolled after all.

Once on the set, the Idealist realized that presenting this proposition to Seagal would be no simple task. The actor was wrapped in a cocoon of fantastic egotism and cushioned by protective layers of managers or handlers. Two in particular—an Englishman who might have been enunciating protocol at Buckingham Palace and a New York thug or agent (not clear which) ready to off you—ensured that not much unwanted reality penetrated Seagal's consciousness. "One must understand," the Englishman patiently explained, "that Mr. Seagal's name is a commodity, and as a commodity it must be preciously . . . ," while the thug-agent snarled, "We've been fucked over before, and we're not gonna be fucked over again." Seagal himself entered the discussion when he finally understood what the Idealist wanted.

"What! Me, Mara? I should play the Buddha!" Seagal yelled. "I am the Buddha! The Tibetans say I was put on this planet to save the world."

Later as Seagal drove with the Idealist through the urban desolation, he pointed out two scrawny hookers on the barren street. Seagal then made a suggestion that shocked the Idealist, coming as it did from a man who had just announced he should be the Buddha. The Idealist in the car had invested too much money and sense of himself to give up, but for a moment he tasted despair: "Here, the millennium, Hollywood," he thought, "is where Buddhism ends."

IN FACT BUDDHISM, especially the Tibetan variety, was only beginning in Hollywood. After *Little Buddha*, two movies about the Dalai Lama—*Kundun* and *Seven Years in Tibet*—were released in 1997. Other movies—*Jacob's Ladder*, *Ghosts*—had quasi-Buddhist themes; even a few movies made by Tibetans—*The Cup*, *Windhorse*—received national distribution. The new idea of Buddhism eddied out in circles through the entertainment industry . . . until at Free Tibet concerts a punk-rock group, The Beastie Boys, were leading fifty thousand people in singing "The *Bodhisattva* Oath."

What is your greatest wish in life? Jennifer Sky of the TV soap opera *General Hospital* answers, "To meet the Dalai Lama!" When the Dalai Lama comes to town, the stars come out at night. They stand patiently in line, finally greeting him with a smile meant to be humble and a sense of occasion that would befit two houses of royalty uniting in simple majesty. Richard Gere, Sharon Stone, Goldie Hawn, Steven Seagal, Bernardo Bertolucci, Spaulding Gray, Harrison Ford, James Coburn, Pierce Brosnan, John Cleese, and Oliver Stone are among those who appear to have made Buddhism and/or the Tibetan cause something more than a photo op and a check for charity. When the Dalai Lama gives a public talk in Los Angeles ten thousand people, many from the entertainment industry, attend. Dickie Samdrup*, a young Tibetan filmmaker, says people in Hollywood always ask if she is a monk or nun, for what else could a Tibetan be. She is often surprised by how little they know about Tibet but how much they

*This is not her real name.

know about Buddhism. Neither on Wall Street nor in Congress will you bump into an equivalent number of budding half-Buddhists or hear such frequent talk of lamas and meditation.

Hollywood is hardly the place in America where Tibetan Buddhism is the most popular, but it may be, for good or bad, the place where it is the most conspicuous. Its adoption of Buddhism is, however, a recent conversion. A decade ago a producer rejected a film script about the Buddha, explaining, "Buddha, Smuddha. Nobody gives a damn about him. All even I know about the Buddha," the producer added, "is that he was fat, Japanese, and lived in the nineteenth century." The producer fingered the script. "Look. If the audience doesn't want to fuck him in the first five minutes, the movie's lost." Today, you will not hear such a flip dismissal. In the men's room at production studios guys as they zip up ask each other what they're working on. In contrast to even a few years ago, "a project on Buddhism" is now as respectable an answer as teenage vampires or a police buddy thriller.

BY CONCENTRATING ON HOLLYWOOD, journalists often dismiss a whole surprising turn in contemporary religion simply as "Tibet chic." In *Virtual Tibet* (2000), for example, Orville Schell ignored the hundreds of Tibetan Buddhist centers across the United States and wrote as if only Hollywood mattered, which not surprisingly reduced Buddhism in this country to a shallow, silly affair. If a study of American politics restricted itself to which movie stars were Democrats and which Republicans, it might also achieve the considerable feat of making our public life more preposterous than it is. *Virtual Tibet* spends its pages tracking down stars like Brad Pitt, who played the lead in *Seven Years in Tibet*. When journalists demanded Pitt's view of the political situation in Tibet, he wondered, "Why ask me? I'm a goddamn actor."

What is "Tibet chic"? It is topping someone who boasts, "Stephen Spielberg said to me . . ." by confiding, "As the Dalai Lama told me personally . . ." The Tibet-chic explanation of Buddhism's appeal: A Jew worships a wrathful God, a Christian is instructed to give to the poor, but all that's required of a Tibetan Buddhist, Hollywood version, is to consider the Dalai Lama cute.

If Tibet-chic critics needed conclusive evidence of superficiality, they found their man in June 1997. That month Steven Seagal was declared a *tulku*, the reincarnation of one of Tibet's great religious figures. Among *tulkus* Seagal is probably the only one who can get the words *Dalai Lama* and *motherfucker* into the same sentence. He may also be the only *tulku* who is reported to carry a gun to meetings. He has starred in action movies (*Hard to Kill*, *The Glimmer Man*) that for excitement never equaled the movies unreeling in his own head, in which he has been—he claims—a Green Beret, a member of the Japanese Mafia, a Zen adept, a CIA agent, etc. As his career declined in the mid '90s, he compensated by fantasizing his greatest role of all, one that would take place offscreen, in which "people all over the world would come up to me and recognize me as a great spiritual leader."

The only slight hitch in his becoming a great spiritual light, possibly a living Buddha, was getting anyone else to believe it. He broke off relations with Kusum Lingpa, an exiled lama in Los Angeles, when Lingpa refused to recognize him as a *tulku*. Seagal then went to India, charted a private plane, and met the Dalai Lama. According to Seagal, during that interview the Dalai Lama prostrated and kissed the actor's feet—revealing that Seagal was little less than a deity. "I don't think he has given such a blessing to another white person," Seagal noted. The slight problem, once again, was that nobody believed Seagal's story. Finally, Seagal met Penor Rinpoche, the titular head of the Nyingma lineage, and began contributing to the Rinpoche's teaching tours and dharma centers. It was Penor Rinpoche who in 1997 recognized Seagal as a noble *tulku* reborn.

The world should have applauded, but instead it laughed. Journalists had a field day lampooning Seagal, his recognition, and his religion. This was, incidentally, the same Penor Rinpoche who had anointed Jetsumna a decade earlier, and Seagal's recognition now made her own look questionable, if not tawdry. (Penor Rinpoche merely *recognized* Seagal, however, and did not *enthrone* him as he had Jetsunma, indicating that Seagal may at present lack the ability to act upon his *bodhisattva* potential. For public consumption, though, that distinction was too subtle.) Hollywood, F. Scott Fitzgerald wrote, is where our intimate dreams cheapen into clichés. In Hollywood, with Seagal, the dream of a pure Tibetan Buddhism coarsened into the image of a corrupt medieval church selling indulgences. A religion that would curb the excesses of egotism had landed in the town of inflated egos, and the unequal contest appeared to reach its foregone conclusion as, amid laughter, the ethos of Tinseltown triumphed.

YET AFTER A FEW YEARS nobody was talking about Seagal. Curiosity focused instead on a different movie star. Perhaps the question most asked about Tibetan Buddhism among outsiders is, "What's the story on Richard Gere?"

The story? Every day for more than twenty-five years—for more than half his life—Gere has meditated between forty-five minutes and two hours, as other commitments get shifted around to allow him to do so. The number of days he's missed meditating in a quarter of a century could be counted on the fingers of one hand. Most years he has gone on retreat in India, where he can meditate day and night. He has published a book of his photos from Tibet, *Pilgrim*, which might be called "Studies in Blurred Photography," but his written introduction exhibits a mastery of Tibetan Buddhism that would do credit to a university professor. Even so, unlike Seagal, he has refused to become a spokesman for Buddhism, feeling unqualified; and if he speaks on behalf of the Tibetans politically, only the Dalai Lama's urging motivates him to do so.

Gere may be an exemplary Buddhist, but he is also, according to *People* magazine, "the sexiest man alive," formerly married to the model Cindy Crawford, one of the sexier women alive. For decades Gere has been a highly paid, big-box-office actor, yet he does not seem to invest much of himself in his acting. A generation ago movie stars who started out as male bimbos, Burt Lancaster, Kirk Douglas, even Tony Curtis, all would have sold their souls for the praise of critics and demanded (successfully) to be cast in ever-better movies. But, except for *Chicago*, Gere has rarely clamored to act in a critically acclaimed film and he has never been nominated for an Academy Award. Of course someone who says, as he does, that acting is "pretty low on the scale of spiritual things" might not master the ascent into the celluloid version of heaven.

Gere thus poses to some an enigma, though a rather bland enigma. In the beginning the Hollywood gossip mills added excitement by painting him as a "Bad Boy." The rumors about his dark mischief included the standard—drugs (white powder, cocaine); the semi-exotic—bisexuality (the young men with him at openings were labeled his boyfriends); and the weird—bestiality (with a gerbil). On national television Barbara Walters demanded of Gere, "Where does this story that won't go away about you and the gerbil come from?" while Gere shook his head. "I just do not know." The story has gotten repeated so many times—so many people claimed to know someone working in the Emergency Room where after the incident with the gerbil Gere supposedly had to go—that as with Catherine the Great and her horse, the tale surely must be invented nonsense.

But suppose the rest were true. It all happened a long time ago and doesn't add up to much anyway, perhaps only to this: Gere was once a Hollywood Bad Boy but through Buddhism has come to lead a rather exemplary life. His co-workers state this explicitly: that he used to be arrogant to the point of offensiveness, his egotism filling all available space, but now every time they see him he is kinder, more gracious, even "lighter" to be with. From someone self-centered he has gone on to become someone endlessly generous: The projects he funds through the Gere Foundation range from installing climate controls in the Tibetan Archives so irreplaceable materials will not disintegrate to insuring thousands of destitute monks and nuns so that the last Tibet-educated teachers can live and instruct decades longer than they might have otherwise.

In interviews Gere sometimes wonders how a kid who grew up in Syracuse, New York, in the 1950s wound up as this strange set of contradictions—sometime *enfant terrible*, part-time political activist, full-time actor, overtime Buddhist practitioner. About the Buddhism in particular, when he assumes the lotus position in meditation, he may puzzle, "Where did this come from?" He thinks back to the confused high-school student carrying around Sartre's *Being and Nothingness*; he recalls the alienated adolescent protesting the Vietnam War; he remembers the young man practicing Zen and never being able to come up with a single answer to the *koan* (Zen riddle) presented him. In his early twenties he holed up in his cheap apartment all day straining to achieve a Zenlike no-mind. What a relief, when he finally discovered Tibetan Buddhism: its emphasis on compassionate warmth let him finally exhale his breath (or so it felt), after having sucked it in for years in the dry stoicism of Zen. But such undramatic reflections are not what interviewers want to hear when they turn on their tape recorders and fire their gossip-hungry questions in rapid succession. So Gere has his answer prepared when the inevitable question comes, "Why did you become a Buddhist?" "I was fucked, totally fucked, and I didn't know how to make it stop. So I started asking, 'Why am I unhappy, and how can I get out of this?' " Totally fucked up? That's updated phrasing for the first truth of Buddhism: suffering. (Despite his blue-collar language, Gere worries that his response is too "B.C.," too buddhistically correct, and sometimes asks interviewers, "Try to make me look interesting.") Unlike Seagal, who entered Buddhism by appointing himself savior of the world, Richard Gere's entry was quieter, in the quiet 2,500-year tradition of unhappy people trying to do something about their unhappiness, about their mess.

Gere thus does make an advertisement for Buddhism, and possibly the only regret for most people would be: The world already has enough Buddhists and cannot afford to lose another Bad Boy, at least not of the handsome and harmless kind.

II

MOVIES, AND THE ELECTRONIC media in general, have been called our contemporary church. But film and television in fact "are realer than the priest," John Updike observed in *The New Yorker*: "We are surrounded by entertainment more completely than medieval man was by the church and its propaganda." In those remote Middle Ages, itinerant preachers thundered their sermons, whose heaven and hell and purgatory crammed life with awe and terror and meaning. By analogy, what "sermon" or message does Hollywood preach? And why have its preachers—actors, directors, scriptwriters—proved receptive to Buddhism to a degree that their counterparts on Wall Street or in Congress have not?

Interviewed on the Larry King TV show, Steven Seagal observed, "A lot of people who come to Hollywood—and I would not exclude myself—are slightly delusional." Unhappy childhoods, neurotic upbringings are, infamously, the spur that drives people to want to become writers and actors, which are themselves highly charged, unstable professions. "Tibet chic" is thus easy to dismiss: "Slightly delusional" egomaniacs have hit upon a better (i.e., worse) delusion. Buddhism may be, ideally, a system for correcting egotistical fantasies of the self, but you have to focus on the self to make the correction. Buddhism and Hollywood—a perfect marriage, critics charge: Self-centered people in the name of lessening self-centeredness have found a way to think even more about themselves. Richard Gere had a problem, a malaise and—unlike politicians and business people who are supposed to get on with their jobs anyway—he demanded a remedy, ordered from the universe an ointment of relief.

But extravagant needs can make people more attuned to new social trends than those whose antennae are not so thoroughly exposed. From its beginnings Hollywood's off-hours were filled with experiments in alternative gratifications that ranged from sex and intoxicants to swamis and self-help nostrums. In the early 1960s Cary Grant (the man), puzzled by the fabled CARY GRANT (the star), extolled in *Life* magazine a marvelous new drug, LSD, that revealed there were depths inside him, not a void after all. The drug dealer who supplied Grant and director John Huston with LSD in the 1960s was forty years later supplying Hollywood with something else—a new message. LSD might shake people out of their complacency, the ex-dealer said, but a more meaningful life could be achieved in only one way—through Tibetan Buddhism.

The private lives and idiosyncratic interests of the people who make the movies matter, especially when Hollywood takes on an "offbeat" subject like Buddhism. Before 1970 popular movies that portrayed Eastern religion, such as *Lost Horizons* (1937, remake 1973) and *The Razor's Edge* (1946), came out of the studio system, from producers and writers for whom the film was merely one more project. But recent movies that treat Buddhism, like *Little Buddha*, *Kundun*, or *Windhorse*, were made by people with a personal involvement in the subject, willing to risk all the obstacles (skeptical commercial forecasts, economic threats from the Chinese government, etc.) so that their passion might stir general audiences in America.

How Hollywood (and, in a larger sense, America) got from a pre-Buddhist 1960 to a Buddha-friendly 2000 is told in the biographical twists and turns of numerous people such as Bruce Joel Rubin. In the early 1960s, when Cary Grant was announcing the new wonder drug LSD in *Life*, Rubin had graduated from college and started working at NBC News. A friend of a friend of Timothy Leary's friend had temporarily stored in Rubin's refrigerator a bottle of the purest LSD ever made—of such potency that, had it, say, spilled into New York's water supply, human society as we know it would have done a St. Vitus dance straight into the locked section of the loony bin. Rubin had been reading *The Tibetan Book of the Dead* for six months when he decided to sample the goody in the refrigerator but misjudged the amount he should take. During the next twenty-four hours he felt he lived a billion years and a million lives. He was subsequently seen not back at work at NBC but living among the Tibetans in Nepal and northern India.

Rubin arrived so early among the Tibetan diaspora that he had little trouble securing a half-hour interview with the Dalai Lama, who was still a relatively neglected figure. The half-hour interview stretched out to three hours, at the end of which the Dalai Lama expressed his pleasure: Previously only officials had come to discuss the refugee problem, and never before had a Westerner asked him a *spiritual* question. The Dalai Lama volunteered to adopt Rubin as his first non-Tibetan student, but Rubin had something else in mind.

Rubin had always wanted to write and make movies, but had faced a small obstacle—he had nothing to write about. His involvement with the Tibetan Buddhist worldview now gave him a subject: to depict a person in the deeper mysterious universe of which one's normal visible life is only a surface expression. Although not a practicing Buddhist, Rubin had an explicitly Buddhist goal—to get audiences to turn from looking outward to looking inward, turn from the hunger for experience to considering where experience itself comes from. His ambitions were rewarded in 1991 with an Academy Award for *Ghosts*, but a less popular film he wrote that year may be more relevant here.

Viewers complained about *Jacob's Ladder*—Rubin's movie about a Vietnam vet troubled by flashbacks and paranoia—that it was confused, undramatic, and hardly the horror suspense movie they'd bought a ticket to see. But to Rubin *Jacob's Ladder* had less to do with the Vietnam War than what he had first glimpsed on his LSD trip and then grasped through his understanding of Tibetan Buddhism. Though most of the audience failed to get it, the soldier actually dies at the beginning, and the movie follows him though the *bardo*, that state Tibetans describe as between death and rebirth, with the city of New York, his oversexed girlfriend, etc., all being projections of the character's psyche whirling through the postdeath process. *Jacob's Ladder* was thus something unheard of, unprecedented: a mainstream movie about the Tibetan *bardo* state, based on *The Tibetan Book of the Dead*. When the movie showed in then-still-communist East Europe, and was discussed on radio, listeners called in declaring, "At last. We can talk about spiritual questions of life and death in the open."

Are there other mainstream movies, then, that are quietly or quasi-

Buddhist in content, which passed by unremarked upon? The hugely successful *The Matrix* (1999) is a sci-fi movie that uses a Buddhist-like paradigm (similar to *Jacob's Ladder*): Daily life is a projected dream state, while our deeper self abides in a larger reality. Other recent movies from *Pi* to *The Sixth Sense* evoke that hidden universe that Rubin hoped cinematically to colonize, while producer Michael Phillips, a collector of Buddhist art, claims his *Close Encounters of the Third Kind* offers a deeper message than merely science-fiction entertainment. Even hard-boiled directors whose typical fare was street violence (Martin Scorsese) or sensuality (Bernardo Bertolucci) turned, in the new temper of the times, to the unlikely business of making movies about Buddhism. Had the demons from *The Tibetan Book of the Dead* been unlocked, as Allen Ginsberg said, and managed to find employment in Los Angeles?

Not exactly. Buddhism in films is like a little hamlet you can detour to, while the highway zooms toward regions of Romantic Comedy, capitals of Suspense Thrillers, industrial parks of Futuristic Fantasies, and metropolitan centers of Good Date Movies. The few films like Bertolucci's *Little Buddha* and Scorsese's *Kundun* are socially significant only as a *Good Housekeeping* "Seal of Approval" that Buddhism is now a legitimate subject in American life. But just as few or no one became a Gandhian watching the movie *Gandhi*, probably nobody became a Buddhist from seeing *Little Buddha* or *Seven Years in Tibet*. The Idealist (who tried to recruit Steven Seagal for his film) has an idea. When his movie about the Buddha finally gets made, he will color-code the scenes: Scenes of worldly life will be shot in ugly garish colors, those of spiritual enlightenment in beautiful hues, so that, imperceptibly, the audience will become disgusted with worldly existence and seek refuge in Buddhism. But it doesn't work that way. Almost no individual movie, which takes ninety or so minutes to run and then is forgotten in an hour and a half or a day and a half, has much lasting influence on anyone's life.

Yet, taken all together—in ways elusive to pinpoint—movies and television have altered our culture and changed historically the way people think. The novelist Larry McMurtry has described, for example, how over-all the Hollywood films of the 1930s and '40s changed the outlook of his generation living in the Southwest. Those black-and-white movies now look in retrospect so coy, even repressed in their sexual content. But at the time they showed youth on the hardscrabble prairie that sex is not a duty but a pleasure—a lesson McMurtry hadn't learned at home or church, and which his overworked parents seemed unaware of. "If we [his rural generation] escaped permanent imprisonment in an obsolete sexual orientation," McMurtry wrote in In a Narrow Grave, "I think much of the credit for that escape must go to the movies."

One could ask the analogous question about what films have shown about spirituality. What "spiritual messages," or interpretation of life, has Hollywood inadvertently preached? For thousands upon thousands of films have, taken all together, depicted human existence in ways that most earlier societies would hardly have recognized, much less assented to.

A curious coincidence: The movies arose and Buddhism arrived in the United States in the same century. The movies did not usher in Buddhism, or vice versa, but their simultaneous landing in America may be a histor-ically significant coincidence nonetheless. The level of technology and the moral teachings of a culture are not as unrelated as at first seems: Each tends to create the other. Scattered in a few medieval manuscripts, for example, lay hints on how to build a sort of proto-camera, but a world interested in allegories of heaven and hell had little use for the social real-ism that a camera reveals. The invention of the camera—and later of film—had to wait for a more earthbound era, for folks keen on the kind of reality the camera can show and dismissive of the reality it cannot.

In Democracy in America Alexis de Tocqueville described, ahead of time, the new democratic social realities to which, in vastly different ways, the movies and Buddhism in America would both later respond. In his chap-ter "In What Spirit the Americans Cultivate the Arts," Tocqueville came close to predicting the invention of the movies or at least to foreseeing what they would do: "They [the arts] frequently withdraw from the

delineation of the soul to fix exclusively on that of the body, and they substitute the representation of motion and sensation for that of sentiment
and thought." Exactly. The movies cannot film the invisible, metaphysical
soul, but what the camera can record are sensory experiences and motion.
Coincidentally, Buddhism is the one religion that also withdraws from
delineation of, or belief in, the soul. Similarly, Buddhism considers the
ordinary world a potpourri of sensations and motions upon which people project their needs and wishful interpretations. Hollywood calls the
illusions it makes from bodies, sensation, and motion "cinema." Buddhism calls the illusions made from them "conventional reality."

In fact the movies illustrate perfectly what Buddhists mean by "reality." To convey the qualified nature of conventional reality Buddhism uses
nine metaphors, ranging from a reflection on water to a dream, but the
best analogy of all would surely be to film. In both a movie and in Buddhism, "reality" is palpably, sensuously before us, making us laugh one
moment and cry the next, but then vanishing unsubstantially when the
projectionist (or, in Buddhism, our projection) flicks off the switch. It was
something like this that had the Dalai Lama chuckling with Richard Gere,
laughing at how actors—but not only actors—emotionally swear to a situation that another part of their brain knows is imaginary.

Why are more people predisposed toward Buddhism now than a
hundred years ago? More exposure to it, certainly. But also in this century
Americans assemble the human reality—character and identity—according to a different blueprint. Earlier the church, the WASP establishment,
elementary and college education all taught there were eternal moral
truths and each individual had an eternal soul that reflected them. (Society then had just enough stasis, or conventions, to corroborate this static
possibility that an individual's self was fixed.) But by the mid–twentieth
century relentless movement and accelerating change—career and job
shifts, divorces, geographical relocations, new racial mixes—had shaken
many people loose from their original fixed situations and from their first
ideas about themselves. Some of these people were willing to consider a

religion that had not issued from their past and supplied them a new vision of what they could be in the future.

Buddhism teaches that what we call the self is not God given, not immutably fixed, but is an aggregate of qualities that, like raw material, can be refined to different purposes. The movies teach the same thing. The movies and TV, probably more than anything learned in school, have taught contemporary Americans how to see themselves, to present their image, and to imagine for themselves other possibilities. Puritans have always mistrusted the theater because it teaches how to strut and preen, how to assume and discard personae, how to be psychologically fluid instead of morally firm. But a theater could play only to limited audiences, while the movies gave lessons to millions and television to billions in how to imagine being other than what you have been told you are. As for Richard Gere, his Buddhist practice has not made him a better actor, but the reverse may be true. His long experience in the actor's trade appears to have taught him some lightness and flexibility with his own emotions, instead of considering them the brute facts of existence. In Buddhism, what is called the self resembles less a thing than, in fact, an actor who can assume different shapes, depending on circumstances.

This, then, is the coincidence that may be historically significant: Buddhism is religiously unique in that it withdraws not only God but also the idea of a soul, and describes in its place an aggregate of body, sensation, and motion, out of which individuals construct their meaning. This is exactly what, in *Democracy in America*, Tocqueville said the arts in America would do. De Tocqueville's point was that in America art will no longer attempt to evoke the divine or the ideal but concentrate solely on human realities. Likewise, Buddhism is a religion more concerned with the various realities an individual experiences than with a divine or otherworldly theology. In this regard—about the making and unmaking of identities; about the individual's mesh with the world—Buddhism and the movies may be preaching, in entirely different languages, a similar message to a new society in flux.

PEOPLE IN THE FILM WORLD have flirted with Eastern religions before. In the 1940s the enlightenment-of-choice was a refined version of Hinduism called Vedanta. The writer Christopher Isherwood escorted Greta Garbo to meet his Vedanta guru, and the guru joked: Next time, bring the Prince of Wales. Garbo did not stay, however; neither she nor any other major star became a Vedantist, and no movies were made about it. As a consequence Vedanta remains all but unknown in the United States today, with a few thousand adherents.

Steven Seagal or Richard Gere may add nothing to understanding Buddhism; *Seven Years* and *Kundun* may furnish no models of cross-cultural transmission. Collectively, however, they have accomplished one thing: They have helped make the old religion of Tibet nearly a household word in America. Apple computers runs an ad featuring the Dalai Lama—there is no need to identify him. An ad for a sport utility vehicle shows it racing past Tibetan musicians playing on rugged terrain—there is no need to identify them. An infant lama recognizing his previous reincarnations's possessions is now used in an ad for M&M's candy, and M&M's assumes that TV viewers will get it. How different this ready familiarity is from even two decades ago, observes Martin Wassell, a liaison for Tibetan interests in Hollywood. Twenty years ago when the Dalai Lama came to town, Wassell would rent a hall seating two hundred people and then worry about empty chairs. He would call TV stations, asking whether they cared to interview the Dalai Lama, and often got the response, "What did you say her last name was?" Now when His Holiness speaks anywhere in America, four thousand people, or forty thousand, may show up.

So much, so very much hangs in the balance. In 1990 the Dalai Lama hosted a group of Jewish rabbis in Dharamsala, interested in learning from them how you survive two thousand years in diaspora. The rabbis told inspiring stories, but they had no magical key, no clues for the Tibetans cast adrift in the twenty-first century. For most of those millennia of exile Jews lived in ghettos, where if they were persecuted their faith was also sheltered. (Jewish people lived in Poland for over a thousand years, but many of them never learned Polish.) Tibetan youth were already learning English and other languages and mastering the Internet as well as intermarrying. Were they to survive as a people or a religion, they had to survive not in ghettos but in the modern transnational hubbub, including its pop culture.

A recent *Publishers Weekly* featured as its cover story the boom in Buddhist books and Buddhist presses in America. Tibetan Buddhism has evidently faced the either/or ultimatum that American academics know only too well: Publish [make movies, etc.] or perish. And so some lamas in exile (and their disciples) did publish, and a few books even elbowed their way onto the best-seller lists. And so a few Hollywood feature films got made, and rock groups staged Free Tibet concerts that tens of thousands attended. When Jetsunma and Tenzin Palmo were growing up, they had all the makings of Buddhists, but they never encountered the possibility and scarcely the word. Their vague spiritual itch was like an illness that cannot be treated because it cannot be diagnosed. No adolescent in England or America will likely float quite so much in the dark again. The practice of Buddhism in the United States is almost infinitesimal compared to that of Christianity, but its name is nearly as well known, and a few other facts about it as well. In no small part because of the media, Buddhism has become, if not mainstream, a standard alternative selection. Religious adherents make the strangest bedfellows: A few matinee idols and film directors have done more than a thousand monks could have to chant Tibetan Buddhism into general awareness in the American culture.

chapter VIII

The Star

SUPPOSE (as when the Soviets rewrote the past) that Richard Gere were erased from the record? Some issues of *People* and *Us* would require replacement cover photos; Buddhist magazines like *Tricycle* and *Shambhala Sun* would need to devise a few new lead stories. But the number of Tibetan Buddhist practitioners in this country, and the nature of their practice, would likely be no different. The person who has turned thousands of people toward Buddhism is not an actor but a butcher—if we can believe Chinese propaganda. "A butcher, his hands dripping red from his victims' blood" is how the Chinese communists demonize Tenzin Gyatso, the Fourteenth Dalai Lama.

The Dalai Lama has been the real advertisement for Tibetan Buddhism. For many Americans that religion, once ignored or dismissed, has now its whole meaning symbolized in his usually smiling face. By now the Dalai Lama seems like a wonderful uncle or kindly grandfather we've known for as long as we can remember. But beneath the familiarity are aspects of him that are strange or paradoxical. The world's most famous Buddhist discourages Westerners from becoming Buddhists, telling them their own religion is perfectly good. The world's most venerated religious figure (excepting, possibly, the Pope) has even declared religion itself unnecessary. Though acclaimed everywhere, this man, it can be argued, has failed at everything. He has not loosened China's heavy hand on Tibet; he has won no political powers over to nonviolence; after a half century of his gentle exhortation and peaceful example, the world is more strife torn and hate filled than ever. Yet he is probably the most admired person on earth anyway, merely because of who he is. Which raises the question, who is he?

On any day of his life, no matter his age (at least since his maturity), regardless of which country he is in, the Dalai Lama reveals a man seemingly operating on a different principle—a principle that, if nothing else, allows him to do a greater variety of different things and usually do them with some grace. When he first visited Washington, D.C., in 1993, for example (after long being denied a visa to the United States), a roomful of senators met with him—mainly because he had won the Nobel Prize for Peace. The senators were unsure of the politics involved, though, and an awkward silence burdened the room. Then the Dalai Lama began to giggle, and next the senators were giggling, and the meeting went quite well. Afterwards a photographer came to photograph the Dalai Lama but was so nervous he kept dropping his equipment. The Dalai Lama's response was to go over and hug the photographer. Later that afternoon a couple had an audience with him, bringing their two-year-old conveniently at his nap time. The boy remained wide-awake, plucking grapes from a huge bowl of fruit on the coffee table, much to his parents' embarrassment. The Dalai Lama got on his knees and began also plucking grapes, flicking them with his finger across the room, as the child gleefully retrieved them. That meeting went very well, too. He often handles situations with a finesse a diplomat would envy, but the above are hardly the calculated gestures of a Tallyrand or Disraeli.

Or, to take another example, he was the same constantly revved engine of often unexpected action when he first visited Mexico in 1988. Security had to be arranged, but because his visit was privately arranged and funded, that security was quite low budget. Those security guards or *matones* (killers) resembled caricatures of Pancho Villa, swearing and drinking, and boasted nicknames like "El Angel" because they looked anything but. The *matones* had not a clue who the Dalai Lama was, and his Mexican hosts prayed nothing too terrible would happen. By the second day, though, the guards were tearful as they explained to the hosts that the Dalai Lama was the sweetest person in the world. They began fetching their mothers so the Dalai Lama could bless them. By the end of his visit, those mangy lions had turned into pussycats: They fingered their newly acquired *malas* and were chanting *Om Mani Padma Hum*. What is peculiar is that the Dalai Lama did not speak Spanish, nor did the guards speak English. He would pinch their cheeks and otherwise find wordless gestures to communicate with them. His hosts marveled: Those guards offered the Tibetan cause nothing, they had no money or influence, but the Dalai Lama was every bit as interested in them as in the political and religious VIPs he was meeting. (Curiously, there is a superstition in Mexico that its dormant volcano the "Sleeping Lady" will rumble into life and the country with it, once the Tibetans arrive.)

Tibetans believe that the Dalai Lama has such a beneficial effect because he is a living Buddha, a being who inspires such awe that they dare not look him directly in the eye. But in how he thinks of himself, the Dalai Lama long ago traded in his god-king's robes for an ordinary person's. (The actual robes remained the same, of course, Tibetan maroon and yellow.) The Dalai Lama insists that he is a simple Buddhist monk, and his insistence goes beyond words. With his constant travel his home is practically on airplanes, but unlike financiers and politicians with their private planes, he flies commercial airlines and refuses to fly first class. In 1963 when Tibetans in exile drafted their first constitution, the Dalai Lama insisted, against everyone's protests, on inserting a clause that he could be impeached. American presidents and other elected servants of the world's democracies now expect to be treated like royalty, while the monarch of a divine theocracy illustrates how a democratic leader might actually behave.

Every day he meets with people from all walks of life—the powerful and the unknown, the great successes and the miserably defeated. He may have had a larger number of meaningful encounters with more people than anyone else in history. He may also hold the record for the range of subjects, from the nature of the universe to pragmatic politics to domestic advice, on which he's spoken knowledgeably and offered counsel. He has, in a sense, acted as a therapist to the world's suffering, even while his own suffering, or rather the tragedy and sorrow of Tibet, is never long absent from his thoughts. Such a weight would weigh down any man, but the Dalai Lama says he is happy, and he obviously is, really a *bon vivant*, confident that all will work out well. His exuberant spirits, his endless sense of humor and fun, his good cheer despite every reason not to feel it, these have not escaped the notice of the watching world. The character of the Dalai Lama has worked like a billboard for Tibetan Buddhism and created a "market" for it where there was none. If the source of the Dalai Lama's happiness were a drug, it would sell well on the black market, and though not a drug, quite a few customers hope to procure it anyway.

IT WAS HARDLY A straight road that led to his becoming the earth's favorite son. In 1959, when Jawaharlal Nehru announced to the Indian parliament that he had granted the Dalai Lama asylum, the parliament stood up as a single body and cheered. But Nehru, a cultured and visionary politician, inwardly was not cheering. He had a vision that did not include the Dalai Lama: India and China would ally themselves (*Hindu-Chin bhai bhai*), making a nonaligned Third Way, creating for Asia a new sociopolitical future. The Dalai Lama's presence in his country, certain to offend China, was an irritating fly in that ointment. As the price of asylum, Nehru placed a de facto embargo on the Dalai Lama's speaking out on political matters. The news story of the year—the Chinese crushing of Tibetan independence, culminating in the Dalai Lama's flight—thus quietly faded from view.

In 1959 what might anyone have reasonably predicted for that twenty-four-year-old princeling, as he faced exile in an unknown world that wanted to have nothing to do with him? Would he join other dethroned monarchs at luxurious spas, pal up with King Zog and his bevy of beautiful women or accompany King Farouk to the gaming tables of Monte Carlo? Given how little was known about the Dalai Lama, such guesses would not have sounded entirely farfetched. He had scarcely the resources or support to plan anything on a grander, more political scale. The Dalai Lama set up his government in exile in Dharamsala, a tiny forgotten village in the Himalayas, where he was forgotten by much of the world himself. The world's political leaders ignored him, not wanting to offend China with its potential billion-customer market, and the Nixon-Kissinger administration refused him even a tourist's visa. Later, in 1979, when the American government finally admitted him for a visit, no grander welcome awaited him at Kennedy Airport than the Tibet-America Committee, a handful of private people who drove him into the USA in an ordinary midsized car, to confront obstacles as insurmountable as any knight in a fairy tale ever faced. Tibet's struggle against China is likened, metaphorically, to David versus Goliath, but in this case the underdog confronted in China's military the equivalent of an army of giants. And to make this fight still more unequal, the Dalai Lama tied his hands behind his back, refusing to use or countenance violence.

His hero was Gandhi, and like Gandhi he determined to overcome his enemies not with violence but through love and compassion for them. But Gandhi's foe was the British, fortunately, for as George Orwell pointed out, Gandhi's tactics would never have succeeded against a totalitarian power like Nazi Germany or modern China. (Hitler said the foolish British should have simply killed Gandhi, and were that not sufficient, killed the thousand leading independence fighters, and if that failed, then ten thousand more, etc.) Besides, the numbers were on Gandhi's side—hundreds of millions of Indians versus a couple of hundred thousand British on the Subcontinent. During the Korean War Mao was willing to sacrifice millions of Chinese lives, and he was prepared, if need be, to loose a similar avalanche of his countrymen's blood upon underpopulated Tibet. To make matters worse, key political figures like Henry Kissinger, Edward Heath, and Georges Pompidou admired Mao for his rational, efficient government, while they considered the Dalai Lama (when they considered him at all) a holy fool who had no business intruding into their global geopolitics.

So not surprisingly he failed: Today, flooded with government-sponsored population transfers from China, Lhasa is a concrete barracks-like Chinese city, in a country where Chinese is the language of instruction in schools and almost all expressions of Buddhism are prohibited. More surprising, though, is the extent to which the Dalai Lama has succeeded. Thanks in no small part to him, more people may be practicing his religion than at any previous time, and once-unknown Tibetan culture has now become part of world civilization. For centuries China was venerated as a magnificent culture, but most outsiders today consider it mainly a fairly cheerless place to do business. By contrast Tibetan centers, without any national support, have sprung up throughout North and South America, Europe, and Australia. In 1959, as Mao listened to reports of the quelling of the Tibetan uprising, he interrupted, "But what about the Dalai Lama?" When told that he had escaped, Mao groaned, "In that case we have lost." Mao was wrong, in that the Chinese conquered Tibet, but possibly right that they lost the battle of ideas. Vast numbers of knowledgeable people consider that Tibetan Buddhism, once dismissed as hopelessly outdated, actually has more answers—far more than Maoism—on how to live happily today.

When at a moment's notice the twenty-four-year-old Dalai Lama escaped from Tibet, he carried with him few possessions and even less in the way of experience to face what lay ahead. The first Westerners to meet this slender boy-man with hunched shoulders (from overmuch study) thought him sweet but hardly equipped to handle the tasks before him. Years later some of them wondered what they had missed; it was certainly nothing on the surface, nothing obvious, but possibly something hidden or buried in his upbringing, that accounted for his invisible, latent strength.

THE DALAI LAMA'S LIFE BEGINS, according to one interpretation, before he was born. His "prequel" was the man whom Alexandra David-Neel interviewed—the Great Thirteenth Dalai Lama (1876–1933)—whom Tibetans consider the same being in a previous manifestation. Toward the end of his life, the Great Thirteenth issued dire prophecies of a dangerous threat descending from the north, and he warned his countrymen to enjoy themselves now, for soon the time would come when no Tibetan would drink a cup of tea in peace. Then in 1933 the Great Thirteenth, though apparently in excellent health, died suddenly. Many Tibetans believe he consciously willed his own demise, otherwise his successor (i. e., his reincarnation) would be too young when Tibet's time of troubles began. After he died, his body was placed in a meditative position, but his head turned east, and though righted, kept turning east, indicating, supposedly, that somewhere in eastern Tibet the new baby Dalai Lama would be born.

In the spring of 1935 the regent of Tibet along with other diviners journeyed to the sacred lake of Lhamoi Latso, and in the lake's prismatic waves and depths they saw visionary shapes of architectural imagery, a jade- and gold-capped monastery and a turquoise tile-roofed house with a brown-and-white dog nearby, which—they assumed—would identify the house where the small boy lived. When two years of tracking down such clues brought lamas from Sera Monastery to just such a house near just such a monastery, they came disguised as merchants in order not to arouse suspicions. But despite their disguises, the little boy ran out to them yelling, "Sera monks! Sera monks!" They carried with them items belonging to the Thirteenth Dalai Lama, which little Tenzin Gyatso seized upon as rightfully his, refusing to relinquish them for brighter baubles. "He was so excited about the whole affair," his older brother recalls, "and so indignant at what he regarded as the attempt to deprive him of his possessions, that he was near to tears." Even before the monks' visit, the little two-year-old had straddled the windowsill and pretended he was on a horse riding to Lhasa, and, curiously, he spoke with a proper Llasa accent. The "discovery" of Tenzin Gyatso, the boy Dalai Lama, is encrusted with numerous such incredible details.

What seems equally inexplicable was the young Dalai Lama's peculiar interest in the West. Tibetans were xenophobes, so incurious about Westerners that they simply forbade their entry into Tibet. The Austrian mountain climber Heinrich Harrer, who escaped wartime detention in British India by stealing across the Himalayas (as related in *Seven Years in Tibet* [1953]), claimed the fourteen-year-old Dalai Lama had never seen a European before him. But long before meeting Harrer, the Dalai Lama was inquisitive about what lay beyond Tibet's borders and determined to possess its strange knowledge. He had already begun secretly teaching himself English from books, and at his first meeting with Harrer, he shyly showed him some sketchmarks on paper, which Harrer recognized as attempts to write in the Latin alphabet. To arrange that meeting, the fourteen-year-old boy had defied all his ministers, which began a lifetime's willingness to ignore precedents in order to meet the modern world on its own terms. A Dalai Lama any less fascinated by the West would have proved, of course, of little utility to Tibet when its troubles descended.

The young Dalai Lama's pretext for meeting Harrer? He wanted to watch movies, and the foreigner was hired to construct a projection booth. People in Lhasa were wild about movies. Although the city had no cinema, rich families possessed projectors (bought from Indian traders), and their homes were crammed on film nights. Charlie Chaplin was the hands-down favorite, with the dog Rin Tin Tin second. However, the Dalai Lama waved aside such fluff and wanted to watch only movies that could increase his useful knowledge. The available films were soon exhausted, so Harrer went from running a projector to running an unofficial tutorial, dredging up everything he knew from military history to mechanics, from physics to geography, to feed his pupil's insatiable curiosity. Once when Harrer arrived late, the Dalai Lama's mother reproached him, saying her son had so few other chances of enjoying himself. The Dalai Lama and Harrer started planning a new dawn for Tibet, in which a world-class university would be built in Llasa and experts from small neutral countries brought in to establish progressive educational and health-care systems. That pretty dream went up in smoke in 1950, when the Chinese communists invaded, and Harrer had to flee for his life. But the Dalai Lama's education for a modern sphere of action was thus already under way when he followed Harrer into that sphere several years later.

One shouldn't, however, imagine the young Dalai Lama fixated on the horizon, panting for what lay beyond it. He was no Tenzin Palmo in reverse, believing himself born in the wrong country and culture. Around age six he plunged into a rigorous Tibetan education, and with time out for mischief, he took to it as a young Dalai Lama should. In his teens, he began his study of *sunnyata* or "emptiness." Just as an "empty" glass is full (of air, microbes, light, atoms), so a person having realized *sunnyata* is also full—of unqualified, unconditioned being. Later, in exile, the Dalai Lama would reveal his mastery of *sunnyata* whenever he was happy while simultaneously his heart was full of the Tibetan tragedy. He began, too, the Tibetan Buddhist study of nonduality, of identifying or equating oneself with others. Nonduality would also serve him well in exile, when he traveled nine months a year, going, doing, meeting, never stopping. Because the usual friction or resistance did not arise between him and another person, he would not be depleted meeting people constantly one after another but, on the contrary, energized by the exchanges.

Most useful of all, his Tibetan education taught him the Buddhist lesson of equanimity in the face of adversity. The Dalai Lama frequently quotes Shantideva's maxim that if we can fix a problem, there's no sense in worrying about it, and if we cannot fix it, there's no sense in worrying about it. Shantideva's maxim is simplicity itself, but the Dalai Lama counterbalanced it by mastering the Tibetan Buddhist worldview that encompasses eons of time and multiple strata of existence, with its manifold perspectives on present happenings. This simplicity-complexity framework gave him a greater vantage point on difficulties he encountered in exile, more intellectual flexibility, and usually another way of looking at them. "What can a person do when something too terrible happens?" the author once asked the Dalai Lama, and he replied, "Try looking at it from as many different angles as possible. Just one may be positive—and that alone will help." The Dalai Lama was intrigued by the West early on, but it was his Tibetan education that gave him something to offer the West that the West did not already know.

SOME LAMAS WHO FLED TIBET in 1959 felt on entering the outside world that they had been dropped into outer space. Even Lama Yeshe regarded the first Americans who approached him warily, as though they might be—who knew what. But the Dalai Lama never shared this wariness. In Tibet he was considered a near divinity enshrined in punctilious protocol, whom one must never touch or look in the eye. In exile he immediately—without any encouragement—started shaking hands, hugging people, and going out personally to greet individuals and crowds. If Westerners wished to profit from his wisdom, he hoped to learn from them equally or more.

Bruce Joel Rubin, stunned by the Dalai Lama's offer to be his teacher, refused, but in 1964 the Dalai Lama acquired his first Western pupil, the twenty-three-year-old Robert Thurman. (Today Thurman is, along with Jeffrey Hopkins, one of the deans of Tibetan studies in America, although perhaps as often identified as actress Uma Thurman's father.) Thurman was studying with Geshe Ngawang Wangyal in New Jersey, to whom he confided his wish to become a Buddhist monk. Geshe Wangyal thought Thurman unsuited for monkhood, but agreed to present Thurman's proposition to the Dalai Lama. The Dalai Lama thought it a fine idea, and soon Thurman was living in Dharamsala and regularly meeting with His Holiness for instruction. Who was the teacher and who the student, though, is not entirely clear. Thurman would burst in eagerly, with this or that esoteric question about Buddhism practically flying off his tongue. The Dalai Lama would typically respond, "Oh talk to—" (and name some lama), and then pour out his own questions. "Now what about Freud?" the Dalai Lama would ask. "What about physics? What about the history of World War Two?" In a year and a half the Dalai Lama absorbed, Thurman estimates, his whole Exeter and Harvard education.

The young Bob Thurman dazzled all Dharamsala: He learned Tibetan in ten weeks, mastered complex Tibetan debate, and became a Buddhist monk. Evidently Geshe Wangyal erred in his judgment—or had he? After a year Thurman grew homesick, gave back his monk's robes, and returned to America. In Dharamsala Thurman's defection was taken as an inauspicious sign. Some Tibetans concluded that the dharma is wasted on Westerners, but the Dalai Lama seemed unfazed.

Then Harold Talbott, who accompanied Thomas Merton to his meetings with the Dalai Lama, returned to Dharamsala with hopes of studying with the Dalai Lama. Greeting a prospective spiritual teacher, a devotee should show himself composed, having mastered his emotional states, but as he asked to become the Dalai Lama's student Harold burst into tears. The Dalai Lama came and took his hand, and together they walked up and down the veranda. Before accepting Harold as his student, however, the Dalai Lama questioned him closely to ensure that he was *mitendo* ("straight," "reliable").

"Once you begin something," he demanded of Harold, "do you stick to it? Do you persevere?"

"No, not really. More the other way around," Harold answered. Why didn't I just lie? he thought. Evidently the Dalai Lama detected depths of sincerity in Harold that Harold did not suspect he possessed, and he agreed to be Harold's teacher and Harold would become his monk in America.

Which was most odd. A Dalai Lama does not usually accept students at all, having too many other responsibilities. And if he does supervise someone's spiritual education, that person would be a tulku, a high reincarnation, not some layman who happens to stroll by. Whoever's training he supervised would also be of a young and impressionable age, not fully formed adults like Thurman and Talbott. But the Dalai Lama realized that in exile he had entered the unknown, and that many precedents might need to be left behind, if Tibetan Buddhism were to survive.

Robert Thurman and Harold Talbott were merely young men acting on their own, and if they were impressive figures later, they were both "dropouts" at the time. With these two seemingly chance encounters, the Dalai Lama initiated a new era: Tibetan Buddhism as a Western religion.

WHEN THE DALAI LAMA toured the National Air and Space Administration, some NASA astronauts were on hand to answer his questions. "Since there's no gravity in space," the Dalai Lama asked, "what happens to your eggs at breakfast?" The astronauts told how they sometimes grabbed their scrambled eggs floating off into midair. "In that case," the Dalai Lama asked, "what happens to your poop?"

These are the questions of a child, not the pontiff of a great religion. The Dalai Lama often moves through the complex modern world as someone mainly curious about it. When, years before, Harrer (successfully) tutored the teenage Dalai Lama in modernity, the Dalai Lama had attempted (unsuccessfully) to convert Harrer to Buddhism. That effort— of making Buddhist converts—is the last thing he would attempt today. In the early '80s a man from California traveled to Dharamsala, intending to perform the most dramatic act of all, conversion, and he challenged the Dalai Lama to put him to the test, for he would endure the agonies of a martyr if need be to become a Buddhist. "Okay," the Dalai Lama replied matter-of-factly, "you're a Buddhist." Usually he won't even go that far. The Dalai Lama tells potential converts to look for whatever benefits they have discovered in Buddhism in their religion of origin.

Once during an interminable drive through south India, in a flyspeck of a village by the road, the Dalai Lama had the ten-car entourage halt, as he jumped out, his robes flying in the breeze. He had spied behind a statue of Dr. Ambedkar (the Untouchable leader who converted to Buddhism, to avoid caste stigmas) an empty room, evidently used as a Buddhist temple. The Dalai Lama hurried into the room, deposited some Buddhist texts there, then hurried back to the car, as the dust of the village settled behind his speeding-away entourage. The Dalai Lama does plant the seeds of Buddhism, where appropriate, but he believes that the seeds of kindness planted in modern secularism are every bit as, if not more, important.

In this attitude the Dalai Lama has come a long way from his own origins. Tibet was steeped in mysticism and mysteries, and as a boy he grew up steeped in them. As a teenager, he read in old Tibetan books about separating the spirit from the body, and planned that one day he would work wonders from great distances. But as an adult in exile, the wonder he has worked is to convert Tibet's magical past to modern respectability. Those of a mystical bent still bait him with such questions as "What makes His Holiness the happiest?" Instead of the quasi-mystical revelation they expect, he answers, "Good food and a sound night's sleep." Or they ask, "What do you remember of your past lives?" He laughs—and in that laughter everything supernatural about Tibet disappears—as he answers, "You know, I can barely remember what I did last week."

The Dalai Lama says that his religion is compassion, which must disappoint every mystic. Indeed, he cannot stop saying it: "My religion is kindness." To dispel the occult, otherworldly aura of Tibetan Buddhism, he could scarcely have hit upon a more effective formula. Who, scientist or secularist, objects to kindness? Yet by equating religion with kindness, the

Dalai Lama risks reducing its power and glory to a Hallmark Cards greeting. When young Tenzin Palmo asked how to become perfect (i.e., enlightened), and was told, "Be good, and be very kind," she thought, Phooey, there has to be more to it than that. We need to catch the Dalai Lama in the act of being kind, to see what makes it more than a cliché.

Whenever he enters a room, invisible magnets seem to draw him straight over to whoever is suffering in that room. The Dalai Lama claims his English is poor and he knows no other foreign language, but with suffering individuals, even schizophrenics, he can connect almost regardless of language. He said that if he gives one person a moment's peace, he will feel he has succeeded. That's a fairly modest definition of success. When asked about his grander achievements, such as winning the Nobel Prize, he replied, "For a religious practitioner, winning it doesn't amount to very much."

Marie L.* has savored the Dalai Lama's kindness. In raising funds in America for the Tibetan political cause, Marie had become close friends with a charismatic Tibetan leader. When she stopped her fund-raising (to try to help Tibetans within Tibet), her political friend turned on her with a vengeance, and she was so devastated she had to seek psychotherapy. Previously, if the Dalai Lama noticed Marie at public events, he would wave. Shortly after her traumatic break with the Tibetan politico, however—though she had complained to no one—the Dalai Lama asked to speak with her. When she entered his room and sat down, he pulled his chair so close that his face was about three inches away, and said: "When I attend the Kashag [the Tibetan cabinet] and hear someone maligned, I try to think of something good about him. When I hear someone praised highly, I think of something bad about him. Do you understand what I am saying?" "Yes," Marie answered. "Good. Start practicing this. Start now!" And the Dalai shuffled over to the bookcase, where he located the verses

*This is not her real name.

in Shantideva that describe how to achieve a view of others infused with equanimity.

Jigme Ngabo tells of the Dalai Lama's kindness to him. Jigme's father was called the "Tibetan Quisling," because in 1951 he signed the Seventeen-Point Agreement that made Tibet officially a Chinese province. (The senior Ngabo, then practically a prisoner in Beijing, had little choice in the matter.) The son did not want to be part of Beijing's "show" Tibetan family, chauffeured about in limousines, and was determined to emigrate to America. En route he met the Dalai Lama in India, a meeting that, given the Ngabo-family history, promised to be awkward. As Jigme explained his plans, the Dalai Lama said nothing but crossed the room and found some pills, and then said, "Take these. They will prevent air sickness on the flight to America." He rummaged in his drawers again and unearthed some other pills: "Tibetans are unused to the food in America and often get ill from it. These pills will cure that sickness." "At that point I thought," Jigme said, "this man loves me more than my own mother does."

In his own mind the Dalai Lama pictures himself not as a world leader but something more preferable: a friend. Most people regard themselves as a good friend, but the requirements of friendship often come second or third (or fourth) in their personal hierarchy, behind job, health, financial security, and certainly behind their families; but the Dalai Lama apparently ranks friendship above all these. A friend, however admirable, is certainly a far cry from those flying monks, levitating lamas, and other marvelous beings the rumors of which produced an earlier generation's fascination with Tibet. The Dalai Lama has swapped a thousand years of magic and mystery for kindness and friendship. Withdraw the magic show, he implies, and Tibetan Buddhism as a religion of compassion can still help ameliorate the world's—and an individual's—travails.

AND YET. Though the Dalai Lama downplays the mystical elements of Tibetan Buddhism, they still hover quietly in the background. Speaking at

American universities and other progressive forums, the Dalai Lama expresses a faith that could hardly sound more commonsensical and contemporary. But monks and advanced practitioners hear him give teachings that might astonish a subdued Episcopalian or a proper Unitarian. As Robert Thurman circumambulated Tibet's sacred Mount Kailash in 1995, he recalled the Dalai Lama's words: "Sixty-two superbliss deities are always present at Mount Kailash. The palace doors are always open there and its radiance is always emanating." At one talk someone questioned the Dalai Lama about reincarnation: "How can there be six billion people on the planet now, when once there were only six hundred thousand?" (In other words, the numbers are wrong.) He laughed and gave an answer as unexpected as it was humorous: "I like to think of it as a kind of tourism." The audience laughed with him, at the image of other beings from elsewhere lately taken to hanging out on planet Earth. Other beings, hidden dimensions, a multistrataed universe—Tibetan Buddhism still keeps in reserve a fantastical mythology. But Buddhism is one religion that does not preach a single "sermon" (or rather rules and guidelines) for everybody, but adapts to meet the capabilities and understanding of a particular audience, and evidently the Dalai Lama does not consider the old Tibetan aurora borealis of marvelous lights and wonders the most useful display for contemporaries.

And yet. Tenzin Palmo felt a seismic quake in her being upon meeting her guru, and though he hardly publicizes it, the Dalai Lama can have this effect on people when he wants. Marie L. (the fund-raiser) attended a benefit for Tibet in Los Angeles, where she remained in a corner content to observe the famous and the fawning. "Come on, do something," she exhorted herself. "I'm supposed to be here promoting the Tibetan cause." Across the room the Dalai Lama was shaking hands with Sharon Stone, when Marie approached Shirley MacLaine and Jon Voight to ask if they had any questions about Tibet. Shirley MacLaine let loose a torrent of abuse at Marie. How dare this little twerp approach her pretending to know something she didn't! Marie felt like crawling into a hole and shriveling up into a ball of nothing. Just then a hand tapped her shoulder, and there was the Dalai Lama saying, "Hello, Marie-la!" The Dalai Lama then pressed his forehead to hers, and she felt such an explosion of bliss and contentment that she barely knew where she was.

There are dozens, hundreds of similar stories that, out of respect for the Dalai Lama's wishes, usually never get publicly told. When the photographer Leslie DiRusso visited India in 1983, she obtained an audience with the Dalai Lama in Dharamsala, which was pleasant enough but nothing remarkable. The next day, having nothing better to do, she attended his public teaching. At one moment he stared directly at her, and smiled, and Leslie felt hit by a bolt of lightning. Her body shuddered with a force that would have put a mere orgasm to shame. After the teaching she hurried to a friend, worried. "Does this mean I have to become a nun? I don't want to be a nun!" Her friend reassured her, "It only means the Dalai Lama has taken you into his mandala." The Dalai Lama had evidently taken her into *something*, for, surprising herself, she subsequently devoted her life to the Tibetan cause, most recently mounting exhibitions of Heinrich Harrer's photographs of Tibet that a million people have viewed.

The Dalai Lama sees himself as a friend, but quietly he considers himself something else, a seeker (as in one committed to the spiritual quest), and he feels kinship with seekers everywhere, even those who expect from him prodigious acts that he cannot, or will not, perform. He wants from religion what Tenzin Palmo and Jetsunma hungered for, what the wildest-eyed hippie who sat at Lama Yeshe's or Chögyam Trungpa's feet hoped to learn, and he has done more and gone further than any of them to find it. When a visitor told him about her father's death, the Dalai Lama sympathized, "You know, I meditate upon my own death five times every day. But when the times comes, I am afraid I will . . ." and here he turned to his translator for help. "What is that word in English? *Botch? Botch?*" As for what he wants from religion, besides a good death, consider the fact that he wakes every day at 4 A.M. to practice four hours before "business" starts, and he steals time for practice throughout the day, which would hardly be necessary if he were merely fine-tuning his kindness.

In Mexico the Dalai gave teachings, participated in the country's first ecumenical conference, met with the president of Mexico, talked with one interviewer after another, and before leaving Mexico finally had a couple of hours to relax. Instead, he confided to his hosts he wished to do something that must be kept secret. He hoped to visit the shrine of the Virgin of Guadalupe. The dark-skinned Virgin of Guadalupe is like the mother goddess of Mexico and to many Mexicans the most moving of all religious symbols. One wonders how the Dalai Lama even knew about her, since none of his briefings had mentioned her. When he quietly paid homage and prayed to her as though she were a *dakini*, sacred feminized "energy," what was he doing really? Honoring his host country, or beseeching its native deities? (Traditionally, Tibetan lamas placated the local spirits when they traveled to a new place.) A shrewd politician visiting Mexico might well choose to visit the shrine of Guadalupe, but that politician would want his visit ballyhoo'd in the media. If the Dalai Lama went secretly to pray to the *dakini* of Mexico, though, such an act of worship would be the last thing he would want publicized.

Any investigation into the more mystical side of the Dalai Lama's religion must end where it started—with a discussion of what he means by kindness. He means what anyone would by it, but also something more: He is referring to *bodhicitta*, cultivating that rare state of mind that doesn't think primarily of oneself but puts others' happiness first. The Dalai Lama often states that he is only a simple Buddhist monk, which causes some speculation on the possible esoteric meaning behind his statement. But all he means is that he has taken two hundred and fifty-three vows of monkhood. Those two hundred-plus vows are not to create an ethical person (ten would do for that), but to make the mind supple for *bodhicitta*, for putting others first.

Bodhicitta possibly accounts—there seems no other explanation—for the most inexplicable, mysterious characteristic of the Dalai Lama. Around age seventy he has begun slowing down a bit, but he has been a perpetual engine, a human dynamo who does not stop, who can interact with scores of people and do hundreds of things a day, day after day after day. The fuel he runs on, evidently, is helping others, and the more he helps the more energy he has. *Bodhicitta* is the opposite of "self-cherishing," and self-cherishing—upholding one's self-image, pursuing a personal agenda, worrying about the future—apparently uses up a lot of fuel. By ceasing self-cherishing to the extent that he has, the Dalai Lama seems to have unlocked the source and unblocked the flow of his energy.

Tibetans say that the Dalai Lama is "sincere," by which Westerners would mean that he is "natural." He will blow his nose, scratch his head, or cry profusely, not stopping to judge whether the occasion is appropriate. He usually doesn't judge: He does not consider whether this person is worth helping, for each person is worth it; or whether that person is important enough to meet, for every person is important; or whether to accept an invitation, be it from the United Nations or a children's club, because all have their merit. (His secretaries and administrators, beseeched with endless invitations and requests, often, however, make such judgments on his behalf.) His biographer John Avedon has accompanied him through twenty-five countries and—as they traipse out into the Indian desert, say, to meet a would-be producer of an unfinanced film script on some Buddhist subject that likely will never get made—Avedon often thinks, "If I were the Dalai Lama, I would not be doing this." But the Dalai Lama does it, and appears to have uncovered the secret of doing (almost) everything. He has mastered tantric practices for controlling the body's energy, but his real secret, the alchemist's stone that mystics have sought for centuries, may simply be his unlimited compassion. Or so he makes it seem.

HOW CAN RELIGION PROSPER in a contemporary, more secular society? The Dalai Lama's answer, hinted at in the previous pages, sounds ironical: by recognizing that religion is not more important than everything else but, in many ways, is less important. Like Gandhi, he believes that the sacred resides less in religious books and divine laws than in an individual's honesty and compassion. Gandhi held that the atheist, if passionate and considerate in his convictions, is a holy man, and the Dalai Lama appears to value a secular truth over a religious one. "If the words of the Buddha and the discoveries of modern science conflict," he has said, "the former have to go."

Dr. Herbert Benson of the Harvard Medical School, reading Alexandra David-Neel, decided to measure tummo, body-heat control, scientifically. Dr. Benson realized, though, that even if he could locate the appropriate hermit-adepts, they would hardly sit still while he stuck rectal thermometers up their anuses, etc. . . . unless the Dalai urged them to. When they met in 1979, the Dalai Lama refused his request as Benson had feared, explaining that the practitioners were in retreat for religious reasons. The Dalai Lama spoke to Benson in Tibetan through a translator, but in midsentence he changed his mind—and changed a millennium's worth of precedent—as he switched to English: "Still . . . our friends to the East [meaning, the Chinese] might be impressed with a Western explanation of what we are doing. Perhaps there is some worth in allowing your study to be done." In a lecture not long thereafter the Dalai Lama told Tibetan monks, "For skeptics, you must show something spectacular because, without that, they won't believe."

The Dalai Lama arranged Dr. Benson's experiments, which proved under laboratory conditions that some lamas can regulate their body temperatures consciously. But the Dalai Lama's own emphases, as he expressed them publicly, lay at the other end of the spectrum from marvels like tummo. The most spectacular feat, he saw, might be the least spectacular one: a religion without the supernatural supporting wires, a faith as ordinary as daylight, as common as kindness—that might impress skeptics even more. Tibetan Buddhism won its late place in the modern world by becoming the first religion that apparently can, when necessary, dispense with religion. The distinction between religion and spirituality sounds rather flaky or New Age, but the Dalai Lama subscribes to it.

Religion involves creeds of salvation, and ramifies into dogma and ritual; those, he says, anyone can forgo. Spirituality, or what he calls "qualities of the human spirit"—e.g., patience, tolerance, contentment, loving-kindness—are, however, everybody's business, monk and atheist alike. Once when the Dalai Lama was asked to name his spiritual peers, he thought for a long time and finally answered, "Actually every person in the world is my spiritual peer." His spiritual kin extends beyond rinpoches, beyond Tibetan Buddhists, beyond even Catholics and Mormons and Jews. When he and his religion arrived in the West, it thus did not have to compete with those faiths but could draw its clientele from the religiously disenfranchised, from those who did not have and in many cases did not want a religion.

Perhaps religions should be contradictory, flip-flopping from the communal to the individual; one moment mystical, the next utilitarian; now gentle and pliant, then flinty and firm; sometimes of an angelic beauty, while other times plain as dirt. For "reality" itself, which includes both life and death, sickness and health, youth and age, is contradictory, and human character no sooner arrives somewhere than it heads off again in the opposite direction.

The Dalai Lama may emphasize kindness, but the mystic powers Alexandra David-Neel desired and the mysteries Dr. Benson investigated appear hidden just behind it. To one audience (in London, say, or Los Angeles) he preaches simple kindness, but then he gives esoteric initiations to another (to advanced practitioners or in a Tibetan monastery). But like the Dalai Lama's approach, bodhicitta—"the mind of enlightenment"— is itself double. In relative terms, bodhicitta is kindness and compassion, but in absolute terms it is wisdom, seeing the ultimate nature of things. In stressing kindness the Dalai Lama resembles a suave old diplomat who speaks in soft conciliatory terms, confident he has his country's hidden power and absolute might to back him up.

The Dalai Lama's final act before he fled Tibet was passing with "first-class honors" his *geshe* examination, for which he had studied *sunnyata* (emptiness) and nonduality—the Tibetan keys to wisdom. Although applauded as brilliant, the Dalai Lama says his understanding in Tibet had remained on an academic level. But apparently all the pressures in exile matured the nature of his learning. To bear so much responsibility and not be overwhelmed, to witness so much sorrow and not be made hopeless, to observe the Chinese holocaust in Tibet and not hate its perpetrators—all his earlier training now had to prove itself in action. If he could not have understood the emptiness or nonpermanence of what he opposed, its overwhelming cruelty would have crushed him. If he could not have sympathized or identified with the obstacles facing him, their descending avalanche might have buried him. Adversity, the Dalai Lama says, is a good school, for it tests our tender sentiments and ensures they won't vanish when we need them most. That he talks of sweet peace yet shows a martial resilience, that he speaks of kindness yet hints of a greater power evokes Shakespeare's figure in Sonnet 94:

> They that have pow'r to hurt, and will do none,
> That do not do the thing they most do show,
> Who, moving others, are themselves as stone,
>
> . . .
>
> They rightly do inherit heaven's graces,
> And husband nature's riches from expense. . . .

Is the Dalai Lama enlightened, then? People ask him that, all the time: "What's it like to be enlightened?" Out comes the hearty laugh, the skillful sidestepping of the question, as he answers, "I wouldn't know. Go ask—" (and in the past he'd name some revered teacher like Kalu Rinpoche). Once at a lecture in California, however, a man in the audience demanded, "Tell us in simple, plain words the quickest way to obtain enlightenment." The Dalai Lama looked at the man, and then studied him more closely, and burst into tears. Was he weeping for such innocence? Or crying for all the travail and misery that shall be endured before, eons hence, every being realizes that final luminous liberation (for such, indeed, he believes will happen)? Whatever else, amid his own experience of sorrow and tragedy, he has demonstrated how to hope and be of good spirits regardless. If that is not enlightenment, it has made Tibetan Buddhism an acceptable nonreligious religion in the West, and made him a priest for these, our dark times.

Book V

IN SEARCH OF
THE ORDINARY:
3 VISITS

Introduction

HOW DO ORDINARY AMERICANS become Tibetan Buddhists? Usually not by spontaneously replicating the corpus of Tibetan Buddhism, as Jetsumna once did; definitely not by sitting bolt upright in an icebound cave, as Tenzo Palmo did; rarely by meditating in between celebrity flashbulbs going off, as Richard Gere does. And if the only description of what a Tibetan Buddhist is were the Dalai Lama or even Lama Yeshe, it might be like a budding writer knowing only Shakespeare and Henry James, discouraged by models too lustrous to copy. To uncover the meaning of Tibetan Buddhism in America, one must embark on a journey into the heart of the ordinary, which is, after all, where every religion must ultimately prove itself.

Ask any other question—how people chose their spouse, or got into their line of work, or furnished their apartment in that particular style—and you can likely trace the answer step by step back to their parents or other early influences like school. But a generation ago no American homes or textbooks taught anything that resembled Tibetan Buddhism. More often than not, a Westerner's first encounter with "Tibet" seemed a fluke, and to catalogue each one's blunderings into Buddhism might result in a volume called (except the title is taken) *A Comedy of Errors*.

One shy young man, for example, got a job that required him to make public presentations, at which he was so painfully inept he decided to take a Dale Carnegie course on business speaking. He did think it a bit surprising that the course instructor wore a long robe, but by the time he realized he'd strayed into the wrong classroom, where "Buddhism for Businessmen" was being taught, it was too late. He'd swallowed the bait; a few years later he was seen in his own monk's robes, wandering about India with a begging bowl. Another young man during the 1970s used to watch the popular TV series *Kung Fu*. In one episode a boy asks the old Kung Fu Master why they are sheltering an obvious scoundrel. "Ah, little grasshopper," the Master answers, "the sun shines not only on the good man. We are here to help whoever comes." Thus inspired, our young viewer determined to follow that precept, and at one point he let an escaped murderer stay in his room. Later he learned about Tibetan Buddhism's idea of compassionate *bodhisattvas*, and when Kalu Rinpoche offered the first three-year retreat in North America, he signed up for it. He built his own cabin and slept upright on a meditation box. By his third year in retreat, when he mended his torn robe, he took such loving care with each stitch that he could have been tending the injured body of the Buddha.

Stories like these abound, some comical, others poignant, but altogether they make American Buddhists seem as random an assortment of quirky individuals as ever assembled under the same label. But certain patterns run beneath this supposed randomness and certain social groups seem hardwired to have more of their numbers become Buddhists.

A current joke concerns a woman from Brooklyn determined to seek out the wisest Tibetan guru in the world, although she must travel to the remotest Himalayas to do so. After months of hazards and ordeals, she finally reaches the holy man's cave on the cliff's edge. In her Yiddish accent she salutes the venerable sage: "Lenny, it's your mother. Come home now!" The joke reflects the fact that American Jews represent a disproportionately high percentage of Buddhists in this country—so much so that they even have their own name: "Jew-Bus." They often reported, when interviewed for this book, to having imbibed a religious inclination early, from watching their mothers light the Shabbat candles or at family Passover seders. But as they came of age during the latter part of the last century—the heyday of "secularism triumphant" in America—they often came to think that Judaism, as practiced in this country, resembled an ethnicity more than a religion. It was a matter of community and close families, which was good, and of certain foods, which were tasty, but finally it left them spiritually undernourished. To satisfy their spiritual hunger, they began to seek sustenance elsewhere. The Zen roshis and Tibetan lamas they sought out never demanded that, to practice Buddhism, one had to repudiate the old faith or convert to the new.

Rabbi Zalman Schachter-Shalomi, the founder of the Jewish Renewal Movement, teaches today at, of all places, Chögyam Trungpa's Naropa University. When asked what a nice rabbi is doing teaching at a Buddhist university, Reb Zalman is at no loss for words. He recalls how he read every Tibetan Buddhist work he could get his hands on even before the Dalai Lama fled Tibet (and after 1959, he wrote Israeli president David Ben Gurion to propose that Israel offer the exiled Tibetans a homeland). All the once-heady matters of Judaism—meditation, other dimensions of being, even the possibility of reincarnation—that went underground during the Jewish assimilation to modernity Reb Zalman found living on the surface in Tibetan Buddhism, ready to greet him like an old friend. He quotes an old Hassidic paradox: "You must invent your own religion, else it shall mean nothing to you. You must follow the religion of your fathers, else you shall lose it." For American Jews, Reb Zalman points out, Tibetan Buddhism is so alien to everything they knew growing up that they might as well have fabricated it themselves. Yet in its meaning and mystery, it has a recognizable feel to it, as though Tibetan Buddhism causes to echo in them the piety and desire for holiness of their ancestors.

At the opposite end of the spectrum are those Americans propelled toward Buddhism because, unlike their Jewish counterparts, few or no spiritual seeds were planted in their childhood. These are men and women like Jetsunma, reared in so-called dysfunctional families, where religious education was minimal and belied by the abuse they suffered. Hurts and harms of their youth left them, as they did Jetsunma, in need of healing—left them wanting something elusive for which they had no name or image. Reaching maturity, many tried to self-remedy their wounds, according to the softer wisdom of the era. They worked at "meaningful," if frequently low-paying jobs in social services or the arts; or they developed their artistic talents, even if they couldn't earn a living by them; or they enrolled in yoga and self-help courses; or they tried psychotherapy—and still they were left unsatisfied. Formerly the good (or just the sufficient) life was handed to a person on an heirloom platter by the church or community or family. But an increasing number of young men and women like Jetsunma and Michael Burroughs and Richard Gere felt they had to construct a meaningful life on their own, and nobody had handed them the instruction manual. When they finally stumbled upon Buddhism, it looked promising with its claim to being a system of healing as well as a religion; and Tibetan Buddhism in particular was so gorgeously exotic, unconnected to the emotional knives that had scarred and marred their childhood.

Coming from opposite directions, Jewish-origin and dysfunctional-origin Buddhists (and most other American Buddhists as well) have arrived at the same point, which point might be called the End of the American Dream. The American promise, in one recent version, held that economic opportunity and rewarding work, a love partner and family, and enough possibility for self-expression would create a secular version of salvation. But that promise, this salvation, did not come true, or true enough, for the participants in our story. In the 1940s the novelist Christopher Isherwood, then working in Hollywood, quit a more glamorous version of the American Dream when he left the company of Greta Garbo and Charlie Chaplin to consort with doughy, scrubbed seekers at the local Hindu temple. Isherwood considered the spiritual meeting of East and West the last human frontier and the most important adventure on which he could embark. Threescore years later American Buddhists often thrill to a kindred excitement that they are going to where nothing in their past pointed them, where no one they personally knew went before. Their yoking together an antithetical New World past to an incongruous Buddhist present, their swirling old Tibetan precepts in with the electronic U. S. of A., may make these otherwise inconspicuous people pathbreakers of sorts.

They may be more pathbreakers than even they suspect. In Buddhist Asia, some scholars claim, lay people did not really *practice*. They observed holidays and said prayers, but ultimately it was the monks' job to bless them into salvation. But Westerners who seriously take up Tibetan Buddhism are attempting to do on a small scale what Chögyam Trungpa or Lama Yeshe did on a vast one. Trungpa and Yeshe recognized this novel situation, and they treated their unusual new disciples as though each were a "lay monk" or a "lay nun." A half century ago, "American Buddhist" sounded like a contradiction or an incongruity, but it is hardly as much an oxymoron as is "lay monk." Here, at this intersection of ancient Asian monasticism and modern American individualism, is a new frontier—a new frontier not only for American practitioners but also for Buddhism itself.

Tibetan Buddhism showed itself surprisingly able to meet this novel situation. Social critics who identify the traditional with the communal have faulted lamas like Trungpa for abandoning their communal traditions and catering to their new self-indulgent American clientele. But Buddhism was already an individualistic religion in Tibet: There the ideal training was one-to-one transmission, guru to disciple, and best of all was for a monk (like the great Milarepa) to seek isolation to practice on his own. When the lamas in exile first observed Americans at Zen centers meditating in groups, they were slightly perplexed, because in Tibet meditation was usually a solitary activity. An individualistic religion had accidentally stumbled into a time and place (the 1970s, America) whose citizenry were all supposedly doing "their own thing": It was not a bad fit.

Before 1975, Zen had been the only form of Buddhism that had interested Americans, and no one suspected then that the Tibetans could ever rival its popularity. (At that time few lamas spoke English, and they had been xenophobes in their own country.) A quarter century later Tibetan has supplanted Zen as Americans' first choice of Buddhisms. One reason is that Japan sent over only an occasional missionary Zen priest, while after 1959 Tibetan Buddhism half relocated to the West. But, in addition, Zen Buddhism takes places on the "Ph.D. level," as John Blofeld observed, by which he meant that its limited number of approaches are all as demanding as, say, graduate school in the sciences. But Tibetan Buddhism is the religion of a thousand ways to meditate, of a seemingly infinite number of methods, one of which was likely to suit an interested American, whether he or she was well educated or self-educated, introvert or extrovert, ardent or lax. In the 1950s when Americans practiced Zen, they often felt like they were traveling to Japan (that was part of its appeal); by the 1980s Tibetan Buddhism had enough approaches and knew enough routes that it could come to them.

Nearly all Americans who become interested in Buddhism, Zen or Tibetan, do share something in common. They are wrestling with an everyday problem: How does one make a good life, when work may be unsatisfactory, marriages often end in divorce, and psychotherapy is finally inadequate? The people profiled in the following section—from an inmate struggling with prison life to a professor wondering whether she is a Buddhist—are all asking, albeit in different vocabularies, How do you achieve fulfillment when the guidelines provided by elders and early teachers no longer suffice? The media, with their emphasis on political news, spotlight religion mainly when it incites social acts of hatred, terrorism, or civil war. The ordinary practitioners in these chapters are making a human news quieter than newspapers report, however, as they show the other face, the sweeter side of spirituality in our time.

chapter IX

●

The Buddhist Gatsby
and a Modest Old Friend

AMERICAN BUDDHISM HAS BEEN reckoned such an incongruous phenomenon, and its participants cut across most social lines, so that stereotypes about them have been slow in forming. Perhaps only three generalizations are at present in circulation about native-born Buddhists in this country. Unlike in Asia, they become Buddhists as fully formed adults; they must wedge their practice in amid other activities, behind their jobs and family; and their pre-Buddhist preparation (as in Jetsunma's and Richard Gere's instances) was early deprivation or youthful hardship. The subject of the present chapter, however, is the living contradiction to these assumptions. He decided to become a Buddhist when he was still in kindergarten; he has made it his first priority now for nearly half a century; and his background was one of luxury and privilege, where servants were plentiful and wishes usually granted. This exemplar, at once ordinary and atypical, is Harold Talbott (b. 1939), the very man who guided Thomas Merton around Dharamsala and subsequently became the Dalai Lama's only Western student.

If Harold Talbott's later life demonstrates what can happen when an American takes up Buddhism and goes the distance with it, his early life, on the contrary, reads like a page ripped out of F. Scott Fitzgerald. *The Great Gatsby* contains a fictional character who fixed the World Series, and though Harold's father (also named Harold) never did that, he did arrange legendary deals, such as the merger of the Chrysler and Dodge motor companies. Otherwise Harold senior, dashing and handsome, occupied himself playing polo or safariing in Africa or serving as a pillar of the Republican Party. Gatsby's quest was to wed the beautiful status symbol Daisy, and Harold senior married the Pennsylvania socialite Peggy Thayer, stylish, intelligent, beautiful, and charming. With perfect Gatsbyesque parents, young Harold grew up in a vast apartment on Fifth Avenue, attended to by maids in uniform. Harold was born, if anyone was, into the American Dream, or the Scott Fitzgerald version of it.

But in him the American Dream goes askew, into something Fitzgerald-Gatsby never heard of: Tibetan Buddhism. In 1943 the U. S. Army sent a Major Brooks Doland on a mission to Tibet, to secure a wartime land route from India to China. Although Major Doland failed in his mission, he did snap some choice photographs, which later appeared in *National Geographic*. (One such photo shows Doland on horseback, with a lhasa apso pup in his saddlebag, wittily named Miss Tick.) The youngest reader of the *National Geographic* could not actually read, but he could gaze at the pictures. The five-year-old decided his future: He would spend his life among those wonderful-looking people in the photos. Young as he was, little Harold already sensed that he might be an oddball phenomenon himself. Harold senior expected the son who bore his name to bear his likeness, to become a practical man of the world, a businessman, a sportsman, instead of a namby-pamby with artistic leanings and sensitivities. The bluff, outgoing father would apply a manly starch of discipline and stern example, which toughened up young Harold not at all. It did make him think, though, that he was a misfit, different in a negative way. In those photos of Tibetans he saw people who seemed different in a positive way, and in childishly identifying with them indulged an unconscious version of If I am not wanted here, I will go there where I might be.

But it wasn't so easy to get from Fifth Avenue to Tibet, especially for an underaged kid. So he proceeded to invent his own junior-size Buddhism. He persuaded his mother to buy him a Japanese bathrobe, which furnished his monk's regalia. A little later from Rudyard Kipling's Kim, he learned the Tibetan mantra Om Mani Padma Hum. With his mantra and monkish robe, the young Buddhist-manqué was on the path, even if the path circled only around his bedroom.

Harold's nest of luxury emptied out a few years later into its own sort of privileged misery. His father, serving as secretary of the Air Force in Eisenhower's cabinet, was charged with a minor scandal, and though exonerated, died of a heart attack not long thereafter. Harold's mother, whom he adored, never got over the scandal, and manic-depressive besides, she jumped out a window and killed herself. Reeling from these shocks of his teenage years, Harold decided he needed a real religion, and not some invented concoction with a Japanese robe and a mantra found in Kipling. Tibetan Buddhism was not on offer then, so he settled on the most majestic faith that was. Perhaps something too fervid characterized his conversion to Catholicism, like those Oxford aesthetes in the nineteenth century who converted to the True Faith for its beauty, incense, and authority.

Classmates and friends remember Harold as brilliant, his mind like a high-octane engine revving too rapidly. Despite his recent conversion to Catholicism, those photos seen long ago in National Geographic, and his subsequent reading of Alexandra David-Neel, had a lingering hold on him. While still in prep school, Harold thus initiated a correspondence with Alan Watts, the famous popularizer of Zen. He eventually invited Alan Watts to lunch, and Watts recalled in his autobiography In My Own Way

(1972) his astonishment. Harold took him to the best French restaurant, knew the headwaiter, and, though underage, ordered the perfect wines to accompany the meal. Watts was further impressed when Harold launched into "a theological discussion of quite amazing profundity." Harold remembers the occasion differently and himself as a prig, grandly pronouncing that though he admired the conception of many Buddhas and bodhisattvas, he upheld the singularity of the divinity of Jesus Christ. "In that case," Watts said genially, "I'd better turn you over to my friend Dom Aelred Graham."

Dom Aelred was the prior of a Benedictine priory in New Hampshire, and after numerous letters back and forth, he and Harold agreed to meet on the platform of the Portsmouth train station. Harold easily recognized Dom Aelred (he was the one wearing a priest's collar), but Dom Aelred was searching for the learned old gentleman who had brooded a lifetime over the philosophic questions discussed in their correspondence. Dom Aelred was a most unusual priest who practiced yoga and Zen meditation. A few years later he received permission from the Benedictines to travel in Asia, where he served as the Pope's unofficial representative to Buddhism. Dom Aelred remembered then the young man who had so impressed him and invited him along, as Harold puts it, "to pack his bags, deal with the tape recorder, write his letters, and get him to appointments on time." And thus in 1967 Harold found himself among the exiled Tibetans in Dharamsala, only a few years after they themselves had arrived, and by a year later he was such an "old Tibetan hand" that he could serve as the best (or only) available guide for Thomas Merton there.

During that Asian trip his life detoured from its predictable course. Harold soon encountered the Dalai Lama when he accompanied Dom Aelred to an audience. After that meeting, he quickly returned to the United States, tidied up his affairs, and then returned to Dharamsala to become the Dalai Lama's student. He lived in an unheated hut and slept on a rope bed, although for ceremonial occasions he would emerge from that hut in a suit and tie, as though stepping out on Fifth Avenue. A far-fetched childhood dream, from when he had first gazed at those *National Geographic* photos, had come true.

When a young person gets implanted in him the notion that he is different, he has three recourses: He can attempt the herculean self-metamorphosis into normality; he can hide his difference; or he can act out that difference defiantly. Given his theatrical, rebellious flair, there was little question Harold would act his out. The way he did so, by chucking the West and diving into Buddhism, established a model for American youth over the next two decades. Like Harold, many of the alienated young would create through Buddhism or Hinduism a self-definition untainted by their parents' society waging war (in Vietnam) and measuring success by too material a yardstick (as Harold's father had). Some went into radical politics, but others like Harold opted for religions that promised them a better citizenship in a sacred universe.

"Tibetan Buddhism," Alan Watts observed at the time, "is Roman Catholicism on acid [LSD]." Though hardly the type to take drugs, Harold felt the heady pull of what was most intoxicating and mystical in religion; whatever was most challenging had always attracted him. This was a trait he shared with Thomas Merton. So he took it to heart in 1968 when Merton told him he must, absolutely must, study *dzogchen*—the most advanced practice in Tibetan Buddhism—an approach that can lead to "enlighten-ment" or Buddha-hood in a single lifetime. "You've got to get this straight, kid," Merton told him:

> If you want to spend the rest of your life being trained to be a cur-ial diplomat and reading sutras and tantras for the next forty years . . . go right ahead and stay in Dharamsala. But if you want to know where it's at, find a *dzogchen* yogi."

But what—as Thomas Merton earlier asked Sonam Kazi—is *dzogchen*? It's said of *dzogchen* that when you first hear it described, if you don't think it's insanity, you have missed the point. Merton was proposing for Harold to immerse himself in a system that, like contemporary physics, turns common sense on its head. As Namkhai Norbu explains in *Dzogchen: The Self-Perfected State* (1989), "the world," what our five senses register, seems solid, deceptively so, like the objects reflected in a mirror. Learn the character of the mirror, or rather of the mind, and why it registers experience the way it does (so *dzogchen* teaches); learn how consciousness itself, like that mirror, remains inherently "empty," shining, and undefiled. Our usual mental states are like the audience in a theater that gets caught up in the drama it beholds. But a mind trained in *dzogchen* resembles the playwright who exults in the creative play with which he maneuvers his imaginary puppets. For Harold to become a *dzogchen* practitioner, he would have to cease being caught up in mental judgments, in likes and dislikes; his mind would have to remain in a state of free play, in nonjudgmental, total presence. If he could do that, he would reason not only by inference and analogy, but register the ebb and flow of sensations *unmediatedly*, the way in some respects a baby does. Could Harold advance from the sometimes painful world of the senses to realizing that his nature, underneath all its manifestations, was inherently perfect? That would certainly be a great leap, from American high society to the highest pinnacle of Tibetan Buddhism.

Harold had promised the Dalai Lama, however, to follow a much more graduated path of slow, sure, incremental advances. He was young, the Dalai Lama was young, and though the tragedy of Tibet haunted everyone's thoughts, an exciting new world in exile was being built from the ground up before them. In the excitement of living in Dharamsala, of being His Holiness's only Western pupil, Harold could forget Merton's advice to take the short path, to attain *dzogchen* enlightenment in the brief moment of a lifetime.

Harold got relieved of his pledge to the Dalai Lama, against his will: he received a Quit India order. Nehru's government had granted the Tibetans asylum in India, but it did not want to risk offending the Chi-

nese by having a prominent American, the son of a former cabinet officer, cozying up to the Dalai Lama. Harold managed through pulling
strings to have the order rescinded, but on two conditions: He must not
set foot in Dharamsala again, and he must withdraw from being the Dalai
Lama's student. Through none of his own doing, Harold was now free to
become the first American to begin an apprenticeship in *dzogchen*.

Cast out of Dharamsala, Harold searched India high and low, and in a
remote corner of the subcontinent he managed to locate his goal—a
dzogchen yogi. Lama Gyurdala (1910–1975), a recent Tibetan exile, was the
kind of person the poet Yeats fantasized all his life about meeting: a sage
dressed in rags, anonymous, unnoticed, eating whatever came his way. If
someone gave Lama Gyurdala money or gifts, he thought, "Oh, good,"
and immediately gave it away to some person in need. He hardly slept and
spent all his waking hours meditating (with breaks to make prayer wheels
and prayer flags). Years later when Harold saw a book titled *Heaven's Face
Thinly Veiled*, he remembered this beggar hermit and thought, "Yes, I have
seen it."

Although Lama Gyurdala accepted Harold as a student, he was too
humble to give him the necessary initiations. Instead, to receive those
empowerments, he sent Harold on a pilgrimage to Dudjom Rinpoche
(1904–87), the head of the Nyingma lineage. The mind-to-mind transmission that Jan Willis received from Lama Yeshe Harold obtained from
this living legend as Dudjom lay on his sickbed in the hospital. From his
reading of Zen and the Beats, Harold knew what to expect: The Master
would slap you with his shoe or point to a barking dog, and the bolt of
lightning would descend, *satori*, the masked ripped off the face of reality.
His initiation from Dudjom Rinpoche was disappointingly undramatic: If
this was the nature of one's mind, the difference afterwards was barely
perceptible. Before the transmission, his normal mental state was a
"stream of consciousness," thoughts drifting randomly in and out like
clouds on an overcast day; afterwards, they somehow lightened, became
less opaque, more sunlit—nothing easier to put his finger on than that.

Always after his pilgrimages to various rinpoches and high lamas, Harold returned to Darjeeling to study with his beloved Lama Gyurdala. By 1975, however, Gyurdala was dying of hepatitis. On his deathbed, he encouraged Harold to seek out the greatest *dzogchen* master alive, the Dodrupchen Rinpoche (1927–), although securing those teachings in Sikkim where the Dodrupchen Rinpoche resided might present a problem. Harold thought of John Blofeld, the famous English Buddhist, who had journeyed to Sikkim a generation before to receive initiations. The route to Sikkim, a rough path at the best of times, had under torrential rains become a stream infested with blood-sucking leeches. Then when Blofeld finally arrived, the great lama spoke no language he knew. Yet it had all worked out for Blofeld . . . still, Gyurdala's warning was hardly encouraging.

But Lama Gyurdala died, and instead Harold returned to America, adrift. "When younger, I was like a child who never thinks of the future," Harold recalls. "It never occurred to me, 'You have to earn a living. You have to have a profession.' " Consequently, he returned to the United States a thirty-six-year-old man, without a profession, without prospects, and with no place to go. After an initiation (such as Harold had received from Dudjom Rinpoche) one's inner difficulties are supposed somewhat to dissolve, and oddly enough, Harold's problems solved themselves, without his doing much of anything. A childhood friend Michael Baldwin, now an investment whiz, rented him a house in Marion on the Massachusetts coast so, Baldwin joked, "at least Harold won't wind up on the street." Baldwin shared his interest in Buddhism, and together they started the Buddhayana Foundation to translate and publish Tibetan books, which provided Harold a job, indeed a rather ideal job. With his head away in the dharma clouds, the problems of the body—how to feed and clothe and have a roof over it—had taken care of themselves. Still Harold was disappointed in himself: He hadn't followed Gyurdala's dying advice; he hadn't gone to Sikkim; he had not met the Dodrupchen Rinpoche, from whom a shower of blessings might have come that he would now never receive.

Some months after moving to Marion, Harold received a bit of unexpected news: The Dodrupchen Rinpoche was visiting America and actually staying nearby. Was that what Gyurdala had meant—the difficulty would not be obtaining the teachings, but obtaining them in Sikkim? The Dodrupchen Rinpoche was generally reclusive, but he greeted Harold quite amiably: "Everyone knows what you did for Lama Gyurdala." (When Gyurdala was dying, the understaffed Indian hospital required some friend to be in attendance, and Harold stayed at his bedside night and day.) The Dodrupchen Rinpoche said disappointingly little else, however, until Harold was getting into a friend's car to go and an attendant rushed up to say that, if it was agreeable, Dodrupchen Rinpoche would come visit him. "How very nice," Harold said, "I hope he can stay the whole weekend?" "Perhaps longer," the attendant replied.

"Perhaps longer" stretched out to nine months, as the great *dzogchen* master occupied an upstairs bedroom in Harold's house, or rather part of a bedroom, a large closet with a window, which the Dodrupchen Rinpoche converted into a kind of Himalayan cave. From that closet-cave Harold let the wisdom of this brilliant, funny, adorable man wash over him. Gradually as he put the Dodrupchen Rinpoche's instructions into practice, the oldest perplexity in religion—the relation of sacred to profane—ceased to be so confounding. (The Buddhist version of that perplexity: How do you connect "meditational reality," in which everything seems wonderful, with "daily reality," where everything promptly turns into a mess?) Unlike Christianity's infinite distance between deity and human (bridged by Christ's intercession), the difference in Buddhism between what the Buddha is and what an ordinary person is is ultimately zero. But Harold did not see how this could possibly be true for himself. Half of the time devotion for Buddhism infused him, but the other half it was as though the first half never existed. He drank, smoked, and dashed down from Marion to New York City for parties, the wilder the better. But gradually, during those nine months, this split within himself ceased to be the chasm tearing life down the middle. The Dodrupchen Rinpoche's presence somehow relaxed his mind so that the hope for the good things seemed less necessary and the dread of the bad less justified. Harold stopped being the scarred partisan—favoring some phenomena, opposing others—and turned into a friendly, neutral observer. With his concentration at once more relaxed and more directed, it seemed not merely that his fixating on drinking or sex or sophisticated parties lightened, but that those activities themselves became more transparent and had less of a magnetic hold on him. At times his mind became suffused with a clear and joyous calm, independent of concepts and sensations entirely. It was like the sweet and tasteless taste of cool, fresh air—this awareness free from the extremes of desire or aversion.

A Tibetan would think that having guides such as Lama Gyurdala and the Dodrupchen Rinpoche would surely bear fruit. Harold has now passed his sixtieth year, however: a time to assess one's accomplishments. And here is his verdict on his: "A life that was waste and ineffectuality." The wonderful seeds planted in him produced nothing. Harold enumerates the ways in which he's incompetent: He can't read a map or drive a car, and the catalogue of impracticality extends from there. He has not written a single book, and whenever asked to give interviews or lectures, afterwards he invariably thinks, "Well, that was useful. It showed I don't understand an iota about anything spiritual, and now I must at last try."

This is a fairly damning self-critique, but how accurate is it? As Tibetan Buddhism established itself in this country, its success was often measured by an American gauge—rather the way Harold appears to judge his achievements by his father's yardstick of success. Someone else might judge it quite differently. A Tibetan might focus, for example, on the year when Harold borrowed a friend's cottage in the English countryside and there performed the *ngondro*—the hundred thousand prostrations, the hundred thousand mantra recitations, etc.—with such concentration that he did not even hear the tractor in the field and only occasionally the birds loudly squabbling over the worms the tractor unearthed. Nor was his single-minded effort confined to that year. Harold's twin brother, John, recalls a visit when Harold would appear at breakfast, take his cup of tea, and return to his room to practice. He would appear at lunch and take his broth back to his room to study and practice. He did have dinner with the family, but even then his thoughts continued to be preoccupied with his practice. "Next time you come visit, you son of a bitch," his brother said jovially, "why don't you bring your mind as well as your body?"

The Tibetans believe such effort does not evaporate in air but sows seeds in the unconscious that will bloom prodigiously years (and life-times) hence. Perhaps Harold's accomplishments are already bearing fruit, although he is not possessive or vain enough to recognize them.

Practically, at the Buddhayana Foundation he and Michael Baldwin started, Harold has worked for twenty-five years with Tulku Thondup, whose *The Healing Power of Mind* (1996) and *Boundless Healing* (2000) have been translated into a dozen languages. At first they had not merely to translate Thondup's books about Tibetan Buddhism but to devise expres-sions for ideas for which there existed no English equivalent. His efforts in preserving a whole Buddhist lineage has turned his brother John's opinion of him around. When Harold became a Buddhist, John thought, "Always knew Harold was nuts. Now he's meditating on the sound of one hand clapping. He should just look up in the dictionary what clapping is." Today John, an Episcopalian minister, likens Harold to one of the ancient Hebrews in Babylonian exile who codified the Old Testament and pre-served it for future generations. "And somewhere along the way Harold has reached depths of awareness and being," John believes, "that most people do not even know exist."

Harold's second achievement: He hasn't killed himself. Around age eighteen he began suffering from bipolar disorder (manic-depression), in which his mental engines outran the speed of thought and then slowed to a moody standstill, similar to those highs and lows that drove his mother to suicide. During his years in India and subsequently, though manic-depression hindered him from doing many things, he always hiked out to see Lama Gyurdala and later he worked steadily on Tulku Thondup's manuscripts, even if during the depressive lows he felt like a cripple hobbling along at half speed. He attributes his emotional well-being today to a nifty little cocktail of Depacot and Wellbutrin. Elsie Mitchell, founder of the Cambridge Buddhist Society, observes that those drugs are often not completely effective, but after all Harold's years of meditation it required only a slight pharmacological tilt to effect his present equanimity. Even before the right pharmaceutical cocktail came along, his friends noted that Harold seemed to observe as much as to suffer his mood swings: The highs and lows disheveled the surface, while underneath he remained calm and clear.

Harold's greatest achievement, though, may be a "negative virtue," an absence which if he focused on, much less boasted of, might cause it to vanish. Harold is not overly preoccupied with himself; he has largely eradicated what Tibetans call "self-cherishing." Consequently, he is not prey to petty vanity, never shows anger or jealousy, and rarely has a bad word to say about anyone. Given his background, he should have become someone like, say, the poet John Berryman, brooding over himself endlessly and making art out of his brooding, even as it led him into alcoholism, wrecked relationships, and finally suicide. Harold started out that way and ended up exactly the opposite. When the Dodrupchen Rinpoche, not liking officialdom, refused to head a Buddhist center in western Massachusetts, he proposed Harold in his place. The Dodrupchen Rinpoche suggested that, with no internal walls separating Harold from others, or from the flow of experience, the center under Harold's care would run without friction (as it has now for decades).

Whatever Harold has achieved in this way, it hardly came naturally. From Madame Blavatsky and Annie Besant to W. Y. Evans-Wenz and Alan Watts, there was always something theatrical or forced about Western explorers of Eastern religions. Given his internal divisions, he too should have become a split creature, half this and half that—a centaur or sphinx—yet he comes across as natural as a dog or cat. As the modern age began, Jean-Jacques Rousseau defined what makes a person modern: He has a civil war raging in his breast. But Harold has instead an unmodern, unhurried ease within himself; it is as though he has altered the desiderata of cultural identity. In the milieu in which he was born the ideal "self" was considered to be what his father Harold Sr. was—heroic, striking, and romantic. Harold Jr.'s accomplishment was to show there can be a different but equally satisfying way of being—which is unforced, sweet, and considerate. The wealth and social prominence of his background have elsewhere left, as an unwanted by-product, a record amount of neuroses, substance abuse, and familial dysfunction. But over such neuroses, over those tormented Rousseauean inner divisions—in Harold's case between Christian and Buddhist, and between religious devotee and secular sensualist—a truce has been declared, and he is noticeably at peace. The civil war is over.

Unlike Harold, many Americans cram their Buddhism in amid a dozen other obligations and ambitions, and surprise themselves by how much they achieve anyway. But all Harold does is mainly practice: Working on Buddhist translations at his job could be considered practice, but even when he is merely photocopying or sending out a mailing, he chants or uses the time to memorize texts. No matter what the activities, below the words, the same ineffable melody is playing. It is the melody of the world become Buddhist practice: For him there is nothing external left over, so he has no exterior window through which he might gaze back and appraise what he has accomplished. Others, however, seem to recognize it. At the western Massachusetts center and elsewhere, acquaintances say that if you have a problem, Harold is so nonjudgmental and judicious, so light and solicitous, there is no one better to discuss it with. The number of people who seek out this man to whom one can say anything and by whom be soothed grows longer each year. He is like that figure described by Yeats: People come to him, because he is of the thing he dreams.

chapter X

●

Into the Closet

BUDDHIST AMERICA IS a landscape of contradictions, full of ifs, buts, and maybes. Sociologists scratch their heads perplexed when tallying how many American Buddhists there are, unsure of the criteria by which to count them. For every American who has given him- or herself wholeheartedly to Buddhism as Harold Talbott has, there are hundreds if not thousands who are curious about it, discuss it, read about it, and possibly even experiment with meditation. Most of these individuals probably would not announce that they are Buddhists. A joke about the ambiguous nature of light says that it is waves on Monday, Wednesday, and Friday and particles on Tuesday, Thursday, and Saturday. More than a few Americans feel a similar ambiguity about Buddhism. Hearing a dharma talk, or reading Tulku Thondup or Lama Yeshe, they sense their affinity for Buddhism, but a day or two later ask, What is a Buddhist anyway, and wonder, "Me?" They might be called, for lack of a better name, Buddhist fellow travelers.

Christine Cohn-Alexander* may read Buddhist literature and attempt what amuses her to hear called "sitting practice" (you don't have to practice to sit; meditation is a different matter), but she draws the line at using the "B" word. Her mother used to dismiss her latest enthusiasm, when she was growing up, with, "It's just a phase you're going through." Perhaps Buddhism is a phase she is going through, she speculates, and why embarrass herself later by proclaiming it now? Why risk being thought a kook by friends and professional colleagues?

Christine recalls a party where she eavesdropped on a curious conversation. It was between a Tibetan lama and a photographer who was verbally inept and could never say quite what he meant. He would ask the lama about various people not whether they were Buddhists, but whether they were Buddhas. "Is Richard Gere a Buddha?" he asked. "What about that basketball coach, Phil Jackson—is he a Buddha?" Good question, Christine decided. Who cares what people believe, but if someone is actually becoming a Buddha, that would be worth taking notice of. The photographer was evidently about to ask about another possible Buddhist, but checked himself: "Oh, never mind. It's just life." Excellent, Christine thought; if Buddhism is just life, if it is a complement to or part of everyday existence, even she might be interested. "It's just life." The phrase tickled her fancy.

When she was growing up in the 1950s and '60s, religion was ceasing to be a part of life, or the part of it that mattered. Religion was a crotchet that farmers and old fogeys held on to, even as history was discarding them and their faith on the refuse pile, along with cars with gear shifts and one-piece bathing suits. A streamlined, more sensible future was being erected out of the materials of modern education and economic prosperity, in which religious superstition had no place. As Christine

*This is not her real name.

reached adulthood, religion began to make a comeback of sorts, although she equated it mainly with right-wing politicians who used it to disguise their self-serving agendas—hardly something to interest bright people like herself. Young and confident, she was prepared for whatever tricks the future had up its sleeve; she expected her ideas about politics, art, and even romance to change and change again. The shock, the entirely unanticipated, however, is that religion has finally come to interest even her.

"IF YOU WANT TO make a case against Christianity, T. S. Eliot suggested, call the poet Christina Rosetti to the witness stand. Her saccharine goodness would condemn it. Well, to make a case against Buddhism," she said, laughing, "consider a different Christina. My shoddy practice— prime evidence for the prosecution."

Her literary allusions are a professional tic: The woman mentioned above, Christine, is an English professor at Princeton. She knows that teaching at an Ivy League university is hardly heroic, light-years away from the triumph it was for a woman to become, say, a doctor in the nineteenth century. But no other girl born in Vandalia, Illinois, in the early 1950s has ended up teaching at Princeton University, and sometimes it seems to her that, starting at age fifteen, she screwed up every intellectual muscle and for thirty years never relaxed to get where she has arrived. At times she wonders whether, for the good of her psyche, she should have spent the whole time otherwise occupied. Occupied how? "Sex sounds nice," she jokes. Instead of debauchery however, Tibetan Buddhism has become her "secret vice," as she calls it.

Her Buddhism is an incongruity in Princeton (although, if you try, you can scare up a Princeton Buddhist Fellowship and a budding undergraduate Buddhist here and there). Although in recent years chain boutiques have usurped the old soda shop and replaced the two-hundred-year-old hardware store along Nassau Street, she still finds Princeton fetching. The underused university chapel looks like a miniature European cathedral washed up next to the stone library. Such handsome old buildings make a suitable backdrop for human dignity, she thinks; they enhance the person strolling past them. Though she rarely goes into Nassau Hall, she knows the first American Congress did, and its history now extends to include her. But that history, these buildings, date from a period that knew nothing of Buddhism. Could those mute stones speak, they might ask: What is a Buddhist? and what is one doing strolling through our august campus?

Oddly, to colleagues with whom she has argued politics late into the night, and even confided intimate details of her erotic life, she has not confessed her interest in Buddhism. To the departmental friend to whom she confided about her first marriage, "Only a saint or a fool should marry a poet, and unfortunately I wasn't and I did," she has yet to say a word about her interest in Buddhism. Certainly no professional repercussions would ensue upon her announcing she is a Buddhist . . . except probably most of her colleagues would begin to have quiet doubts about her. Their likely question—What is a postdeconstructionist feminist critic doing chasing strange gods?—is, in fact, her question too.

Five years ago, in the Strand used bookstore in New York, idly browsing through the store's orphaned volumes, she noticed a curious title, *The Tibetan Book of Living and Dying* (1992). She casually began reading the book, and five months later she was still reading it. Typically she dispatched books as though they were cocktail canapes, but this one she reserved for when she was relaxed and the world was calm, on luxurious Sunday mornings. Besides, most chapters of this curious volume were not simply to be read, but *lived*. Obtain a Ph.D. in literature, and you will have done a Grand Tour of Western culture, its literature and its history, on the well-trodden path of many before you. Of course there still remain commentaries to write, theories to set forth, theses to argue, but there are few genuine knock-you-off-your-chair discoveries left to be made. For Christine, this introduction to Tibetan Buddhism was her ticket into the unknown.

Back when she was a student, "the tragic view of life" had been in fashion, and she preferred those authors—Sophocles, Dante, Shakespeare,

Dostoevsky—who stared catastrophe in the face and made meaning from it. But reading *Living and Dying* she thought that Buddhism trumped those literary masters. In it the circle of suffering seemed encased in a larger, benevolent circle where everything could be put to good use. Tragedy (or even dying) was not the final station-stop, but a layover on the way to a further destination. The ampleness of this view, which annexed even death into one's personal story, beguiled Christine. And best of all, she thought, it isn't religion. "I have found that modern people want a path shorn of dogma, fundamentalism, exclusivity, complex metaphysics," the book's author Sogyal Rinpoche wrote, and proposed to set in their place a path "that can be integrated with ordinary life and practiced anywhere." Like a magician's wand, the book thus made theology and dogma disappear, yet nearly everything discussed in it, from dealing with difficult emotions to sharing another's happiness, approached being a sacred act. Like storybooks read to you in childhood, the volume left Christine with the conviction that we live spellbound, in a world of wonder.

The unexpected doorway that Tibetan Buddhism opened for Alexandra David-Neel had led her far way, but Christine discovered a last frontier in an even more unlikely place, in her bedroom on Sunday morning, reading books omitted from her graduate course syllabi.

Had "spirituality" been the missing element, then, during all those busy career years when she could barely look left or right? Funny, she had thought that what was missing was spelled M-A-N. But if religion was the missing element, no one she knew had ever missed it. Faith had not sold well in her childhood, in the postwar, prosperous America of the 1950s. Although her father was Christian and her mother Jewish, she grew up (except for holidays) essentially areligious. The Passover seders spent with her mother's family had exuded an appealing warmth rather like Thanksgiving, but with a faint hint of something holier. The hint never became less faint. Christine saw that American Judaism produced good families, good morals, good communities—admirable but nothing you, or rather she, could actually believe in or worship.

Her mother's Judaism not so much rejected as simply not found, she tried the new, improved version. In her early years in Princeton she shopped Christianity and settled upon Quaker meetings, which had the benefit of being held in a two-hundred-year-old log cabin where a fire blazed in the fireplace. There everyone sat in silence, and that autumn as the leaves fell outside, cares of the world fell away inside. Only after she had discovered Buddhism did she understand why this charming scene had not yielded her more solace. Quaker silent meeting was not strictly meditation (it was more your everyday thoughts, left to settle), whereas Tibetan Buddhist texts demonstrated how to quiet the mind and redirect it. During one such Quaker meeting, thinking about Christianity, she recalled an anecdote about William Blake. "Do you believe," a concerned friend had tried to pin that mystical poet down, "that Jesus Christ is the one and only begotten son of God?" "Yes," answered Blake. "And so are you, and so am I." Blake's response was heretical, but its equivalent in Buddhism would be considered the right answer—you are your own Buddha. When Christine later began to read about Buddhism, she liked that, instead of being a supporting character to a messiah figure, each practitioner occupied center stage—the central character of his or her own drama.

Having taken one baby bite of Buddhism, Christine wondered how to proceed. She wasn't going to join a *sangha* or Buddhist group, where she would have felt trapped in some Rotary Club of the Spirit. The books she read all advised the novice to find a guru who can explain exactly what to do. Should she look under G in the phone book? She hardly relished the thought of some Buddhist priest telling her to stop doing everything she enjoyed—rising as late as possible; indulging in bright, stylish clothes; drinks at the end of the day; lively sexual fantasies—to cease everything, that is, which made life bearable. She did like to read, however, and it turned out she liked reading about Tibetan Buddhism. Unlike the novels devoured late at night in bed, Buddhist works were morning books, to be read upright and with concentration, as though you were solving the human equivalent of a mathematical theory.

American popularizers often reduced Tibetan Buddhism to clichés, but the Tibetans themselves could surprise her intellectually. Judging books by their attractive covers, she picked up two volumes by someone named Thinley Norbu. So strange were the ideas in them and so eccentric the prose that Christine felt she was reading knowledge imported from over the edge of the world. In *Being and Nothingness* (read in graduate school) the French philosopher Jean-Paul Sartre had declared, "Consciousness is ego-less." Thinley Norbu took off from there: The contents of our mind that we identify with—our thoughts and our feelings—are not our true identity at all. Refusing to identify with or clutch fast to what we are thinking, he suggested, will release us into a different order of experience entirely. Norbu must be talking about the imagination, Christine decided, and in her discipline the imagination is admired for creating literature but considered otherwise an unreliable guide for conducting one's life. Thinley Norbu thought differently. If we don't get bogged down in our thoughts or feelings, then we pass through them and enter directly the imaginative free play of the mind itself. In what Norbu called "play-mind"—which becomes active when we do not get stuck in heavy moods and seriousness—we enjoy a light, subtle perception that can register any event as luminous. Breathing in and out, for example, is hardly noticeable, but once it gets suffused with mental attentiveness in meditation it becomes as pleasurable (so experienced meditators claim) as chocolate or sex. In his other-planetary prose Thinley Norbu thus conducted his readers into a back-door entrance into experience, where everyday obstacles and fixations decompose and recompose in untampered-with awareness. Freud had claimed that most of our assumptions about the world are merely projections, but Norbu's *Magic Dance* and *White Sail* demonstrated, as it were, how to run the projector. He did not segregate in apartheid subjective from objective, but like a true poet, or post-Einsteinian physicist, he considered that phenomena *out there* reorder themselves to corroborate the changing shape of the "I" *inside us*. Christine found his wild vision which made artistic play and material reality interchangeable refreshing, but still she was glad she did not have to teach it to undergraduates.

Her colleagues would have dismissed Norbu's Buddhist thinking as muddled mysticism or worse. So Christine lived out her little experience of Buddhism privately, book in hand, coffee cup nearby, as the Sunday-morning sunlight through the window shades lay down in stripes across the page. She vacated her privacy once, however, when she saw a flyer announcing a talk by a Tibetan lama that night. The lama's picture on the flyer (it was Tulku Thondup) showed him, unlike most Buddhist monks with their shaved heads, actually having hair and looking ruggedly handsome, so she decided to risk wasting an evening.

In person, my goodness, he was short (and she'd heard Tibetans were supposed to be strong and tall). From that large stage his speech sounded soft, by its very gentleness holding the audience's attention. His equanimity was almost disconcerting. The books Christine read invariably said to find a guru, and though he caused no shock waves to shoot down her spine, Tulku Thondup seemed to her one she might trust. During the questions, it was evident that others were entertaining the same possibility, but he objected that he was not that kind of teacher. "In Tibet, I'd have no choice," he said (referring to the fact that he is a rinpoche), "but in America just say you're a writer, and people think you're odd and leave you alone." Obviously, people weren't leaving him alone, but he had hit upon this gentle formula for not taking disciples. Christine surprised herself by standing up and asking, "There is no big crush of lamas here, you know, and what do we do, if we can't find a teacher?" Half inaudibly Thondup said the word *pratyekabuddhas*, people who reach enlightenment on their own. Since Christine was already standing, she asked, "And what about *sanghas*—what if you don't belong to a *sangha*?" He said that way you would avoid infighting and rivalry, so possibly it was better, your practice would not be distracted. There, on that stage, stood a man who clearly did not fight against whatever is. At first his responses disappointed Christine, giving her no push; but upon reflection, she was encouraged that any positive approach was valid, including probably her own. That evening Tulku Thondup led a long guided meditation (subsequently published as *Boundless Healing*), and afterwards the gray-haired woman next to her exclaimed "Marvelous, marvelous, marvelous" as they were leaving the auditorium.

After Tulku Thondup's talk, she ceased to doubt so much the value of her armchair Buddhism. In old Tibet a hermit-sage might meditate away his appendicitis and thrive on a diet of nettles. But Christine had learned meditation from books—which may be like learning to swim while in a desert by reading a manual—yet she was grateful for its small brightening of her dark moods. And occasionally solutions to problems that had loomed intractable did come to her during meditation. She recalled, for example, an argument within her department, after which she kept going over and over what the other person had said, also what she had said. Or should have said. But finally all the repetitions and echoes of that argument in her head fell quiet during meditation, and then as though out of nowhere came an idea how, without either accusation or exactly apology, to approach her colleague afresh. Was that what Socrates's half trances in the marketplace were, a silencing of the outer voices in order to hear the inner?

But meditation, and Buddhism itself, may face in her their acid test, she adds, since beneath her social veneer she is possibly the most self-centered person this side of the Mississippi. She can check self-preoccupation in the classroom, where her maternal instincts surface, hovering solicitously over each student's development. But the life of a professor hardly matches its old romantic image of it—i.e., teach a class in the morning, compose a scholarly page in the afternoon, smoke a pipe (or screw a student) in the evening. Now it's "seven/twenty-four," all the hours of the week are barely enough for the endless committees, endless meeting with students, interminable departmental politics, infinite letters of recommendation, ceaseless papers, eternally recurring conferences, until there's hardly a moment left over for spontaneous human decency.

And everything is *post*—postdeconstruction, postcolonial discourse, post-postmodernism—as though we are inhabiting the aftermath of Time and killing the few minutes left by chattering shrilly. The supposedly noble profession of teaching would now try anyone's patience, and Christine feels that even with Buddhism she is too often failing the test. She is amazed how at one moment, during meditation, peace can prevail, permeating her being, while later during the day she gets irritated by the triviality of university conversations or upset at mere trifles. If she doesn't advertise she's a Buddhist, she says, maybe it's because she would be a bad advertisement for it.

Yet, without knowing about her Buddhist interest, her friends remark that she is softer and more enjoyable to be with now than a few years ago. When that observation was relayed back to Christine, she waved it aside. "Age tends to tame the shrew." But, in fact, there are different criteria or opposing schools for evaluating a person. In the academia/intelligentsia school of character assessment, someone like Christine scrutinizes her every trait under a microscope and magnifies every slight flaw, which should result in self-aware persons who don't harm others, at least not blindly. By contrast the Buddhist school or approach views everyone, starting with oneself, as generously as possible, which results not in people dissected to inconsequence but potential Buddhas capable of magnificence.

Not all that long ago—though in excellent health, though mortuary tables projected for one of her demographic group a good quarter century left to live—Christine felt that, in some way, her life was already over. This was not exactly a morbid thought: She anticipated writing two or three more books, serving as chair of her department, and, with luck, having yet one last romantic fling. But the line between her present life and her death seemed to run straight, without any major surprises or wonderful detours. Since her chancing upon Tibetan Buddhism, the line scans differently, more resonantly.

This is Christine's interpretation of the matter. By middle age our routines have become closed, everything is solid, arrangements fixed in place. Her own life-approach became fixed in place, she believes, earlier than most. As a teenager in Illinois Christine was called "brainy," meaning that she reasoned out with her head what others knew by instinct or emotion. Her sense of Tibetan Buddhism is that it pries apart the artificially glued-togetherness of the mature person and returns you to a self in flux before it hardened into that "self." Since she began meditating, her intuitions have become stronger and her emotions more fluid. She is no longer Princess Hamlet, endlessly deliberating before doing; she just does it, and usually it turns out to be the right thing to have done. Consequently, some of the sense of unknown possibilities she had when she graduated from high school and also when she was twenty-seven and newly divorced, she now feels again.

Perhaps you don't have to be a hermit in a Himalayan cave, she concedes, to get a boost from Tibetan Buddhism: Amateurs and armchair Buddhists may apply, too. There are glorious mornings when Christine thinks her whole inner landscape has been transformed, but then come gray days when she feels nothing has changed and not a thing she has done mattered. But at long last she can accept that the elated times and the dead times don't invalidate each other and that the "truth" (so-called) flows in between, and floats her along with it. Recently she met a long-time practitioner who could no longer meditate after a head injury, much to his dismay. During his convalescence he equated Buddhism, not with meditation as before, but with the pliant coming to terms with what is beyond one's terms. So it is just life after all, Christine thought—but life with more flexible concepts, more malleable moods. As in those dreams where you stumble upon an unsuspected extra room to your house, Tibetan Buddhism has opened up for her more living space, an extra room of possibility for now, for this lifetime . . . until she wakes into another dream.

Of course, everything is going her way—for the time being. Christine wonders how she would handle a catastrophe like a head injury or any other of those reversals of fortune that fill the novels she teaches. One pin-prick, and possibly all the air, the beautiful thoughts, will go out of her, like a burst balloon. . . . But she recalls reading C. S. Lewis's saying that a Christian should not manufacture hypothetical tragedies and then imagine his faith insufficient to withstand them. Christine translates this cautionary warning into the language of Tibetan Buddhism. All right, she has buddha-nature; one of these lifetimes, give or take a million years, she will become an enlightened being herself. And in the meantime, when or if the worst happens, she will watch with curiosity how an embryonic Buddha bears it away.

chapter XI

•

To Hell and to Jail

TIBET'S MOST BELOVED YOGI was a criminal. When young, to revenge harms done to his family, Milarepa learned black magic and rained death and destruction down on his enemies. But afterwards he repented, and atoned by performing Sisyphean labors, until his heart softened into a source of wisdom and songs that have inspired Tibetans for a thousand years. Reading *The Life of Milarepa*, Christine reflected about the relation of past deeds to present experience. In academia, revisionism is the name of the game, and rewriting the past provides jobs for each new generation of scholars. But Milarepa knew he could not undo the past intellectually, not by a jot, not by a fraction of a jot, but only by changing himself could he change his relation to the past. Later when Christine chanced upon a small book about a convict in San Quentin, she concluded that the prisoner would have to do as Milarepa did, or else the deadly sequence of cause and effect in which he was caught would eventually strangle him. Everything in the past had gotten him to this present point, a dead end, and how was he to devise a different way to enter what lay ahead?

When that prisoner, named Jarvis Jay Masters, entered San Quentin Penitentiary, invisible chains linked his childhood to the recent past, which linked again to the present in a way that practically ensured he would go from bad to worse. During that wayward and abused childhood, Jarvis Masters learned to commit petty crimes; for those crimes, he was sentenced to jail; in jail, he learned the malevolent ins and outs of a criminal career.

There is an explanation for every bad thing he did, but the explanations will explain him into hell, into death; the only alternative is for him somehow to will himself a new purpose outside that biographical cause and effect. Jarvis Masters's "reason" for being in San Quentin, dictated by the state, is to commit no further crimes and—since he is on death row and should his appeal be denied—on a designated date to die. But if he creates in his mind through the Buddhism he adopted in prison a different goal—to grow in compassion, say, or to help other inmates—then his "purpose" in prison will diverge from his reason for being there. The chain of causality will then be partially severed. Then like Milarepa, he might possess not only the benevolent teachings but also certain reformed darker forces to do a good that mere innocence cannot imagine doing.

The success or failure of Buddhism in the West may ride, in an odd way, on people like Jarvis Masters. The Dalai Lama and even Lama Yeshe are like Gandhi or Joan of Arc, beings whose moral grandeur seems unrelated to an ordinary person's daily allotment of small pleasures and tiny disappointments. But Jarvis Masters is at the very bottom of the social and ethical ladder—San Quentin, death row—and if he can get somewhere anyway, that would be news to take to heart. His past, in which he was first abandoned by his parents, then raised pell-mell with little education and less love, was of an almost unrelieved bleakness. His present, confined to a tiny cell, suspended under a death sentence, is even bleaker. If Buddhism can temper that direness, and infuse this hopelessness with hope, it will have proved itself. Though only one man, Jarvis Masters, is thus a kind of ultimate test case.

WHEN JARVIS, aged nineteen, first entered San Quentin in 1981, two surprises were in store for him. He never suspected he would end up on death row, and he never expected to become a Tibetan Buddhist. But everything else, as noted above, seemed foreordained from day one. A fish swims in the sea, a bird flies in the air, and ill-treated, cast-off boys like Jarvis inhabit the correctional institutional facilities of the United States. The child of drug addicts, by age five he began making his way through a series of foster homes; by twelve he was a ward of the state, subsequently in and out of detention homes and reform schools, never thinking life could be any different. He once saw a little tree sprouting up out of the concrete sidewalk, which filled him with wonder, and then he tore it out, because its beauty was a lie or everything else he knew was. Much later, when he began to educate himself in San Quentin, he figured out that prison extends a welcome mat for boys (and men) full of rage. Many are African-American, as Jarvis is, but for all races prison life forms an extension of their violent inner lives. Only there are they not abnormal.

In 1985 an officer, Sergeant Burchfield, was stabbed to death in San Quentin. Although many prisoners were suspected of having conspired in the killing, eventually three were brought to trial: the twenty-one-year-old who had stabbed him; an older convict who had ordered the killing; and Jarvis, who was accused of sharpening the metal later used to make the murder weapon. The other two were sentenced to life, and in one of the longest trials in California history, Jarvis, only two years older than the killer but with a violent record, alone of the three was given the death penalty. Since the trial ended in 1990, his home has been this side of the gas chamber, death row, where he waits the outcome of his appeals.

"The thought of death has saved many a man's life," Nietzsche wrote. During the trial, Jarvis panicked as never before. He might die and die soon, he realized, and he had not a clue about what his life had meant or why he had done anything he had done. When Melody Chavis, the investigator who works on death row cases, met Jarvis, she could barely see him, with his stocking cap pulled over his forehead, eyes hidden behind sunglasses, a ballpoint-pen tattoo across his face. She did feel, however, the sullenness and resentment radiating from his angry body. Nonetheless, for the first time since he could remember, Jarvis willingly cooperated with someone and not, he said, because he wanted "to justify the things I had done. I wasn't cooperating now just to save my skin." He desperately needed time, time to understand—though his trial judge told him he should never have been born—why he had been.

One day Jarvis was leafing through a magazine Melody Chavis had given him, where he chanced upon an article by a Tibetan lama, "Life in Relation to Death." "Wow!" he thought. "This is right up my alley!" As his various trial dates were set, he would prepare himself, and then a postponement would send his terror spiraling. He asked Melody how to keep from going crazy, and all she could think of was what had helped her through a difficult period: the meditations she had learned at the Tibetan Buddhist Institute in Berkeley. Have I got anything to lose? Jarvis thought. For an hour before dawn each day his prison cell became his shrine room, his folded-up blanket his prayer mat, as he meditated before the prison erupted into a madhouse of noise and other prisoners might spy him doing it. Melody worried that she had acted like a colonial missionary, forcing Tibetan meditations on an African-American man. "Are you sure you don't want me to find some other kind of teaching for you?" she asked him. "Maybe there's an African-based tradition you would like better."

"Well, you're not from Tibet," Jarvis answered. "I want to do whatever works, and this is helping me." It was helping, Melody surmised: Jarvis had stopped wearing his stocking cap and dark glasses, and she noticed that an "expressive light began to shine in his eyes." "Jarvis," she teased him, "you look more like a college student now than a gang member."

In the years since the trial, Tibetan Buddhism has helped Jarvis maintain an optimistic outlook as he awaits his life-or-death appeals' verdict. The lama who wrote "Life in Relation to Death" has become his teacher (by mail). Daily Jarvis wakes to practice a sweet meditative quiet as if, for an hour, he were not in prison but meditating in a temple or on a mountainside. "Such periods of silence, of breathing softly into a state of relaxation," he says, are "the most rare and wonderful experiences in all my years of incarceration."

But being a Buddhist in San Quentin is not exactly easy. If he waits past dawn to meditate, someone a few cells down will be yelling, "Come feed me, you fuckers," and somebody yelling back at him, "Shut up, Motherfucker!" Another convict screams, "Who you calling a fucking punk," and is answered, "When this cell open, I fuck you, Bitch." No, this is not the tinkling of temple bells. Elsewhere on death row prisoners get to use phones and typewriters and cassette players, but because he is accused of murdering a guard, Jarvis is denied such niceties. Confined to his bare cell except for a few hours a week in the exercise yard, he is denied the basic choices of *what* and *when* (what to eat, when to shower, when to turn off the lights, etc.)—a condition sure to infantilize nearly any adult. Against these odds Jarvis has managed to mature and—although he would not word it this way—deepen his humanity.

Although nearly illiterate when he first entered San Quentin, Jarvis has now written a small book, *Finding Freedom:Writings from Death Row* (Padma Publishing, 1997) that evokes better than many large volumes do the reality of prison life. The book was not composed on a computer, or even with the benefit of a fully functioning ballpoint pen. Jarvis was allowed only the pen's flimsy inner tube of ink, deprived of its plastic casing, to record what it was like to be a Buddhist where there never had been a Buddhist before. To practice on death row depended on his being resourceful. When he requested a *mala* (Tibetan prayer beads), he was denied permission to have one. So he extracted the staple from a *Sports Illus-*

trated and sharpened it into a needle; unraveled his prison jeans for the thread; and during one long night bored excruciatingly tiny holes in one Tylenol after another and strung all the pills together to make his own mala. (The painstaking work induced such a headache that he nearly broke the mala to get a Tylenol, but meditated instead.) Another night he woke to find ants crawling all over his body, which defying instinct he did not swat or slap. He dissolved sugar cubes in a cup of water, and dripped a sugary trail for the ants to follow out of his cell. "I've done too much practice these past days," he thought, "to destroy the well-earned karma by killing ants." The putative killer on death row would not murder an ant!

In San Quentin all religious inmates are distrusted and the few Buddhist ones openly despised. To call yourself a Buddhist there could actually jeopardize your life. A religious convict is assumed to be working some scam, or else he's a weakling, hence more vulnerable. Consequently when his Tibetan lama came to initiate him, Jarvis requested that the initiation be done in private, away from the other inmates' hostile gaze. Request was denied. There in the neon-lit hall where prisoners and visitors were hollering through the glass partition, the lama in his Tibetan robes—out of place as though he had flown in from another planet—gave Jarvis his vows, and Jarvis repeated those vows to harm no one and to help everyone. "Helping others could cost me my life in here," Jarvis said. "Can I qualify my vow by common sense?" Buddhism has a different common sense, the lama replied, in which life and death come and go and return again, while helping belongs to a more enduring reality than either. This could be a suicidal vow, Jarvis thought to himself.

He tried to be a good Buddhist on the sly, meditating and praying in secret, as the anger of San Quentin raged around him. One day, as yet again a fight broke out in the exercise yard, the tower guards aimed their automatic rifles and ordered all the prisoners to lie facedown. Jarvis knew somebody might die then and there, one of the men fighting would kill the other, or a guard could open fire on them both. "Shit!" he thought.

"How long can I go on trying to be a Buddhist in this prison? Who am I kidding?" Lying there facedown in the dirt, Jarvis determined to live out his Buddhist principles, no matter the risks.

Exactly how risky it was he soon learned. One day shortly thereafter, an unfamiliar prisoner—at first he looked like a woman—entered the exercise yard. Hair in a ponytail and Vaseline on his lips, the man swished in tight jeans alongside the yard fence, oblivious of the hatred directed at him. No yard in San Quentin detested homosexuals more. Jarvis eyed the tower guards, who obviously knew what was going on, their guns already pointed into the yard. (This would hardly be the first time a sadistic official had set up such a ploy to get a prisoner killed.) According to prison ethics, none of this was Jarvis's business. But he couldn't just stand by while an innocent man died, or—as his friend Dan walked deliberately over to the poor queen, a sharpened shank emerging from his sleeve—could he see a second man whom he knew die for killing the first. Without thinking Jarvis darted to the fence, inserting himself between Dan and his prey, and asked the gay inmate, "Got a spare cigarette?" He saw, felt, the adrenaline coursing through Dan's body; Dan's frenzied eyes were those of a ferocious animal, not even registering Jarvis, only seeing somebody in his way, a substitute target for his blind murderous hate. At the last second Dan snapped to, recognizing Jarvis, and he walked angrily away. The gay man, clueless about the near execution and the reprieve that had just transpired, said to Jarvis, "Hey, Daddy, did you want this cigarette or what?"

"No, I don't smoke," Jarvis said. The queen was confused. Jarvis was, too, wondering why, damn it, such things were happening to him more often since he had taken his vows.

On the Fourth of July that year guards from another unit were covering his tier. They were waiting until their shift ended so they could go home to their parties, and to make the time pass more quickly they baited the prisoners. They refused the inmates basic necessities like toilet paper and eating utensils; they slopped food all over the trays as if they were feeding animals; they refused some prisoners any dinner at all. The tier was seething with only one thought—revenge. Kill those fucking asshole guards when they next make their rounds. The guards had behaved stupidly, Jarvis felt, but not enough to deserve to die. He had to think quickly, think how to deflect the rage mounting all around him. He had an inspiration. He got the other inmates to stuff towels into the cell toilets, and flush and keep flushing till the whole tier flooded. As the toilets began flushing, the inmates started laughing and joking; this was their party, their Declaration of Independence. The two guards would have to work overtime and miss their parties, and they stormed back in, mad as hell. They waded through calf-deep water to Jarvis's cell, and angrily accused him of inciting the flooding: "Mister, you are going into the Hole [solitary confinement]!"

"You sure it was me?" Jarvis said innocently. "Man, why would I do something like that?"

"Oh, we know it was you! And while you're in the Hole, you'll have a very, very long time to ask yourself why."

Jarvis smiled at the guards. The Hole was bad but worth the pleasure, he thought, of seeing those two men still alive.

Being a Buddhist has thus made Jarvis's life in San Quentin both less and more bearable, more dangerous but more meaningful, and, at certain moments, even beautiful. When faced with a difficult situation, he sometimes wonders, what would people on the outside do? Would they smile and sweetly agree, "Let's all be Buddhists and put our knives away and love one another?" Occasionally he fantasizes raising his hand amid the madness and commanding, "Stop! A Buddhist is here." But in San Quentin the madness wasn't stopping. Every day there was worse violence, more hatred, new stabbings. Jarvis is haunted by memories of a night some years back when a new prisoner was thrown into the cell next to his. Brian, not even out of his teens, panicked as he realized that, with his life sentence, he would never leave there. Jarvis tried to stay awake all night, in case Brian needed to talk, but at a certain point he fell asleep, and when he awoke, Brian had hanged himself. For years, for the hundredth time, he wonders what he could or should have said to him. Perhaps:

> Brian, I know what you're feeling. But all of life is precious—even yours in prison. No matter how difficult your life seems tonight, no matter how isolated you feel, you're not alone. There are so many babies dying, homeless people in the streets, millions of people starving. There is much suffering, a lot worse than yours. Sometimes we have to challenge ourselves to survive. I love you, dude. Don't kill yourself. . . . Don't kill yourself.

Maybe the right words would have stopped Brian from taking his life, but at the time Jarvis didn't know them. Now, years later, he has found these words: *Life is precious*, which at San Quentin (and elsewhere where human beings are valued cheaply) seems patently, plainly, a lie. That a young man as ignorant and angry as Jarvis could enter San Quentin, and discover there life's preciousness, and live it out amid hate and deprivation, makes it true, however, even were it not so before.

JARVIS MASTERS IS A FREAK, the only Tibetan Buddhist on death row. Were he elsewhere in San Quentin, he might enjoy some like-minded company, for most American prisons now have Buddhist inmates. Their temples are lessons in impermanence, bare rooms where the inmates meet that served another purpose an hour before and will serve a different purpose an hour hence. Buddhist teachers and volunteers work with prisoners; there is a national Prison Dharma Network and a national prison newsletter, *The Bodhi Seed*. Quite a stir of activity, considering that the number of Buddhist prisoners is small, and small for good reason. Other prisoners are hostile to the Buddhists in their midst, calling them "idol worshipers" or worse. Some prison chaplains encourage this hostility. Yet, despite the antagonism, regardless of the small (if growing) numbers, prisons are a testing ground. No faking it, no sugar-sweet sentiments here. A Buddhist at the shopping mall, say, or Christine teaching Lit. Crit. may not know if (or mind that) their practice is at that moment relevant. But here Buddhism must prove itself—make a hard life more tolerable, and do so quickly—or those prisoners won't be hanging around for next week's dharma meeting.

What can make life in prison somewhat more bearable? The following attitudes apparently make a difference: An inmate who can take responsibility and say, Yes, I did such-and-such and so I'm here, usually fares better than one whose resentment turns into unbroken bitterness. It also helps to accept that prison is the reality for now but know that one day it will be otherwise, that prison is not the final truth of the matter. Even knowing that, an inmate must somehow live in the present, the hard present, instead of dreaming of what once was or counting the days of his sentence left, because, as one inmate said, that's just counting off the days till death. The Buddhist's terms for the above understandings are karma, impermanence, and mindfulness. If a prisoner masters them in some form or another, he will probably have an easier time doing time.

One inmate worries about his infant son and frets that years hence when they finally meet, his son will hate him for being an ex-offender, a two-bit con, not the kind of father any boy should have. But at rare times he realizes that his ideas about his son's future reaction (and even what a prisoner is) are contrivances of his own mind. For a moment then he stops thinking about it and savors a momentary peace. Almost every prisoner who has attained some degree of peace has realized something about his own mind: that it was his distorted thinking that at least partially caused his troubles. "I want," "I'll do," "I'll have" were the spurs that motivated him into action, but a maimed background had produced a warped "I" whose decisions got him into hot water—and into prison. Sometimes in the cell simply to cease mentally rehashing over regrets, to let painful memories go blank, can feel like a gift from heaven—what a Buddhist would call *sunnyata*.

In the pen, as one inmate put it, every day is unique but unique in the same way. What's constant is how, in many prisons, the inmates live under tensions resembling in some aspects those of war. In those conditions every prisoner wants something similar: not to get stabbed, killed, humiliated, etc. "Me against them" can be a self-protection in prison, but even so, if an inmate can sympathize with that common plight, then the second prison that a defensive, isolated sense of self creates may begin to unlock a little. Thus in addition to the karma, impermanence, mindfulness, and *sunnyata* mentioned above, he may generate his own homespun version of compassion (or nonduality). All together, that's almost the whole Buddhist kit, minus the meditation. Meditation, which requires no gadgets or permission, would seem heaven-made for prisoners, but with all the crowding, noise, and preset schedules, meditation is impossible for many inmates. Unless they rise before dawn to do it, as Jarvis does.

Some remarkable prison inmates, struggling to bear their sufferings, have re-created nearly the whole Buddhist path entirely on their own. Very ill people, coping with their pain, have been known to do it, too, sometimes oblivious that their efforts have any kindredness to Buddhism. Their stories, from both the sickbed and the prison cell, indirectly support Buddhism's claim that it is not a religion but something that occurs "in life"—not a man-made, synthetic medicine but a plant with healing properties that grows of itself. Although other inmates have achieved relief on their own, on his own all he would have achieved, Jarvis feels, is fury and despair. He is grateful to his Tibetan lama and the Buddhist map of deliverance for getting him out of hell and leaving him merely in jail.

BEFORE JARVIS TOOK HIS vows from the visiting lama, he had, out of self-protective caution, kept his Buddhism a secret untold to any other inmate. But much against his wishes, the taking-of-vows "ceremony" took place in the prison's Visitors' Room, under the glare of neon lights, where the other prisoners and guards could witness it. Afterwards, while he waited to be escorted back to his cell, another inmate yelled out to him, "Are you a Buddhist-man?" A guard hovered nearby to listen, so he was on the spot. What should he do? Lie, after just taking vows? Jarvis stalled, before finally answering, "Sure I am." He looked the guard directly in the face, "There may be just a taste of Buddha in us all."

c o n c l u s i o n

For a Future to Be Possible

WHEN THE STORY TOLD in these pages began, had most Americans tried to locate Tibet on a map, they would have pockmarked half the globe with bad-guess pinpricks. By the time the story ends, some Hollywood stars know more about Tibetan Buddhism than the Dalai Lama does—or at least they act that way. Perhaps never in history did another country undergo such a reversal in its image and meaning in so brief a time. In one generation Tibet's culture went from being considered religion's fantasyland to becoming a well-documented and grim reality.

Before the 1950s, in the tiny space it occupied in the world's consciousness, Tibet evoked the ultimate over-the-rainbow. The ditzy flapper in *Gentlemen Prefer Blondes* (1925) complains about a boyfriend, "All he does is talk about some exposition he went on to a place called Tibet and after talking for hours I found out that all they were was a lot of Chinamen." Before the time of Thomas Merton's visit to the Dalai Lama, most people knew as much about Tibet as that flapper did; it was geographical white space on which charlatans and cranks could scribble their fantasies. In the nineteenth century Madame Blavatsky had founded a quasi-religion, Theosophy, based on her experiences in Tibet, although in fact she had never set foot there. Later the writer James Hilton fashioned a fictional Himalayan utopia called Shangri-La, in a novel so popular that Franklin Roosevelt named his rural retreat after it. (And forever afterwards anyone who wants to dismiss Tibet calls it Shangri-La.) The Russian painter Nicholas Roerich roamed the Tibetan borderlands trying to locate the lost kingdom of Shambala (the model for Hilton's Shangri-La) and discovered nary a clue until he showed some Mongolian herdsmen photographs of New York City. "That's it!" they exclaimed. "That's Shambala!"

In retrospect Blavatsky, Roerich, Hilton, and other Shangri-La-esques appear like children frolicking in a playground, which a holocaust would later decimate. After 1959 Tibet became a real-world matter of statistics, accurate knowledge, and factual information, but at the price of its near-extinction. Yet from the political defeat of Tibet rose up the cultural triumph of its religion. The fortitude and equilibrium the Tibetans displayed under foreign domination and in exile attracted curiosity about Tibetan Buddhism—evidently the source of their resilience. For overall those people suffered the trials of Job, but they behaved like a tribe of Walt Whitmans. Their buoyant spirits suggested that they might know the secrets of outwitting tragedy. It was a positive image of religion, and the image came at the right time.

At mid–twentieth century, as the old utopian image of a fantastical Tibet was dying, another utopia was also ending—that heaven on earth of the social scientists. Those social scientists, and earlier secularists as well, had envisioned the world progressing into a rationality and prosperity that would have no need of the ineffectual balms of religion. Theirs was a wonderful vision, and more's the pity that the opposite of it transpired. In the past few decades the poorest one-fifth of the Earth's population has seen its share of worldly goods reduced by two-thirds (from one-thirtieth to one-ninetieth of what the wealthiest one-fifth possesses). Even in the United States the discrepancy between the rich and poor has widened troublesomely. Poverty, hunger, famine, war, terrorism, and racial inequality have not evaporated like dark clouds on a sunny day, as the social forecasters predicted they would.

Such commentators now acknowledge the dire politico-economic conditions that dominate much of the globe but go on to point out that religion is not a solution but, rather, a major contributor to the blight. In Belfast, Beirut, or the Balkans, or wherever Protestants are killing Catholics are killing Jews are killing Muslims are killing Hindus are killing Buddhists (the sequence can be ordered differently), the very idea of faith may turn a person's heart to stone. But the Dalai Lama repudiating violence and accepting the Nobel Peace Prize; Lama Yeshe taking on everyone else's problems and forgetting he is supposed to be dying; Tenzin Palmo exiting her beloved solitude to assist underprivileged Asian women; American dharma centers with their encouragement of compassion: These are also pictures of religion at work. Compared to other politicians, what a clean odor he left behind, Orwell said of Gandhi, and the same words would describe the Dalai Lama and the incense of freshness Tibetan Buddhism still exudes. It may not change any socioeconomic structures, but Tibetan Buddhism can change their lives, some Western practitioners have discovered—even change a secular individual's life and, oddly, change it for the better.

Religion in the modern West, during the time this story takes place, has undergone a sea change. Picture a large cathedral symbolically dominating the landscape; then picture a modest American home or urban apartment with a little sunlight streaming through the window. Buddhism was, peculiarly enough, one of the forces that helped rehouse religion from the first sort of dwelling to the latter. As the lamas made their unfamiliar way in America, their kind of Buddhism shifted from monasteries and monastics, its reference point in old Tibet, to being at home in lay life and among lay people. In the process they uprooted religion from its old habitat in churches and Sundays and priestly sacraments and relocated it to any day and everywhere and something one mainly does for oneself.

"I like to joke that religion is a luxury item," the Dalai Lama occasionally says, and then chuckles before adding, "Kindness is not." His religion is kindness, he declares; compassion is his faith. But kindness makes a more ambiguous guide to conduct than, say, the Ten Commandments, and at one lecture someone asked him, "How do you know then, what is right and what is wrong?" A minister (or rabbi or imam) might have opened his holy book and cited precept and precedent, but the Dalai Lama found the question not all that easy to answer. "Something that is good in one situation may be bad in another," he replied. "Generally speaking, though, if it promotes happiness, it is good."

What makes you happy is religion? (To promote others' happiness, Tibetan Buddhism says—as does common sense—you likely need to be happy first yourself.) A contemporary may no longer believe in sin enough to expiate it (Christianity), or in an upright soul enough to sacrifice for its purity (Judaism), or in houris in paradise (Islam), or in uniting self with Self (Hinduism), but, generally speaking, everybody wants to be a little happier. Human happiness, rather than God, may be a good starting point in a society that in many ways is secular even when it is religious. Earlier, when Dr. Herbert Benson of the Harvard Medical School measured the effects of Tibetan esoteric practices on the sympathetic and parasympathetic nervous systems, he hardly expected any religious leader to endorse his reducing spirituality to physiology. The Dalai Lama's enthusiasm caught him off guard: "Your way of identifying the physiological impact of spiritual forces," he told Benson, "is doing a thousand times more to bring the religions of the world together than all the philosophers are." At such moments Tibetan Buddhism displaces religion from its heavenly mansion into the studio apartment of the ordinary human body.

THOSE ADAPTATIONS OF Tibetan Buddhism to the contemporary situation are transpiring in other religions as well. The heavenly choir has dimmed in Christianity and Judaism, as those faiths likewise increasingly emphasize individual and direct experience. But such re-formations, because prepared in a historical pressure cooker, have taken a more visible, dramatic form in Tibetan Buddhism. Contemporary Tibetan Buddhism is also unallied with any political power structure, which may be why it shows a present-day religion in an unusually favorable light. We might then inquire: What does its unexpected success in Europe and America imply for the religion of the future—if religion is to have a future—a future, that is, other than promoting hatred and violence? Can we extrapolate from its successful adaptations the ingredients of cur-rently workable spirituality? Three ingredients in particular—three trends illustrated in Tibetan Buddhism's career in the West—may be necessary for religions overall, if they are to be a positive force in days and years to come.

The first exemplary trend that Tibetan Buddhism in exile has illus-trated is *universality, nonpartisanship*. At this very moment people are slaugh-tering other people in the name of religion. When terrorists flew hijacked planes into the World Trade Center and Pentagon on September 11, 2001, they surely thought they were honoring God. When George W. Bush invaded Iraq in March 2003, he assumed he was morally, if not divinely, in the right, which made the realistic considerations that innocent people would die or world terrorism increase or the American economy be hurt by it irrelevant. No one can entertain a more dangerous idea, possibly, than that he or she is right, if that sense of rightness is based on national or ethnic division. Until recently almost all religions were located in national/regional or ethnic bases. When the Dalai Lama and his followers fled Tibet in 1959, Tibetan Buddhism severed its national roots. When Westerners began practicing it, it lost whatever was ethnically Asian about it. Tibetan Buddhism in exile—not by its comparatively small number of adherents, certainly, but in its orientation—may have turned into, in one sense, the first universal religion. It does not sigh, homesick, for some one place—Rome, Mecca, Jerusalem, or India—as being special above all oth-

ers. It is universal not because it sends out missionaries to convert heathens regardless of race or ethnicity, but because it makes no fundamental division between "missionaries" and "heathens"; it is learning to be at
home everywhere.

Increasingly our world, this planet, is becoming for good or bad a
single place. It can be quite good: Individuals from disparate corners, Rus-
sia, India, South America, meet and instantly connect on a deep level, and
the handicaps of a provincial upbringing (unlike, say, in *Winesburg, Ohio*)
are shed with fair ease. But it is bad when an economic disaster or political upheaval or environmental destruction like ozone holes ramifies
across half the globe. The Dalai Lama begins his day, he says, "with [his]
ears busy listening to BBC World News," believing that a solicitude for less
than the whole Earth is like an ostrich, its head buried dangerously in
some national or ethnic hole. For if this planet is a single unity or being,
as some idealists claim, it is a being ailing and wounded, whom only a
nonpartisan physician can heal.

The second ingredient in Tibetan Buddhism, and for a civilizing religion of the future, is *individual responsibility*. In most religions the Author of
all life is indirectly God, and the final authority on it, the Bible or the
Church. In the Buddhist idea of karma, however, individuals are considered to create the situation in which they find themselves. In the Tibetan
version of Buddhism, final accountability begins and ends—not with the
laws, not with community—but with the person, since everything else is
a karmic reflection of how he or she experiences it. Does such a metaphysical premise make any practical difference? In fact Buddhist practitioners in America tend to approach personal problems differently. In
psychotherapy (which Buddhism in the West resembles) the client comes
in a victim blaming, blaming—blaming the mother or father usually or
the spouse or anybody else, for unfairly causing his suffering. Buddhist
practitioners are overall more inclined to suspect that they themselves are
feeding into the problem, instead of casting blame for it. "With our quarrels with our neighbors, we make rhetoric," Yeats said; "with our quarrels

with ourselves, we make poetry." In the religion of the future the individual may be left, if not to make the poetry of the world, at least to take the prosaic responsibility for it. For if the gods are "projections" (as they are in Tibetan Buddhism), and if sacred texts are less authoritarian dogma than helpful "guidebooks" (again as in Tibetan Buddhism, especially in exile), then there is no separate power outside the individual person that could tidy life into livability.

The third potential ingredient or element for religion as a positive force in the coming time: *heightened capabilities*. For a mere individual observing it, there can seem no way to stop the destruction—that is, to counterbalance the desolation of species, of environmental habitats, of civil societies, and of dear humans, too. If all the world's good and all the world's evil were counterpoised in a huge Manichean scale of balances, those latter evils would surely outweigh all prospect of redemption. Common sense, and hope, become frustrated before the irrationality of destructive power, finding logic cannot dissuade it. But is there another way of looking at it that might, partially, influence what we are looking at?

Some scientists claim that human beings use approximately 15 percent of their brain capacity, which leads fantasticists to speculate: What would happen if we could use 20 or 25 percent? Many lamas Alexandra David-Neel met in old Tibet seemed to possess clairvoyant mental powers, as in a more modest way Chögyam Trungpa and Lama Yeshe did as well. Gandhi undertook his "experiments with truth"—such as in old age sleeping chastely with a naked young woman—in order to increase his *siddhi*, to enhance the powers in his own person sufficiently to be able to counter British oppression in India. All Gandhi's experiments, and those of other visionaries, too, were to activate the greater potential within their own minds. What possibilities beyond our present limited view, they in effect ask, would we see if we developed our mental power or saw with an increased range of acuter vision?

The Dalai Lama and other Tibetan teachers in fact downplay the notion of *siddhi*, of achieving unusual abilities through meditation; you should practice Buddhism, they say, to increase your kindness and compassion. But behind this realizable goal of achievable goodness, they have never abandoned the promise of enlightenment: the promise that people can become more clear-sighted and effective than anybody but a Buddha can presently imagine. Although it is no longer the wild 1960s and '70s, this sixties-ish hope of becoming the idealized self of one's dreams or beyond one's dreams is still what draws people to Tibetan Buddhism. If Buddhism offered only its beautiful ethics, one could just as well read Marcus Aurelius or the Christian philosophers. In addition to creating ethical persons (the goal of all religions), the rather unique goal of Tibetan Buddhism is to create *bodhisattvas*, even Buddhas. And one definition of a *bodhisattva* is a capable being who realizes more of his dormant abilities, in order to help others. The hope is that such a man or woman, no longer so restricted by self-absorbed considerations, would be infused with the courage and insight to charge where few now go, whether to right a mess in the immediate vicinity or to act on some larger plane of noble endeavor. Human beings into *bodhisattvas*—that is a frail hope, but it is a hope.

AND WITH SUCH HOPES Tibetan Buddhism continues to attract new followers today. But tomorrow? Without a crystal ball, who can say? After a longer habitation here, the *Tibetan* in Tibetan Buddhism may switch to some other adjective. Indeed, some scholars like Robert Thurman and Stephen Bachelor have playfully suggested that even the word *Buddhism* can go, for its alien sound may impede integrating the dharma into our culture. Since anything is theoretically possible, we could wake up tomorrow to discover that Tibetan Buddhism had been a passing fad here after all. But we shan't wake like the revelers in *A Midsummer Night's Dream* to discover it was only a mirage. Even if Tibetan Buddhism disappeared tomorrow, it would have meanwhile enriched numerous lives and renewed appreciation for what spirituality is.

Odds are, though, it won't disappear, not *tomorrow*. Tibetan Buddhism is a good religion for history's darker hours. In exile its followers have furnished an instructive study in how to lose everything and lead lives of fulfillment and humor regardless. The Dalai Lama has watched his country and culture erased from the board, yet few can demonstrate better than he how to be of good cheer. Such has always sounded the message of Buddhism: We live in a world of suffering, yet we can remake it (or if not "it," ourselves) and experience auspiciousness nevertheless. And in history's brighter hours, when material plenty, peace, and choices abound, Tibetan Buddhism teaches how to maximize that good fortune and use it as a preparation against eventual sickness and dying. So long as anyone falls short of a satisfying life or dies in pain or fear, there will likely be some role for what we for the time being are calling Tibetan Buddhism.

Thirty-five years ago Thomas Merton took his seat on a plane, expecting that within twenty-four hours he would reap, simultaneously, his first glimpse of and a homecoming in Asia. His expectations were too low, for a religious enchantment he had dreamed of his whole life soon enveloped him in the Buddhist Himalayas. But not he, not anybody prophesied the larger surprise: that Tibetan Buddhism would board the return flight— crossing a millennium, via a route improbable—and then, landing, disembark into its own homecoming in the West.

Bibliographical Note
and Acknowledgments

A NOTE IN LIEU OF A BIBLIOGRAPHY

As I was writing this book I compiled the usual standard bibliography, which at a certain point, I realized to my dismay, was becoming longer than the actual text itself. This overly plump bibliography was not due to unprecedentedly inordinate amounts of research—although, working on the book for seven years, I might be tempted to think so. Rather the book branches into several quite different areas, some of them in the contemporary period where popular and journalistic accounts cancerously multiply. In fact, most of the book derives not from written accounts but from firsthand research and interviews, while the written accounts it is based on are often second-rate materials or transient journalism that would likely interest no reader. Eventually I conceded that the book would be easier to hold in one's hand and less ungainly overall unencumbered by such a bibliography. Of course a Select Bibliography containing only the first-rate writings of interest would be possible, and in fact indirectly the book does provide just that, in the text itself where I cite, at appropriate places, books that someone might want to consider for further reading. As for the old-fashioned (i.e., pre-Internet) kind of bibliography, however, it might be simplest to say: This is not that kind of book. *Re-enchantment* is not primarily a book for fellow scholars and research libraries, but for the time-honored "common reader," who wants to argue and be stimulated and to gain something to take home personally. Having said that, I would like to add that if any readers wish to pursue aspects of this subject further, and are stymied in their own researches and think that I might be of help, please write me care of the publisher and I shall be certain to respond.

ACKNOWLEDGMENTS

Two people, as though its guardian protectors, helped make this the better book it could be. Molly Friedrich, my agent, evinced such intelligence and gave such support to the book that I can hardly image it would exist without her. Alane Mason performed the most visionary act of all—she bought the book—and later she read every line with a meticulous care that makes her seem less a contemporary editor than one with the great editors of legend.

Writing is a solitary act, notoriously so, but at certain moments I suddenly found myself in the best of company in the most supportive of circumstances. Those better occasions were provided by the Rockefeller Foundation at Bellagio, Italy, the Virginia Center for the Creative Arts in Sweetbriar, Yaddo in Saratoga Springs, New York, and the East-West Center in Honolulu, where (among many others) Terry Bigalke, Betty Buck, Nancy Lewis, Charles Morrison, and Geoff White embody the Center's legendary hospitality while making it a force for improved understanding and cooperation in the world.

So many people provided the information, knowledge, insight, and wisdom upon which the book is based that I shall merely begin my list of those to be thanked here and then continue it further in person. Gratitude, in gargantuan doses, to the following: John Avedon, Tara Brach, Jeff and Cheryl Bragg, Kathleen Bryant, Dan Capper, Nawang Chodok, H. H. the Fourteenth Dalai Lama, Massimo Corona, Harvey Cox, Maura Daly, Leslie DiRusso, Rebecca Redwood French, Winifred Gallager, Carolyn Gimian, Philip Glass, Heinrich Harrar, Jeffrey Hopkins, LiAnne Hunt, Wilson Hurley, Darcy Jones, Kamptrul Rinpoche, Jarvis Jay Masters, Pat Masters, Ken McLeod, Richard Melton, Fabrice Midal, Wib Middleton, Mike and Dan and Ben and Willis, W. S. Merwin, Konchok Norbu, Thinley Norbu, Tenzin Palmo, Tenzin Parsons, Ani Rinchen, Geshe Sonam Rinchen, Nick Ribush, Leslie Robinson, Bruce Joel Rubin, Rabbi Zalman Schachter-Shalomi, Martha Sherrill, E. Gene Smith, Ruth Sonan, Anna de Souza, David Swick, Harold Talbott, John Talbott, Noreen Teoh, Tulku Thondup, Karma Lekshe Tsomo, Nicholas Vreeland, Martin Wassell, Lama Wanchuk, Paula de Wijs, and Jan Willis.

Also, for their practical support and/or personal encouragement, many a thanks to: Alessandra Bastagli, Christopher Candland, Brad Evans, Susan Ginsburg, Rochelle Kainer, Susan Nugent, Bonnie Ram, Katherine Ranken, and Jay Tolson.

DEDICATION

This book is dedicated
to my friend Eloise Goreau,
to the teachers of the various Tibetan lineages,
to the dakini embodiments, C. and M., and
to the happiness and welfare of you who read this book.

Index